How To Make Your House A Home

how to make your
HOUSE a HOME

how to make your HOUSE a HOME

By

KAY HARDY

Illustrations by the author

Decorative Spots by Virginia Whitney

FUNK & WAGNALLS COMPANY

New York

CONTENTS

PREFACE

THIS BOOK is dedicated to the young homemakers who are building a home for themselves for the first time. Most of them have had the plans for this home in their hearts for a long time. They've waited even longer for the dreams to be translated into blueprints than for builders and materials. Most particularly, this book is dedicated to those new homemakers who find themselves faced with their new home—beautiful, a dream come true, but filled with *empty rooms* and a budget that will not stretch too far after the first mortgage is paid. They have the wedding presents to start with—a good lamp, perhaps even a love-seat or an end table. But what next? Modern couples know what they want the rooms they live in to look like. They don't want chi-chi. They don't want the cover of a decorator's magazine with costly antiques and 18-foot ceilings. What they *do* want is simplicity, practicality, livability, *home,* as the author of this book has found from talking with many of them. The book was written to show them how to go about getting the result they have in mind. Most of all, it will try to prove to them that it's not only fun, but *more fun* to have to do it on a limited budget.

When you read this book, we hope you will feel sorry for the poor couple who have all the money in the world to spend on furnishing their home, for they will have no choice but to hire the best decorator in town and let him have all the fun fixing up *their* home. Decorators are fine people, in their place, and this book will tell you how to make the best use of them, *at no cost.* And of course if you were rich, you would miss all the fun of deciding according to "the Hardy plan" which room to do first, which furniture is most important to buy first, which can be left to next month's budget. If you were very rich, you'd have everything delivered at once—oh horrible thought!—and miss all the joy of showering attention upon each piece of carefully chosen furniture in its turn till each chair and table became a real part of the final picture you have in mind.

We feel there is a real need for the book that is written here, because this kind of buying for the home, the piece-by-piece and room-by-room kind that most of you will have to do, takes *know-how* to be successful. You can't go around falling in love with dressing tables and pipe stands at random and expect the aggregation to look like home. Not the home you'd hoped for. This book will help you steer a straight, well-charted course right from the beginning, with practical information on how to get the most for your money, how to buy one piece of furniture this year and have it fit perfectly with the piece you can't afford till next year, how to match one room to the next. We hope you will profit by the wisdom of one who has learned the costly way from experience to avoid the pitfalls of home planning that could turn your dreams into drudgery or disappointment. We hope you'll find useful the many hints on a variety of homemaking problems you will have to face—how to get the most into a closet, how to buy at auction, how to live with pictures, how to refinish, paint, or stencil furniture, even how to monogram towels and linens and upholster chairs. These are the A B C's that will give you the power to make your own house a home. No one can do that but yourself, living and working in your own home every day, but it is our hope that this book will give you the help you need to make the way easier and the result more satisfying. In dedicating this book to you, the new, young homemaker, we can say that we hope your work in this field never ends. For in the making of a home there is no finish. Part of the success is in the continuing, and the day that you stop adding beauty to your home, you can be sure that your heart has left it. If this book can help keep your heart in your home, it will accomplish its purpose.

I

THE PERSONAL TOUCH

AT LAST you have your new home. It took a long time to plan it, and it seems to you that it took longer still to build it. Or, if you found your dream-home ready-built, you had a very long search. Naturally you want it to be perfect in every detail. But you don't want to spend a fortune to make it so, for you must have something left over to pay the butcher and the baker.

If you know how to plan so not a cent will be wasted, if you know how to shop to get the most for your money, you can have a charming home, developed all by yourself within the walls of that new house.

It will take time. You can't expect to do it all in a few weeks, and it wouldn't be nearly as successful if you could. If you can plan the home with just the absolute essentials for the very beginning, the more you live in the house, the more you may find your ideas changing.

Then, too, if you buy gradually you can acquire really good things without going into debt over your ears. So don't succumb to the wiles of a high-pressure salesman who suggests a budget plan, and tells you that you'll have many months to pay. Budget plans are good in their own place. Use them if you wish, but take it easy wtih your planning, buying and doing.

Then there is the creative thrill of doing things yourself for your own home, and the wonderful companionship of sharing this work with your husband. He and you will both take more pride in your home if you have done every step of it together. It's a wonderful way to save money, too. If you wield the paint brush and apply the happy color, if you paste on those lovely lengths of wall paper; if you stitch up the curtains, the bedspreads, slipcovers and dressing-table skirts, your home will take on a more intimate personality than if you hired the most expensive decorator.

Decorators have good ideas. They have spent years training for their craft. They can help you, and you have them if you wish to use them. They are in the stores and they are paid by the stores to advise you, *without cost to you*, if you are buying furniture or fabrics there. Or there are decorators who build display rooms. There are decorators who show you rooms in the magazines or newspapers. Here you can find wonderful new ideas for fifteen cents. Here you can see pictures of new fabrics and furniture. You can tear out the pictures and take them with you to your stores. Then, if you don't find the things you want there, an inquiry to the magazine will tell you how you can get them.

1

If your husband is handy with tools, patterns of furniture to build in his home workshop are to be had for about a quarter. These are similar to the tissues that you can buy to make slipcovers or draperies. If he is handier with a paint brush than with the hammer and saw, you can buy the furniture ready-built but unfinished, and he can spend his evenings sandpapering and painting it to a fine hand-rubbed finish.

Too many young homemakers are so anxious to get settled that they buy a suite of furniture. Maybe these were all right when mother and father started housekeeping, but they have less personality than individual pieces lovingly assembled. Many of those suites are too large and heavy in proportion for the smaller homes and rooms of today.

There is lots of new furniture gradually becoming available which has been styled and sized to fit into these small homes. Some of it is modern in style, for many of the new homemakers prefer a clean break from the styles of yesteryear. Other homemakers prefer traditional styles and there are new pieces designed with them in mind. Even in these traditional type chairs, couches, tables and chests there is a tendency toward simplicity which makes them look well in any room or with any other pieces already on hand.

Many young homemakers have something to start with, and therefore must key the new things they add to fit wedding presents, or bachelor-apartment furniture. This may be done easily; often a new surface finish, or another slipcover, gives new character to a favorite old friend.

One of the most important aspects of home decoration is the color scheme. There are more questions asked on this subject than on any other when a store holds a decorating clinic. Most of the questions start out with such phrases as "I have an Oriental rug," or, "My sofa is covered with wine-red mohair," or, "My walls are tan, and the landlord won't let me repaint them."

These questions are more easily answered by the decorator or lecturer than some of the others, for color is easier to reduce to a formula of north or south exposures, or favorite colors. Many of these color formulas and idea "springboards" to help you make your own color schemes are outlined for you in Chapter VII in much the same way as your individual questions would be answered by a decorator or at a forum. See Chapter VII for suggestions.

It is harder to answer problems of proportion of furniture and number of pieces to the size of the room. To reduce the number of chairs and their size to a formula is impossible. You will find it absolutely necessary to work out your own arrangement with pencil and paper, and this should be done before any new things are purchased.

If you took your problem to an expensive decorator she would take a ruler, square off paper to scale, and make a floor plan. This you can do as well yourself, and Chapter II tells you how. After tracing-paper plans are prepared, you may go shopping as described but be firm in your decisions. Many small stores allow you time to decide, and will hold things for you. Some even go so far as to allow you to take the piece on approval to see how it looks in the room. If you like the piece, you buy; otherwise there is no obligation. This is the best way to do, but the privilege has been so often abused that many large city stores have discontinued the practice entirely.

One of the nicest ideas recently developed is the "add-a-piece" idea. This has been developed for bedroom furniture, allowing the purchaser to buy one piece at a time from the "open stock" of the grouping. Then, as the budget permits, another piece may be

Mengel modern oak add-a-piece set

purchased in the same wood, until the ensemble of beds, chests, dressing-table and chair is all collected. These ensembles have been developed in solid maple, veneered mahogany, tawny bleached mahogany and frosted bleached oak.

Another manufacturer discovered the strength of laminated maple and has manufactured inexpensive modern furniture that will never warp or peel. This is available for either living-room or bedroom furniture. One

of the most progressive art museums exhibited moulded plywood furniture which they believe is the coming development for the small home of tomorrow.

Moulded plywood is suitable for furniture that will last a long time under all atmospheric conditions. These chairs are moulded to the contours of the human figure and are

very comfortable. The housewife would find them light and easy to move when housecleaning. Much of this new furniture is in light-colored wood, for the modern tendency is to prefer light-colored finishes of blond woods.

As the furniture is acquired and the draperies and slipcovers made, the floor coverings and accessories must be chosen. Many people find that the purchase of a large broadloom rug takes a large part of the furnishing money. There is a tendency, therefore, to have well-waxed floors and use scatter rugs of wool or cotton. These are easy to keep clean, and are "becoming" to a small room. They do not protect the fine hardwood in the way a large broadloom does, so you may prefer to plan on this investment.

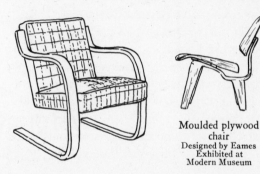

Moulded plywood
chair
Designed by Eames
Exhibited at
Modern Museum

There are many grades of carpeting. It does not pay to buy a cheap one, for the fuzz will rub off or the backing will tear.

The best manufacturers stand back of their broadloom, so it pays to buy a recognized brand from a good store. If this is your plan, determine on the color you will use before organizing the color scheme; but save the purchase until the day you are ready. You need chairs to sit on, tables and lamps for reading, but you can get along without the rug for a little while. See Chapter VI for advice.

Lamps do so much to make the home look cozy that they should be purchased as soon as possible. You can either buy the lamp complete with the right shade, or you can have a lamp made from a treasured jar, or bit of pottery, and buy a separate lampshade to fit. A tendency to buy a small inexpensive lamp should be firmly squelched. Do go a little extravagant and choose one large enough to really give good light and to look attractive when it is lit. See Chapter IX for suggestions.

Other personal accessories such as ash trays, flower bowls, and all the other things that express YOU may be already yours, either as things you have purchased or that have been given you as wedding presents. If you do not already have these things, wait a little before buying them, for as you settle in your home you may find your ideas of what is suitable will change.

A collection of some one item may occur to you as just what you will need to complete the decorative scheme. It may be framed fans of the eighteenth century or pretty bottles of no particular period that are nice in color. Or you may decide that Chinese art will look well in your rather modern scheme and you may gradually acquire a few lovely pieces of Chinese blue pottery.

Part of the fun of decorating a home is that you can string it out over a long period of time. If you keep on improving your home you will continue to love it more and more. When the day comes that you no longer want to add beauty to it, look out, for your heart has left its habitation.

II

PLANNING FOR NOW AND THE FUTURE

WHEN YOU and your husband look around at your new home there seems to be a lot of space to fill with furniture all at once. Fortunately most of us do not have so much ready cash on hand that we can rush out and buy anything that happens to appeal. We must take care and thought in our buying to be sure that we receive full value for every penny spent. The story of the smart young girl who worked on a fashion magazine is applicable to this point. When she received only a small salary, she bought her clothes with care, giving each purchase careful thought. She was always well turned out in attractive ensembles. One day a wealthy man fell in love with her and married her. With unlimited money to spend on her clothes, she bought everything that appealed to her, and without her previous careful consideration, her ensembles were never as attractive as when she had only a fraction to spend.

So you, with proper planning and due thought before each purchase, may have a better ensemble than the hasty buyer who has more money to spend. But it does require careful thought, and often takes more shopping time or a longer period before the home is completely furnished with each small accessory in place.

There are two basic ways of buying. You may decide to buy all that you need now, and buy less expensive pieces in order to do so. Or you may decide that you would rather have fewer pieces and buy them gradually. Then you would start with the minimum of furniture and add to it as time goes on.

If you choose the former method, you may select some inexpensive unpainted furniture, and finish it yourself. (Directions to help you are found in Chapter X.) There are sectional pieces, in maple, walnut or other wood finishes, planned to fit along the wall. These include desks, chests of drawers, open shelves and shelves with doors. These pieces are small enough to fit well into a beginning home, and may be relegated to other less important rooms when you move to a larger home. They are well made and sturdy enough to justify the price charged, and often cost less than "built-ins" that you would have made by the local carpenter or cabinetmaker.

Many of the stores have had special groups of furniture designed and made for them. They keep these pieces in stock in a variety of finishes, either in natural wood, light-color finishes or dark lacquer. This means that one piece at a time may be purchased. When more money is available you can return to

Sectional pieces grouped together

the shop with assurance that you will find the next piece there. It pays to shop in all the stores in your neighborhood and find one that operates on this "open-stock" plan. It is discouraging to purchase a fine chest and return to find that other pieces in the same finish and style are not to be had, or cannot be ordered.

One manufacturer of bedroom furniture makes sets in four finishes. The two modern groups are in frosted oak and tawny mahogany or bleached mahogany. The traditional sets come in solid maple or mahogany veneer. These sets may be purchased a piece at a time, permitting you to buy the bed, or twin beds, with a single matching chest of drawers first. Then another matching chest of drawers, a highboy, or the dressing-table, and the small chests for beside the bed may be added. This means that as many pieces

or as few as desired may be used. Some people like a sparsely furnished bedroom; while others can't seem to have enough drawer space for all their clothes.

Many of the manufacturers of "plywood modern" make attractive and reasonable pieces from laminated moulded wood. It was discovered before the war that "bonding" two or more thin layers of wood together produced a wood of greater strength than a plain piece of wood of twice or three times the thickness. These laminated woods are impervious to moisture. Many of them were used for boats or planes during the war. Used in furniture now, they produce wood that is strong, light to move, and attractive in finish. They are good investments for a long-term buy, and are surprisingly inexpensive. These bonded woods are used in the bedroom furniture described above, and in living-room furniture such as desks, cabinets, bookcases, tables of all sorts, and a variety of chairs.

Sketch a Plan.—After you and your husband have chosen between the "all at once" or the "piece at a time" method, it is time to start sketching floor plans and working out the budget. No matter which method is used, do start with a floor plan and use it as your guide. It will keep you from buying unnecessary things, or from buying a couch that is too large to fit in the space for which it is intended.

The blue print of the house will help you to draw the floor plan of each room. It has been worked out to scale, and the size of each room is clearly indicated. So, too, are the baseboard plug outlets that may be used for lamps or removable electric units.

If you do not have a blue print, use a long, folding, carpenter's rule to measure each wall of the rooms, indicating the doors and windows, as well as the electrical outlets.

Prepare a scaled sheet of paper by drawing off parallel lines at ¼″ intervals, then turn the paper and draw cross lines at ¼″ intervals. This provides a cross-ruled sheet, with each square representing one square foot. Lay a piece of tracing paper over this and count off the number of blocks, first for the length of the room, then for the width of the room. Draw these lines in and mark the placing of the doors and windows as shown. Do this for each room in the house. They may be on one large sheet of paper if you prefer, but they are easier to handle when each room is sketched on a separate sheet. Then, if you are shopping for bedroom furniture, take the bedroom sketch with you to the store. When shopping for living-room furniture you'll need to carry only the floor plan for that room.

Most people start with some things already on hand, no matter how new they are to real homemaking. It may be some furniture from the attic or the room at home, or from the college room, or from the bachelor apartment. Analyze the condition of this furniture. It may look dog-eared on the surface, but perhaps a slipcover or a new paint job will make it as good as new. Don't discard it until you are very sure there is something better available.

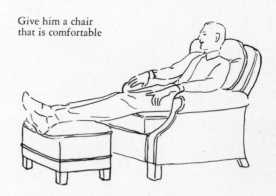

Give him a chair that is comfortable

Here's a Check List of What You Will Probably Want for Your Living-Room

First

A couch, a sofa or sectional pieces that form a couch
Two comfortable chairs
Two or four side chairs
A desk
A large table or a game table

Second

Lamp tables and lamps
A large coffee table
Bookcases or built-in cabinets

Anytime

Pictures, mirror, accessories
Fireplace fittings
Radio, record player and cabinet for records
Rug or rugs

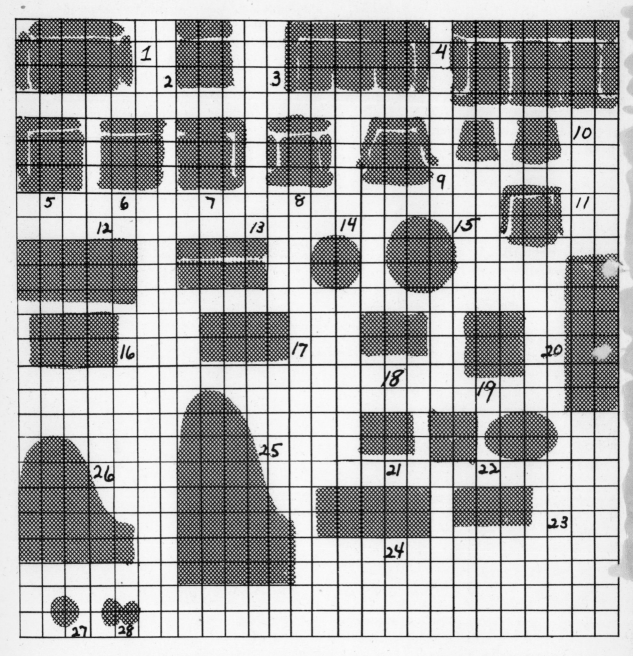

Trace around these living-room pieces, making as many as desired for the room arrangement. Cut out, and shift around on the floor plan to obtain the best possible arrangement. Scale is ¼" equals 1'.

1 Love seat	12 Flat top desk	21 Small chest of drawers
2 Armless upholstered chair	13 Secretary desk	22 Two end tables
3 Couch or sofa	14 Round lamp table or tea table	23 Radio cabinet
4 Larger couch or sofa	15 Coffee table or drum table	24 Upright piano
5-7 Sectional couch parts	16 Slant front desk	25 Concert grand piano
8 Club or Lawson chair	17 Console table	26 Smaller grand piano
9 Wing chair	18 End table	27 Floor lamp
10 Two side chairs	19 Card table	28 Bridge lamp
11 Open arm chair	20 Studio couch	

Here are the sizes you will need to draw these to fit your scaled floor plan. Trace as many as you wish to suit the needs of the room, cut them out of stiffer paper, move them around on the floor plan until you have found the arrangement you like, then either paste them in place or draw around them. Mark the ones that you already have. Then mark the ones that you plan to buy, in the order that you plan to buy them.

Usually you will wish to have two side chairs, one large chair and the couch first. The side chairs may be used for simple dinners at the game table if you have no dining-room. The large couch and the one large chair make a comfortable conversational group for pleasant evenings at home. One lamp and lamp table, or matching pairs, will come next.

Average Sizes of Living-Room Furniture

Sofa—2′ 6″ to 3′ 6″ by 6′ to 7′
Love Seat—2′ 6″ to 3′ by 3′ 6″ to 4′ 6″
Club Chair—2′ 9″ by 3′ 6″
. . . ng Chair—2′ 6″ by 2′ 9″
Bridge Chair or Side Chair—1′ 6″ square
Desks—
  Secretary—1′ 6″ to 2′ deep by 3′ to 4′ long by 6′ to 7′ high
  . . . at Top—2′ to 2′ 6″ deep by 4′ to 5′ long
  Slant Front Desk—2′ to 2′ 6″ deep by 3′ to 4′ long (Height of back approximately 44″ to 48″)
Lowboy—1′ 6″ to 2′ deep by 3′ 6″ long by 30″ high
Highboy or Chest on Chest—1′ 6″ or 2′ deep by 3′ 6″ long by 5′ or 6′ high

End Tables—1′ 6″ by 1′ or 1′ 8″ by 1′ 8″
Coffee Tables—1′ 6″ by 2′ 6″ or 2′ by 3′, or 2′ 6″ by 4′
Bridge Tables—2′ 6″ by 2′ 6″
Console Tables—1′ 6″ by 3′
Circular Tables—
  Lamp—2′ diameter
  Coffee—3′ diameter
  Drum—3′ diameter
  Pie Crust—3′ diameter
  The average table is 30″ high
Pianos—
  Grand—4′ 10″ to 5′ wide by 6′ to 9′ long
  Upright—2′ by 5′

Sectional pieces to be used separately, or pushed together to make a sofa

Many of the accessories will be wedding presents. If not, let them wait and have the fun of picking them up later, perhaps as mementos of travels taken together. You can

buy large dishes for ash trays. They cost little and are more practical than some of the small things sold for the purpose.

Don't forget the living-room is the "entertaining-room," too. It is the room your friends, acquaintances and neighbors see, the room by which they form an opinion of your taste and of the kind of people that you are. Therefore plan it to be attractive. Consider each purchase carefully to be sure it fits in with all the other furniture. Do not buy any garish pieces or any very large clumsy things.

Figure that in this room you spend about seventy per cent of your time. Therefore, plan to spend between sixty and seventy per cent of your furnishing money here. This may mean that other rooms will suffer lack of attention in the beginning, but you can make it up to them later on.

Even with the higher prices of furniture, an attractive room may be made. Recently a leading store furnished a living-room for $760. This room included two sofas, one sectional chair which could later be added to one of the sofas to make it larger, two cupboards, one round coffee table, a corner bookcase, and two side bookcases, one desk, two small chairs, and three chests of drawers to be used as lamp tables.

The lamps and rug were not included in this first price, but were to be added later as needed.

Here's a Check List of What You Will Want for Your Dining-Room

First
 Table large enough to seat four or six
 Chairs (side chairs and armchairs) four or six
Second
 Buffet, cabinet or chest of shallow drawers for storing linen, silver and accessories
 Serving-table
Third
 Chinaware

 Silver
 Glassware
  All these are chosen to suit decorative scheme of the room, and to harmonize in color.
Anytime
 Screen
 Lamps on buffet
 Candlesticks on table
 Rugs

Many of the new small homes feature a dining alcove off the kitchen, and plan on only occasional dress-up meals in a separate part of the house. This is economical both of time, trouble, and steps, and of furniture. For the dining alcove a built-in bench or window seat is popular. Or if the view is a feature, then a window shelf-table is built with stools or chairs facing the window.

If there is no separate dining-room, the area of the living-room that is nearest the kitchen is planned for a dining corner. This may have a built-in corner bench or a table with matching chairs. A screen can be used when desired to shut this corner off from the main part of the living-room. Some of the new dining-tables are made in sections, with a part that can be used for a serving table or a buffet when not needed as an extension.

Many of these new tables are topped with a plastic coating that is impervious to heat, stains or chipping. These are good long-term investments. So are the tables with glass tops, providing the glass tops are thick enough and strong enough. Some of the glass tops are of textured glass, which is rather more pleasant than the transparent glass. It does look odd to see people's feet through a table-top while dining. So unless you have tried them out, and do not mind this odd effect, do choose one that is opaque rather than transparent.

Dining-tables come in various sizes and shapes. The two armchairs and two side

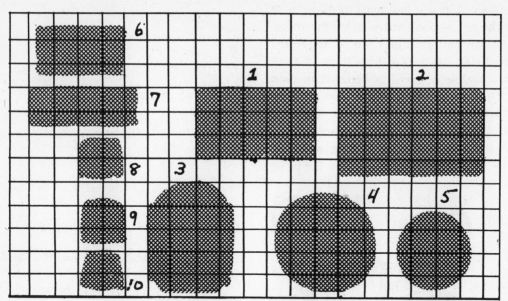

Dining-room furniture. Scale ¼″ equals 1′. Arrange floor plan for dining alcove or dining-room according to this scale. Mark all doors and windows before determining size of furniture to be used.

Dining tables of several sizes and shapes are shown. Trace all and try before deciding on the shape and size to be purchased.

1 Small oblong dining table	3 Oval dining table	6 Serving table or console table 8, 9, and 10 Chairs
2 Large oblong dining table	4 and 5 Round dining tables	7 Buffet

chairs or four to six side chairs are the minimum requirements. These may be purchased gradually, providing the store agrees to hold the group for you; or this is one instance where a group is so desirable it may pay you to go in for a bit of "instalment paying."

AVERAGE SIZES OF DINING-ROOM FURNITURE

Tables—
    Rectangular—3′ or 3′ 6″ by 4′ to 6′
    Round—4′ 6″ to 5′ 6″ diameter
    Refectory—2′ 6″ by 5′ 6″

Armchairs—2′ by 2′
Side Chairs—1′ 6″ by 1′ 6″
Serving Table—1′ 6″ by 2′ 6″ to 3′ 6″
Chests—1′ 6″ by 3′ 6″ to 4′
Cabinets—1′ 6″ by 2′ 6″ to 3′
Buffet—1′ 9″ to 2′ by 4′ 6″ to 6′

In the dining-room a bare floor is often easier to keep clean than a carpet. If you prefer a rug, buy a patterned one to fit under the table, large enough so you can push the chairs back and forth without snarling up the edges.

This may mean a fairly large expense. It may mean that this expenditure is more than the original budget can afford. Don't worry, for it is more fun to add these extras gradually. There is a special thrill with each new addition.

Here's a Check List of What You Will Want for Your Bedroom

First
    A comfortable double bed, twin beds or couches with tailored covers
Second
    Two chests
    Dressing-Table
    Comfortable chair with ottoman, or chaise longue
    Stool
    Two side chairs
Third
    Chests or night tables beside the beds
    Lamps for night tables and dressing-tables
Anytime
    Rugs

Here are sizes you will need to draw these to fit the ¼″ scaled floor plan of the room. Trace them and arrange them as suggested for the living room. If the bedroom is quite small, a double bed will fit better than twin beds. Or in a small room sometimes separate beds may be used if fitted along opposite walls. Couch beds are good space savers. They may be fitted into a corner, with one storage cabinet between to hold a lamp, or

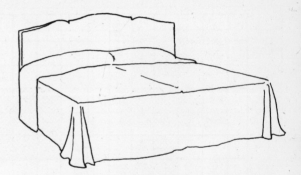

Twin beds against one large headboard—one bedspread

Oval rug in figured pattern for dining-room

they may be placed along the full length of the wall.

Average Sizes of Bedroom Furniture

Beds—
    Single—3′ 6″ by 6′ 6″
    Twin—3′ 3″ by 6′ 6″
    Three-quarter—4′ by 6′ 6″
    Double—4′ 6″ by 6′ 6″
Dresser—1′ 6″ to 2′ by 3′ to 4′
Chests—1′ 6″ to 2′ by 2′ 6″ to 4′
Dressing Table—1′ 6″ to 1′ 10″ by 3′ to 4′
Bench—1′ 6″ by 2′
Boudoir Chair—2′ 6″ by 2′ 6″
Side Chair—1′ 6″ by 1′ 6″
Tables—1′ to 2′ square

Bedside Chests—1′ 6″ to 2′ deep by 1′ to 1′ 6″ wide by 30″ high

Necessary clearance between wall and bed for ease in making bed—1′ 6″

Necessary room for table between beds or between bed and wall—2′

Necessary room at foot of bed for passing—2′

Necessary room between twin beds—1′ 6″ or 2′

Passing space between furniture—1′ 6″ or 2′

Keep space for easy passage or through traffic—3′ wide

Minimum size for bedroom with one occupant—11′ by 13′

Minimum desirable space for two occupants—12′ by 14′

Sleeping couches angled into corner of room

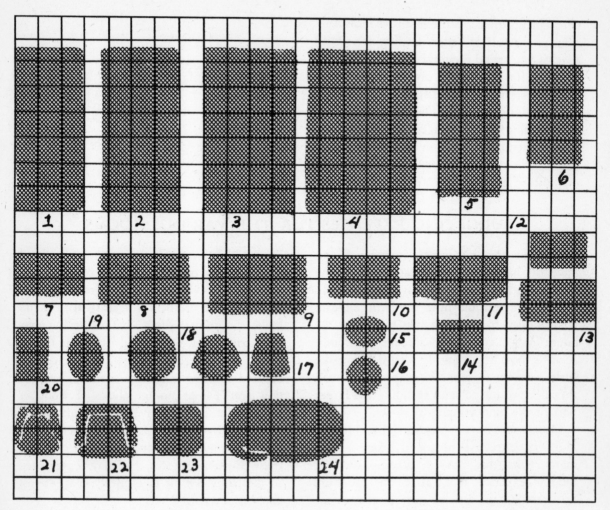

Bedroom furniture. Scale ¼″ equals 1′. Draw outline of bedroom to that scale and place doors and windows before starting to arrange furniture.

1. Single bed
2. Twin bed
3. Three-quarter bed
4. Double bed
5. Youth bed
6. Crib
7. Chest of drawers
8. Larger chest of drawers

9. Chifforobe or high chest
10. Dressing-table
11. Dressing-table
12. Youth chest
13. Youth chifforobe
14. Bench
15. Oval dressing-table stool
16. Round dressing-table stool

17. Two side chairs
18. Lamp table
19. End table or bedside table
20. Bedside table or small bedside chest of drawers
21. Small arm chair
22. Arm chair
23. Ottoman to match
24. Chaise longue

There is a vogue at present for placing twin beds close together, with one large headboard attached to the wall behind them. This is slipcovered with fabric to match the single bedspread that covers both beds with one flat smooth expanse of fabric.

Some of the manufacturers have headboards that fit themselves to the two separate beds. Some people have headboards built with special places for radio, telephone, night light for reading, and all the other necessities. If your husband is clever with tools, design your own and have him build it to hold anything you wish.

Whatever you do, buy comfortable beds. They are a long-term investment, and the ad-

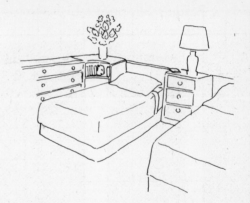

vertisements that feature improved dispositions as a result of better sleeping are right! Even if you spend the total amount you have planned for the initial investment in bedroom furniture on the beds, by all means buy the best spring and mattress available.

A leading store arranged a bedroom for about $430 and included in it two beds, three chests, two cupboards, one vanity base and one mirror as well as a corner bookcase.

BUDGETING EXPENSES FOR THE VARIOUS ROOMS

Without knowing exactly how much you have on hand of savings, and how many rooms you have to furnish, it is pretty difficult to suggest just how you will allocate your money to the different rooms in the house. As we have previously said, the living-room is most important. It is harder to make little economies and stop-gaps look well there. So we recommend spending the larger part of the money there.

Most brides have a very special feeling for a dainty, attractive bedroom. There are so many ways this can be accomplished at modest expense, that, after the beds are purchased, it is wise to start to plan some

"make-dos" for there. It is easy to make a packing case, or a wall shelf, or a cast-off table into a very charming dressing-table. Even one of those bent-iron drug-store chairs looks charming with a coat of strawberry-pink paint and a seat pad of turquoise. A sturdy pine chest may be padded and slip-covered to provide storage space and a window seat. Closet storage chests of wood or composition may be covered in bright chintz or with a coat of pink paint. So plan on some economies here. As you are able to replace these emergency pieces, they may be relegated to the bathroom, or to a guest room, or just thrown out altogether.

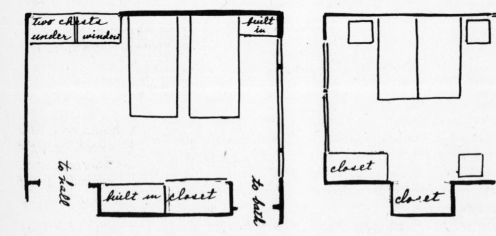

Bedrooms with twin beds and twin chests of drawers

Here Is a Bride's Shopping List with Prices Paid for Each Piece *

LIVING-ROOM

Sofa	$233.50
Upholstered chair	49.50
Comfortable chair	79.50
Webbed chair	29.50
Desk	69.50
Coffee table	19.50
Lamp table	19.50
Bookcase-cabinet	79.00
Side chair	14.50
Stool	8.95
Total	**$602.95**

BEDROOM

Double bed	$ 49.50
(Twin beds would cost twice as much)	
Two chests of drawers	139.00
Mirror and dressing table	99.00
Dressing table stool	12.50
Bedside chests (2)	45.00
Upholstered armchair	49.50
Side chair	17.50
Large mirror for over chest	49.50
Total	**$461.50**

DINING-ROOM

Table	$ 79.00
Six chairs at $17.50 each	105.00
Buffet chest	64.50
Total	**$248.50**

* Since the bride planned on sewing slip covers the furniture was purchased upholstered only in muslin. Prices listed include furniture only, not rugs, lamps and accessories.

One very clever bride spent only $100 on furnishings for temporary rented quarters, yet with this small budget and her husband's help she made a very cozy home. It is not what you spend, but how you spend it, that counts in decoration.

When the husband is handy with tools, any number of clever built-in arrangements will help a dining-room or alcove. Some of these may be purchased ready-built in a lumber yard and installed in place, to add great style to the home. Many of these lumber yards permit instalment payments in order to help finance wise home improvements. Catalogs of these millwork pieces may be had on application at the local lumber yard, and provide many worthwhile suggestions both for the inside and the outside embellishment of your home.

As mentioned elsewhere, paper patterns are available for the home carpenter and for the home sewer. Any work that you can do yourself in making your home more attractive not only saves you money that you would otherwise spend for someone else's labor, but also adds to the feeling of pride in your home.

CLOSETS ARE USUALLY TOO FEW AND POORLY PLANNED

Don't let clutter swamp your home just because you forgot to plan a place to keep everything. It is easy to plan enough closets when you build or, if you have an already built house, to have some "carpentered" in. If your husband is truly a handy man around the house, he can do many of these for you. Or, you may prefer to have him help you plan them, and call a carpenter for the actual execution. Even some carpenters make a mess of built-in cupboards and cabinets. It requires a man with a cabinetmaker's skill. So before you ask for his estimate and give him the go-ahead sign, ask to see some samples of work he has done in similar pieces.

Let's start with the bedroom closets. You are lucky if you and your husband each have one. Then the rods and shelves may be placed

Woman's minimum closet with sections arranged for neat storage

messy and clumsy. You will find that shelves do better for shoes as well as for your hats and bags.

If there is lots of room in the closet you may wish to have a chest of drawers there for lingerie and sweaters. Otherwise plan a cabinet with shallow drawers. They hold more that is easily reached than do deeper drawers where things are piled one on the other. It is smart to use tray sliders such as are found in a man's chifforobe, and have them built right into the closet.

If the closet is deep, the area behind the clothes-pole can have a dustproof curtain attached. Behind this you can keep plenty of moth flakes and store the clothing not in current use. This will keep the rod from becoming crowded and the clothes from being crushed. Suitcases may be kept back there, or they may be stacked on a high shelf above the dresses. An exhibition home, built by a plywood manufacturer, had one side-wall of a bedroom made into a closet by the addition of plywood doors that opened out. In a

to suit the size of your garments. For instance, if you have several evening dresses you will need a rod placed 6′ from the floor so the skirts won't get crushed. Probably you will keep these in dust-proof garment bags, so this can be in a separate section. The day-time dresses need a rod only 5′ from the floor. This same rod can carry short suits and blouses, with a built-in shoe shelf tier below, for they require only 3″ to 4″. If the closet is wide enough, the space above the shoes can have shelf room for hats that are often used, or for pocketbooks. One clever way to handle many handbags is to have a magazine rack of plywood inside the closet door, and file the handbags there. Shoe bags are

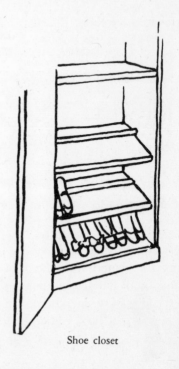

Shoe closet

smaller room, sliding doors would be more practical for such an arrangement. Half of the space was devoted to the clothing for the man, the other half for the woman; and the entire top, out-of-reach area had separate doors that concealed storage boxes or suitcases.

In the area devoted to men's clothing the rod should be about 5' 5" from the floor. This will hold heavy overcoats as well as suits hung with their trousers extended full length. If the trousers are hung at one side and the jackets at another, there will be clearance room left for a tier of shoe shelves. Plan these shelves to accommodate the average wardrobe of shoes. The average is six pairs, including sport shoes. If your husband has

Man's closet

not a special chest of drawers for his shirts, have one built into the closet, with shallow tiers so that only five or six shirts are on each pile. These drawers should be 18" to 20" deep with a width of 18" for each pile of shirts.

He will bless you for racks the full width of the closet door, on which he can hang his accumulation of neckties, and will like it even better if there is a mirror above so he

can tie his tie right there. If his clothesbrush and shoebrush have their own special hooks, then he will be sure you want to be a helpmate. Men are orderly souls once they are given a break with a well-planned closet. It will cut down his dressing time if he has a well-organized place to "work" where all his clothes are assembled.

Child's closet

Children's Closets

The best authorities on child training claim that the reason many children leave things around is that they simply do not know where to put them away. If you help the child by giving him a planned wardrobe closet he will take great pride in hanging up his own snowsuit when he comes in from play. Rods may be placed low for the small child, and raised as the child grows. The wooded upright to hold the rod simply has to be cut with arm supports at 6" intervals, or the metal end supports may be re-attached as desired. If storage space is short in your home you can have a double rod arrangement, and keep his party clothes on a rod above. You can fetch those for him on unusual occasions. Have a tier of slanted shelves for his shoes just like yours. Make it almost as large as yours, too,

Toy cupboard

Your husband can easily build these storage closets along a wall of the dining-room

for it would be extravagant to have to make another for him every few years. Even if the tiny shoes look lost now, they will soon fill up the space.

Build a Toy Cupboard, Too

A toy cupboard is just as necessary to him as a clothes closet. At this stage in his career probably toys are far more important than clothes. If you build a chest with a let-down front it will serve as playhouse on rainy days. Later this can be nailed closed and the chest used for a sweater chest. If the lift-up top is padded with a flat mattress-like cushion it can be used for a window seat, or a play seat pulled up behind the table.

Dining-Room Closets

After you have acquired all the linens, china and glassware listed on pages 123, 124, 128, and 129, and gifts of friends, you will be faced with quite a storage problem. It is amazing just how much space is needed even for the simplest "wardrobe" of vases. Yet if you do not have a variety of sizes and shapes, you will find it difficult to arrange flowers attractively. There should be several shelves

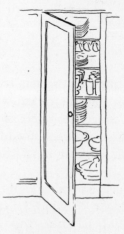

Dining-room closet

Add a breakfast alcove by building a storage cupboard out at right angles to the kitchen wall

for these. Glassware takes up much space, and the set of china for special entertaining, plus the one for every-day use, means more space. Think of the flat platters and trays. They require special consideration.

Linens, too, need a place where they may lay flat, and where not too many sets are piled on top of other sets. Drawers are more practical for these than shelves. You can pull them out to find what you want, while it is difficult to shove your hand into shallow shelf space.

A specially planned cabinet is the answer. Some furniture manufacturers are designing and making such cabinets now. You can design one to suit your needs to build for your dining room, or for the L off the living room where you plan to have your meals.

If you are planning and building your house, you may wish to make such a storage unit form the wall between the kitchen and the dining section. This can then have pass-areas, opening both into the kitchen and the dining alcove. These can be left open always, or have sliding or hinged doors to permit them to be closed. They should be above a shelf on which serving dishes may be placed to be taken through to the side needed. If the storage drawers slide through, too, the silver may be put away in the kitchen and taken out in the dining room. If the cupboards for glassware and china open on both sides more steps will be saved.

Special shallow shelves may be arranged for the glasses. The strips of metal with support angles such as are used for bookcases are handy things to have installed inside such cupboards. Then you may change the shelves easily, adjusting them to fit the accessories on hand.

The best china plates may be stacked with rounds of cotton flannel between each plate to protect them, or, if you prefer, you can buy rubber-bound metal racks that will permit the dishes to rest on their sides. The latter

Built-in storage wall between kitchen and dining section

are recommended, for they prevent the weight of top dishes from pressing on those below, as is inevitable when dishes are piled. In either case the depth between these shelves will be around 12″, with other shallower shelves of 8½″ and 6″ distances for bowls, soup dishes, cream pitchers, teacups and other dishes and glassware.

The Linen Closet

Besides the dining-room linen there is to be considered the bath and bed linen. Perhaps you have a closet for bath linen in the

A Quilts or spreads

B Puffs or comfortables

C Bath towels

D Table linens

E Bed linens

F Blankets

G Blanket drawers

Linen closet

bathroom and another place planned for bed linen, but most homes have a linen closet in the hall. Usually this closet opens wide with shallow shelves, for this is the most practical arrangement. These are built around 18″ deep. The wider the doors open, the more storage space will be within easy reach. If the door is narrow you may wish to have the doors fold like an accordion screen. If your neighborhood is damp, you may prefer shutter doors to regular doors so that the linen closet will have circulation of air and there will be less danger of mildew.

Have 30″ of the lower space devoted to big drawers in which to store blankets and comfortables. Have the top space for extra pillows, spreads or bath mats. Plan to devote the space in between to neat piles of bed linen on one shelf and bath linen on the other shelf. Have shallow bin-drawers or open shelves for the table linen if there is no storage space planned for it elsewhere. See sketch above. See Linen Closet Check Lists on pages 130 and 131.

If several people are using the closet, you may find it easier to keep order if you have labels attached to the edges of the shelves

and the fronts of the drawers. Thus when someone dashes to the closet for guest towels in a hurry, the label tells that this pile is the one. When lunch sets are wanted by that new maid you are lucky enough to have, she will know which of the drawers to pull out to find them.

Cleaning-Equipment Closet

More mundane, but just as necessary, is the closet for the equipment that will keep your house shining bright. While a vacuum cleaner is a necessary implement it does take up a lot of space, particularly if you have one with a tube and all the attachments. Then there is the stiff broom, the soft broom, the dry mop and the wet mop. These will each require its own hanging clips to keep it firmly in place. Hooks will hold the stiff whiskbroom, the soft broom, the dust-pan, and the special brush for radiators and for Venetian blinds. There should be shelves for wax polishes, scouring powders and all such necessities. A plywood "file," attached to the inside of the door, will hold polishing cloths and dust rags.

Hall Closets

Hall closets come to be catch-alls unless stern restraint is practised. If they are so organized that rubbers and umbrellas have their own places, then they will not be tossed in helter-skelter. If there is a properly placed clothes-pole for the small fry to reach as well as the high one for grown-ups, they can be taught orderliness early in life.

Here is another place where a mirror should be put inside the door unless there is a wall mirror nearby. There should be two shelves for hats; for then the closet is far more useful when you have an occasional party. The family hats may be moved up topside, and the guests' hats placed on the easy-to-reach shelf. If there is no special storage spot for tennis rackets and golf clubs, then a place must be made for them in the hall closet. Racks on the wall inside the door take up little room and hold the rackets neatly. For the golf clubs the deep corner of the closet may have a strong bracket.

Other Closets

You may realize that your personal requirements make other closets necessary. If you like games at your house, you will want a built-in cupboard in the living-room, or in the game room, to hold card tables, chess and

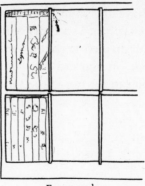

For records

backgammon boards, dart games, archery sets, cards, dice and all the multitude of things. This can be as carefully planned as the other cupboards, and built to your special specifications.

If you have a record player and are making a collection of fine records you will need storage space for them. This is easy to plan by measuring the sizes of the various albums, planning the cabinets to hold them, binding out, for easy use. Because they should never lean heavily against each other there should be a perpendicular plywood panel set into grooved slots to support them about every 8″ or 10″. If you have some records without albums, buy some of the metal racks that hold each record separate. These may be set into the shelves, but you should have doors enclosing the shelves as dust spoils the records.

If you like wine with your meals it will be

Build a record cupboard under the windows

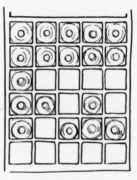

Wine closet

easier to have the right kind if you store a variety in a cupboard specially built. Plywood shelves with dividers keep the bottles in place on their side, or you can buy a metal honeycomb section to set inside the cabinet. These will be cut to size by the liquor supply house that sells them.

Your lumber dealer has a catalog of closets and cupboards or sections which may be put together to make the one you want. Ask him to show you. You will find shallow shelves or perpendicular plywood sections for trays and platters, decorative corner cupboards, tiers of drawers that may be set into the wall, or doors that may be placed in front of shelves to keep out dust. Many of these will help you in your planning, and in your building of practical, well-organized closets.

III

WISE BUYING

IF YOUR money is insufficient for the necessary furnishings after you have made the first payment on the house, then you will probably wish to take advantage of instalment payments on the furnishings. Different stores have different arrangements for this. Some of them require more in down payment, and provide a shorter time to pay; while others permit a longer time to pay, but add an extra amount to cover the interest. It will pay you, when shopping for your furniture, to investigate the various methods. Find out which suit your finances the best. Above all do not sign any papers for payments without carefully figuring out whether the amount charged for the credit arrangement and time extension is fair or excessive.

When you planned to have a home you decided that the amount spent on rent could better be spent toward permanent ownership. It is the same way in buying your furniture. If you were renting a furnished apartment it would cost more than an unfurnished one, for you would pay "rent" on the furniture each month. If you plan to spend a similar amount buying your own, it is a good investment. In a short time it belongs to you, and you stop paying "rent" on it. But it is very

important not to plunge, so that the amount you are spending on payments for the house, and for the furniture, too, does not form too heavy a burden. You must have something left over for food, clothing, medical attention and all the other necessities of life.

If you are moving into a new neighborhood, do investigate the store from which you are making purchases. So much is hidden in furniture construction and in other home-furnishings, that the amateur may be badly "gypped" if he deals with an unscrupulous store. A store that has a good reputation in the neighborhood is anxious to keep it. Their buyers are experts who are anxious and able to obtain the best available for you; and they will tell you what is inside the chair, whether the finish of the table is apt to last or will scratch and mar easily.

The stores have furniture in varying price ranges. It will pay you to dicuss with the head of the department what the differences are in values. Sometimes the reason for the higher cost of a piece of upholstered furniture will justify your paying it. After you have heard what material is in the chair, you will know whether the springs are strong enough to last a lifetime, or whether the chair will soon need re-upholstering. (The latter part of this chapter explains these things to you.)

It will also pay you to choose the oldest salesman on the floor. These older men have spent a lifetime with furniture and rugs. They know a great deal about them. They are perhaps rather garrulous, but they tell you what you need to know, if you have the patience to listen. You will be well rewarded, for your deep interest will often lead them to show you the best articles procurable. They will take more interest in you as a beginning homemaker than the young beginning salesman, who is possibly more concerned in the sale as a source of a commission.

As previously mentioned, many department stores have free advisory service available in the decorating departments to help you with color schemes or with choosing furniture *if you buy the things in that store.* You may wish to take advantage of this trained advice. Inquire about it when making your first purchases.

BUYING AT AUCTION

If you are sure of your knowledge of furniture, and do not need professional advice when you buy, you may prefer to buy your things at auction. Auctions are fun. It is interesting to prowl through an assortment of chairs, rugs, tables, lamps and china, to discard in your mind all the impossible items, and suddenly happen on the one treasure you really must have. But because auctions are fun, sometimes the buyer is carried away on the wings of his own enthusiasm, and pays more for a used chair in somewhat battered condition than he would pay for it in new condition.

The wise thing to do is to study the piece under consideration carefully, then to go to the retail stores and find out what the "new" price is. Then, when the auction is in progress, stick to the price that you have determined you can afford, the price that is well under the store price, or stay away from auctions.

There are all kinds of auctions. There is the country auction, for which placards are posted well in advance of the sale stating that: "Hargrave's Farm at Four Corners is selling out household goods and farm implements on Thursday, June 18th, starting at 10 o'clock." This sale may yield some nice sturdy farm furniture, or it may have Victorian whatnots and haircloth upholstered furniture. It may have some really good Early American pine or maple furniture, or some family antiques. The auction may be far enough out in the country so that only the local people know about it, but it is likely that there will be a half dozen "scouts" from antique shops, who will buy up the best pieces at half the price they know they can charge for them when they take them to the city for resale.

A country auction may be held in some lovely old house, and the furniture will be beautiful. You have seen the sign of the auction, you have even seen it advertised in the local and the not-so-local newspapers. Little do you know that the house has been rented for the occasion, and the furniture brought in from the attics of a furniture dealer. You soon discover that Helen Hokinson dowagers are buying everything in sight at ridiculous prices.

So analyze the situation carefully. You may be able to find bargains at a country auction. You are far more apt to have only an enjoyable day watching the people and eating the good lunch sold by the Ladies Aid of the First Baptist Church.

Every large city has several auction galleries. These specialize in selling off "estates." When a household is broken up, and the heirs wish cash rather than a chest of drawers, all the furniture is consigned to the gallery. The honest galleries will not permit a minimum price to be placed on each piece. Nor will they permit a representative of the lawyer, or of the family, to come in and bid up the pieces to a high price. Therefore these sales are good spots in which to buy old family treasures at low prices.

Sometimes dealers will go out of business. When their things are sold at the same auction galleries, they may have a friend trying to keep the prices up for them at the risk of buying them in for his business. These are less likely to produce bargains, as the professionals aim to keep the good furniture in their hands for larger sales profit.

The best buys are at storage auctions. Here is auctioned furniture that has been stored too long without payment of storage charges. The family has lost interest in their goods and chattels or perhaps have moved to a distant city. Many times the furniture is good, but needs recovering. The tables may need refinishing, the silver may require polishing, but there are many really good buys to be had. Because all of the furniture has been carefully fumigated in the reputable large warehouses, there is no risk entailed.

Furniture that is out of style often sells at low prices, while decorator periods go for high prices. One lady waited all morning for a small Victorian armchair to be put up for sale. The upholstery of cherry satin was tattered, and the whole chair would need a costly upholstery job. Yet, when the chair was sold, the price jumped to $57, because there were dealers present who recognized they could resell it at a profit.

At the same sale a sturdy, well-upholstered love seat sold for $15, and a solid mahogany dining table sold for $1. Out-of-door furniture sold for a fraction of its cost because it was a winter sale, and most of the customers were not thinking that far ahead. The careful planner may, therefore, find real bargains at auctions, especially if consideration is given to refinishing and slipcovering.

There are some "storage warehouses" that buy up old furniture, and sell it at flat prices. Sometimes this furniture is actually furniture that has been previously sold as new, then used only for a short time. The buyers have not kept up their payments, and the furniture company has taken it back for resale. In actual cases where this has happened, good values may be had. Again it is wise to be sure of the honesty of the dealer, and the quality of his claims.

There are "secondhand furniture" stores in small and large cities, even in small towns. In many cases these have good values. If you are a good judge, or trust the claims of the company, many bargains may be had in such shops. Sometimes these firms buy furniture that requires refinishing. They fix it up, adding any pieces of veneer or any molding that is necessary and then sell it. Their mark-up is certainly justified for the time and trouble it saves you.

Some shops make a feature of bleaching furniture. The new smartness that the blonde finish gives to even an old washstand, or an old commode, makes it sell for several times its original cost. Bleaching is such a messy and difficult process that it is often worth your while to pay the charge. Or you can window-shop these places for ideas of what to do with old, unattractive pieces that you can find in a relative's attic, or in a small out-of-the-way shop. If you find a shop run by a man who understands your problem, who knows the sort of thing you are after, it is wise to talk to him quite frankly. He will then be able to find things for you that you might not have the time to ferret out yourself. When he understands your budget, too, he will keep the purchases within your price range, perhaps advising you on restoration methods if you have time to do it yourself.

SHOPPING GUIDE

When buying lifetime investments in furniture it is wise to depend on brand names just as thoroughly as you do when buying food or soap. These manufacturers who advertise widely are producing things of which they are proud. They will stand back of the merchandise if anything happens to go wrong with it, or if a flaw develops where none was expected. These products are apt to be better designed and have a backing of better research in the materials used. You can count on getting the most for your money. Study the decoration magazines and learn who are the recognized manufacturers of furniture, rugs, fabrics, china and glassware before you go shopping. Then ask for those brands by name, and be sure you get them, if you can.

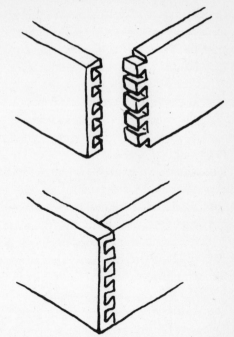

"Half blind" dovetail—very strong—should be at back and front of drawers

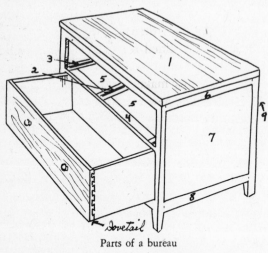

Parts of a bureau

1 Top panel	6 Top frame
2 Center guide	7 Side panel
3 Carry drawers	8 Bottom frame
4 Bearer for drawers	9 Plywood back for dust
5 Dust panel	protection

Chests of Drawers

If the wood used has not been properly seasoned, or if the chest has not been properly constructed it will warp, split and spread.

The drawers will stick and not slide smoothly and easily. Drawers of the new plywood chests have a molded interior construction that eliminates cracks to catch fine lingerie. Also they have a grooved side construction, which insures the drawer sliding in and out smoothly. Some drawers slide on a ball bearing construction, which is excellent, but expensive.

All drawers should have dovetailed joints, at the corners. (See the detail drawing.) Each section should be joined to the other with either a mortise joint or a dowel joint. (See detail drawing.) There should be dust panels between the drawers and the back of the chest should be finished with a plywood panel. If the chest is to stand out into the room, this back panel must be of the same wood and finish as the front and top.

Cheaper furniture will have the lock joint; still cheaper, the nailed joint; and cheapest of all the butt joint, with nails. (See diagram sketches.)

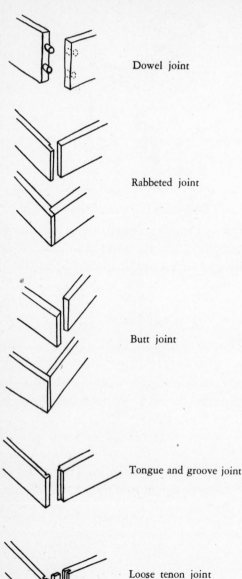

Dowel joint

Rabbeted joint

Butt joint

Tongue and groove joint

Loose tenon joint

Dado joint method of fitting shelves in cabinet walls

Veneer

Veneer is not to be avoided, for in both antique and modern furniture many fine woods are available in veneer, which could never be obtained in solid wood. As has been explained before, modern methods of laminating plywoods make veneer more satisfactory today than ever before.

Such woods as walnut, mahogany, curly maple and birch are found in fine veneers on chests of drawers—applied to gumwood foundation. Many fine antique chests show matched veneers forming attractive patterns. The thin slices of wood have been pieced together to form an evenly balanced design. This matched veneer appears on the doors of cabinets, on the fronts of desks, and on fine chests of drawers or commodes.

Antique French furniture uses wood veneers in a variety of contrast, some in green and soft colors for inlay against a soft-colored walnut veneer background. Many of these attractive pieces are sufficiently "out of style," so that they can be purchased reasonably. They are beautiful works of art, and a good investment. The satinwood desks or cabinets of this period are a pale honey color, and look very charming against a dark wall.

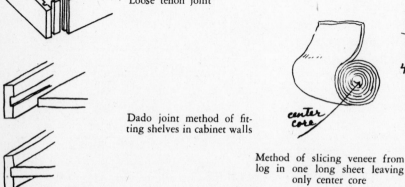

center core

Method of slicing veneer from log in one long sheet leaving only center core

Cutting veneer
Various types of cuts
1 Rotary
2 Half round rotary
3 Sliced
4 Quartered

Bleached Woods

Veneered furniture does not take kindly to bleaching as a rule. *Do not try it yourself on any but solid woods.* Some of the bleached mahogany pieces have had the veneer bleached before being applied, or have been handled by an expert.

Oak is a strong, coarse-textured wood and thus takes kindly to bleaching, as does pine or maple. Bleached finishes are often called "pickled finishes," because they are derived from the vinegar treatment originally used to remove the ground coat on English furniture which had been gilded or painted. Most present-day bleaches are chemical and raise the grain of the wood in an interesting effect.

Some of the modern chemical bleached finishes are not as permanent as others. If a transparent surface finish has been added, this is more likely to prevent change in color than if the bleached wood is left exposed.

These transparent surface finishes are shellac, lacquer or varnish. They may be applied on a stained or a natural wood finish. The open wood pores may be slightly colored with a thin glazing of oil paint that forms a light protective film.

Opaque Finishes

Opaque finishes of lacquer, oil paints, colored enamels and varnishes cover the wood, and are usually used on furniture of pine, or gumwood. Some of these finishes are permanent and are highly resistant to scarring, stain or burns.

Tables

The best way to test a table is to see how steady it is by trying to rock it back and forth. If the legs are improperly braced it will sway. Check to be sure that they have dowel or

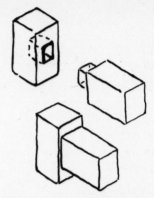

Mortise and tenon construction

mortise and tenon construction in the apron of the table. (See diagram.) See that there is corner support for the legs. (See diagram.)

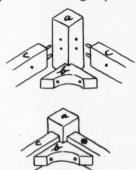

Table corner reinforcement or chair "post" joined to chair "rails"

a Section of chair leg   b Corner block to support assembly
c Chair rails at side of seat

If the table has a supported leaf, see that the hardware is strong and well constructed. Be sure the draw-table mechanism slides smoothly and easily. Check to see that table drawers have corner dowels and that they slide easily.

If the table is to be used for dining, be sure the top has been treated with a heat resistant finish, so it will not mar if a hot dish is placed on it without a pad. If this is not certain, have it treated with an extra coat of spar varnish at home before it is used.

Some of the fabric-like finishes of plastic are attractive for table tops for dinettes. The plastic prevents them from becoming scratched or scarred.

Chairs

The traditional type side chair usually has cross stretchers between the legs to help strengthen them. These are set into the legs firmly with dowels. The seat frame is fitted together with dowel construction, or with mortise and tenon, and there is a corner reinforcement in each corner under the seat pad or upholstery. (See diagram.)

Upholstered armchairs have much the same construction. The back is fitted firmly into the back upright, and into the sides of the seat. Usually the back upright of armchairs is cut in one piece with the back leg. The center splat fits into a slot at the back of the seat and the top rail of the chair back.

Many of the modern chairs made of laminated wood have strong construction of a simplified nature. Some of the other wartime developments made use of insufficiently seasoned wood, and have already started to fall to pieces. It should not be forgotten that unseasoned wood is affected by humidity. Again, make sure the manufacturer will stand back of a new product.

In upholstered chairs or couches a large part of the material is hidden from view. The frame that shows may be of maple, walnut, mahogany, oak, or gum in a traditional type chair, or of oak, birch or natural maple in a modern chair. In most cases the hidden frame is of ash. The seat of the chair has cross-laced webbing of strong jute or linen firmly tacked to the under side of the seat frame. Resting on this are the spiral springs, placed closely together so when the hand rests on the chair no individual one is evident. These are tied in place with strong cord, working across the tops of each spring, to hold it firmly in place in relation to all the others. The best method of tying is from front to back, side to side, and on both diagonals. This means the chair is tied four

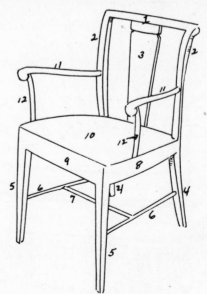

Parts of a chair

1 Top rail	6 Side stretchers
2 Back post	7 Cross stretcher
3 Center splat (chair may have several splats)	8 Side panel
	9 Front panel (or apron)
4 Back legs	10 Pad seat
5 Front legs	11 Arms
12 Arm stump	

ways. Because of high labor costs, few upholstered chairs are now tied more than twice, from front to back, and across from side to side. (See sketch.)

After the cords are firmly tied and tacked to the frame, a layer of burlap is placed on them, stretched taut, but not so tight that it

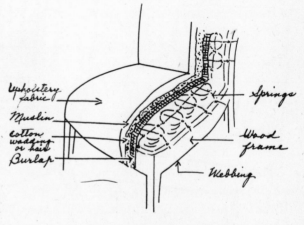

Anatomy of an upholstered chair

Tufted upholstered chair

Shaped cushion wing chair

Lawson chair with straight cushion back

Club chair

Lawson chair

Barrel chair

Fanback (or scoopback) chair

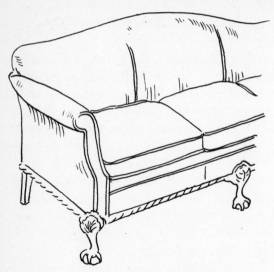

Curved back Georgian sofa—wood frame and
legs carved

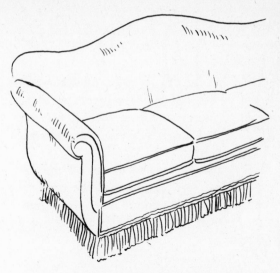

Regency type sofa—curved back and outcurved arms

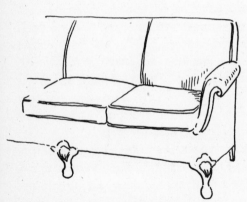

Straight top Georgian sofa—curved legs

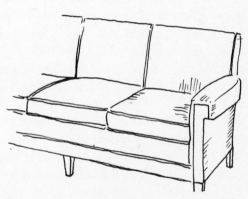

Modern club sofa—simplified squared arms, straight
tapered legs

Federal sofa

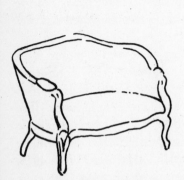

French sofa—Louis XV

Duncan Phyfe sofa

pushes down the springs, and it is tacked in place on the frame. It is then layered with hair, cotton wadding and muslin before the upholstery is added.

Cheap furniture is apt to have stuffing that attracts moths and bugs—so avoid it, using instead furniture with hair stuffing. Moss is used as a satisfactory substitute for hair, but not in the best pieces.

Every chair is required to carry a tag underneath the seat stating that the material used in the upholstering is new, not second-hand. Request this tag if you are buying a new chair.

Beds, Mattresses and Springs

Whether you plan on a separate headboard screwed to the wall, or a wooden bedstead, you will want a firm and steady frame to hold the spring and mattress. The headboard and footboard usually have side splats that fit firmly in place and attach with strong bolted construction. Some bedsteads are made with cross splats as well—for extra strength. This is especially necessary if one member of the family is a heavyweight. If your husband is extra tall, it will pay to order special sleep equipment to fit. Some stores stock longer beds, others have them made to order.

Some people prefer a "hard" bed, some a "soft" bed for sleeping. There are even manufacturers who will provide double bed mattresses that supply one type at one side of the mattress, with the other type of sleeping on the other side. Most people prefer an innerspring mattress. These are made with many coil springs, each contained in a separate cotton pocket, held together by clips or springs. The shapes of these coils vary according to the type made by the manufacturer. So also do the number of layers of hair or cotton-felt padding used to top the coils. Most stores have a small cross-section display unit, which they will gladly show you, so that you may understand the inside construction before you buy.

Other innerspring mattresses have open springs held together by small cross springs, and covered by layer cotton inside the mattress ticking. All these mattresses should have a deep stitched tuck at the edges, with airhole ventilations at the sides. For easier turning it helps if there are tab loops.

The new foam rubber or latex mattresses are excellent. They are very soft and springy because of the millions of air bubbles in the construction. These are recommended for their comfort and durability.

Hair mattresses, made of good quality curled horsehair, are expensive, but are preferred by some people. They flatten out with use, and have to be remade from time to time, sometimes with the addition of extra hair. Blown-in cotton felt and layer cotton mattresses are less expensive, but far less comfortable. The best grades are almost as expensive as innerspring mattresses and consist of blown cotton centers, with felted cotton layers surrounding them.

Kapok mattresses are soft, light and easy to handle. They are moisture and vermin proof, but have a tendency to bunch and form lumps as the material pulverizes. Used for small cushions, kapok has a longer life if frequently exposed to sun and air, or if separated into stitched compartments that hold it firm. It should not be recommended for any but temporary use.

Most mattresses are covered either with ticking or with damask. The former is stronger than the latter, particularly if it is a good grade, but many people prefer the more attractive designs and colors available in the damask. The perpendicular sides of the mattress are usually reinforced for extra strength with quilting or stitching. The edge ridge or roll gives a neat, well-defined edge and appears on better mattresses. Formerly the tuftings were in the form of cotton puffs, or buttons; now they are made of plastic, rubber or metal in such a way as to be firm, but not obtrusive.

Springs

Open coil springs are usually sold with the solid mattresses. They are firm, well supported by a strong metal frame, and springs that hold them in place. Because they are open, they are easy to keep clean.

Box springs consist of spiral springs attached to a frame or foundation, usually of wood, cushioned with a layer of upholstery and covered with ticking or damask to match the mattress. They are usually sold with innerspring mattresses. The "Hollywood bed" consists of a box spring on six legs, with matching innerspring mattress. This is the type that is used with the separate headboard attached to the wall. If preferred such a unit may be purchased and headboards chosen from a variety of styles to be mounted directly on the bed.

Bed Pillows

The most satisfactory bed pillows are those filled with down or the feathers of water fowl. These have more resiliency than the feathers of land birds. Sometimes the content tag that comes attached to all pillows will tell that they have half down and half of some other type of feathers. Some pillows are covered with special covering that prevents the odor of the feathers from bothering those who suffer from allergies. A good pillow may be judged by its bulk in comparison to its weight. A well filled pillow of the standard 21″ by 27″ size should weigh about a pound and a half. Press down in the center of the pillow with the hand. The more promptly the pillow springs back into place when you remove your hand, the better the feathers used and the longer the pillow will hold its shape.

For buying of rugs see information in Chapter VI.

For buying hints for glassware, silver, china or lamps see Chapter IX.

For buying fine fabrics see Chapter VIII.

IV

PREPARING THE ROOMS

SOME HOMES are completely finished inside before you move in, with the painting and wallpapering all complete. In other cases that is left to be done later. If the walls have been plastered it takes some time for them to dry thoroughly. Any painting that would be done or any wallpaper that would be pasted in place would be doomed to spot or peel. It is wise therefore to be very, very patient before attempting finished decoration on plaster walls.

If the walls are surfaced with any of the plaster boards or sheet compositions, these are fused together with a quick drying seam covering composition. These may be painted at once. Before painting, the seams of the boards should be rubbed absolutely flat with fine sandpaper, and then painted with a sizing. This prevents the color drying with a duller sheen in these joinings than on the flat board.

When the wall paint is purchased you will do well to tell the salesman what kind of walls you plan to paint. He will then tell you whether you need to buy sizing for a surface coat. This varies somewhat with the type of the finish paint you plan to use. Many of the new paints have a resinous or plastic base. These dry rapidly, and in most cases require only one coat to cover the plaster, wallboard or old paint or wallpaper. These may be put on with a brush or with a roller supplied for the purpose.

The old kalsomine or water paints are easy to apply, and are made of dry powder mixed with water. This is easy to use, and is a great favorite where the color scheme is to have frequent changes. It is often used for ceilings, especially when there is to be wallpaper on the walls. It is usually applied before the paper. Then you do not have to worry quite so much about spatters.

Oil color is what the term implies; the paint is mixed with linseed oil base. There has been an oil shortage lately, and most of the oil paint to be had is of rather inferior quality.

The colors in any of these paints are shown on color cards distributed by the paint company. Since the large demand is for light shades or for white, the large cans, gallons or quarts, come in white, oyster, gray, buff, peach, pale yellow and sky blue. These colors are used as the base colors when more exciting colors are to be mixed. The strong pigments come in pound cans, and are concentrated in strength. Or the oil colors come in concentrated color, packaged in tubes. The strong powdered colors may be purchased in dry form to be added to kalsomine. No matter what kind of paint you are using, the following color chart will help you in mixing it, and will tell you what colors you will need to obtain the desired fashionable color.

COLOR-MIXING CHART

Since the trade names of ready-mixed paint colors vary according to the ideas of different manufacturers, it is impossible to give color mixing directions based on such trade names. For instance, one manufacturer shows a lovely soft blue-green, with directions to make it by mixing equal parts of aquamarine and almond green. Another color is made by mixing equal parts of Wedgewood green and Jersey cream. Inasmuch as these trade names are not found on other paints, it is impossible to use them in directions. You will have to translate the tint names into the various trade names when ordering paints.

To mix colors add some of the opposite color to soften or gray the tone. Add some white or light tint to lighten the color.

To obtain interesting shades of color mix with some of the adjoining colors as found on the color circle. For instance, more interesting blue shades may be made by the addition of green or of purple. If both green and purple are added to the blue, they will neutralize each other, returning the color to the clear blue, but usually softer in tone than if the true "pigment" blue is taken from the can.

The following mixtures of colors suggest the paint to be included to form a desired color. In many cases the proportion is not stated, for the shade desired will vary according to the person mixing the color. Experiment until the right result is obtained. Beware of mixing too many colors together, for the result may be muddy.

RED

American Beauty—White, Alizerin Crimson (2 to 1)
Baby Pink—White, American Vermilion
Barberry Red—White, American Vermilion, Raw Sienna
Burgundy—Cobalt Blue, Indian Red, White
Cardinal—White, Permanent Red Deep
Cerise or Cherry—White, Alizerin Crimson
Claret—White, Permanent Red, deep
Crimson—Alizerin Crimson pigment or ready-mixed paint
Garnet—Permanent Red Deep, Burnt Sienna
Grape—White, Cobalt Blue, Lamp Black, touch of Crimson

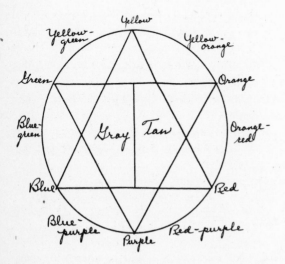

Color circle

Harvard Crimson—Permanent Red Deep, Permanent Red, light

Laurel Pink—White, Permanent Red, light

Maroon—White, Indian Red (2 to 1)

Old Rose—White, Indian Red, Venetian Red

Pink—Tint of Red, White with and Red pigments added to give desired shade

Raspberry—White, Permanent Red, deep, touch of Ultramarine Blue

Ruby Red—Alizerin Crimson, White, touch of Ultramarine Blue

Scarlet—Ready mixed, or American Vermilion or Cadmium Red, light

Strawberry—Permanent Red, deep, White

ORANGE

Apricot—White, Chrome Yellow, Raw Sienna

Brick Red—White, Yellow Ochre, Venetian Red, touch of Burnt Umber

Burnt Orange—Chrome Yellow, deep, with White, Raw Sienna, and Burnt Sienna (4, 3, 1)

Carnelian—White, Raw Sienna, Venetian Red (8 to 4 to 1)

Carrot—White, Chrome Yellow, Vermilion

Copper—White, Yellow Ochre, Venetian Red (16, 8, 1)

Coral—White, American Vermilion, Chrome Yellow, Raw Sienna

Flame—White with Cadmium Orange

Flesh—Many variations possible, tints of red-orange and orange. Most popular mixture: White, Raw Sienna, Burnt Sienna, Burnt Umber

Geranium — White, American Vermilion, Chrome Yellow, deep

Henna—White, Raw Sienna, small amount Venetian Red

Honeydew—White, Chrome Yellow, deep, Chrome Yellow, medium

Lacquer—Yellow Ochre, American Vermilion, Venetian Red

Paprika—Yellow Ochre, Venetian Red, Vermilion

Peach—White, with Chrome Yellow and Venetian Red

Pimento—White, American Vermilion, Chrome Yellow

Pompeian Red—White, Venetian Red, American Vermilion

Poppy—White, Chrome Yellow, American Vermilion

Rust—White, with Raw Sienna and Burnt Sienna

Salmon—White with Yellow Ochre and Venetian Red

Tangerine—White, Chrome Yellow and American Vermilion

Terra Cotta—White with Burnt Sienna and Raw Sienna

Tomato—White with Cadmium Orange and Vermilion

Vermilion—Pigment or ready-mixed color

YELLOW

Amber—White with Chrome Yellow, medium and Burnt Sienna

Banana—White with Chrome Yellow and Burnt Umber

Brass—White with Chrome Yellow, medium, Yellow Ochre, Raw Umber

Buttercup—White with Chrome Yellow, light

Canary—White, Chrome Yellow, Yellow Ochre and touch of Cobalt Blue

Chamois—White, Chrome Yellow, medium, Burnt Umber

Champagne—White, Yellow Ochre, Burnt Umber, Lamp Black

Chartreuse—White, Cadmium Lemon, touch of Cobalt Blue

Citron — White, Cadmium Yellow, Burnt Sienna

Colonial Yellow—Ready-mixed paint color or White, Chrome Yellow, medium and Raw Umber

Daffodil—White, Chrome Yellow

Empire Yellow—White, Cadmium Yellow

Gold—Equal amounts White and Yellow Ochre, small amounts Raw Sienna, and Cobalt Blue

Goldenrod—White, Chrome Yellow, medium, Raw Umber

Honey—White, Chrome Yellow, medium, Raw Umber and Raw Sienna

Lemon—White with Cadmium Yellow

Maize—White, Chrome Yellow, with touch of Cobalt Blue

Mustard—White, Yellow Ochre, Cobalt Blue to gray it

Old Gold—Yellow Ochre, White (2 to 1) grayed with Cobalt Blue

Primrose—White, Chrome Yellow

GREEN

Apple Green—White, Chrome Green and Raw Sienna

Aquamarine—White, Cobalt Blue and Yellow Ochre (2 to 1)

Bottle Green—Chrome Green, deep, lightened with Chrome Green, light or grayed with Venetian Red

Boxwood Green—Cobalt Blue with Yellow Ochre

Emerald — Ready-mixed paint or White, Chrome Green, medium, with Chrome Green, light

Grass Green—White, Chrome Green, light, Raw Umber

Hunter Green — Chrome Green, medium, touched with White

Jade—White with Cadmium Yellow and Cobalt Blue or White with Chrome Green, medium

Kelly Green—White with Chrome Green, light and Chrome Green, medium

Laurel—Chrome Green and Raw Sienna

Lettuce — White, Cadmium Yellow, Cobalt Blue, with touch of Raw Umber

Lime—White, Chrome Green, Raw Sienna

Moss—Chrome Green, Burnt Sienna, touched with White

Nile—White, Cobalt Blue, Cadmium Yellow, Burnt Umber

Olive—White, Cobalt Blue, Cadmium Yellow, Burnt Umber or White Chrome Green and Raw Sienna

Pea Green—White with equal parts of Cadmium Yellow and Cobalt Blue grayed with Burnt Umber

Pistache or Pistachio—White with Chrome Green or White with Cadmium Yellow and Cobalt Blue

Reseda—White, Chrome Green, Raw Umber

Sage—White, Yellow Ochre, and Ultramarine Blue

Spruce Green or Spruce Blue—White with Ultramarine Blue and Yellow Ochre

BLUE

Baby Blue—White with Ultramarine Blue

Bluebird—White, Ultramarine Blue, Prussian Blue, Raw Umber

Brittany Blue—White, Prussian Blue, touch of Lamp Black

Cadet Blue—White, Lamp Black, Ultramarine Blue (Make *French Blue* by adding slightly more blue)

Copenhagen Blue—White, Ultramarine Blue and Lamp Black

Cornflower Blue—White, Ultramarine Blue, touch of Alizerin Crimson

Delft Blue—White, Prussian Blue, American Vermilion touch to gray it.

Delphineum—White, Prussian Blue, grayed with Burnt Umber

Forget-Me-Not—White, Cobalt Blue, touch of Burnt Umber

Midnight Blue—Ultramarine Blue, White and Black (2, 1, 1)

Old Blue—White, Cobalt Blue, Yellow Ochre, grayed with Burnt Umber

Peacock — White, Prussian Blue, Chrome Green, deep

Plum—Ultramarine Blue, White, Black (4, 3, 1)

Powder—White, Cobalt Blue grayed with Yellow Ochre

Robin's Egg—White, Chrome, Green, touch of Prussian Blue

Royal Blue—Ultramarine, White, touch of Alizerin Crimson

Sapphire—White, Ultramarine Blue, Alizerin Crimson

Sky Blue—White and Cobalt Blue

Turquoise—White, Chrome Green, medium, and Prussian Blue

Wedgewood Blue—White, Ultramarine Blue, Lamp Black, touch of Alizerin Crimson

Yale Blue—Ultramarine Blue with touch of White and Black

PURPLE

Amethyst—White, Crimson, Cerulean Blue (8 to 1)

Egg Plant—Crimson, White, Black and Ultramarine Blue (3, 1, 1, 1)

Heliotrope — White, Cobalt Blue, Alizerin Crimson

Lavender—White, Cobalt Blue, Alizerin Crimson

Lilac—White, Crimson, Ultramarine, touch of Black

Magenta—Cobalt Violet, White and Crimson

Mulberry—Cobalt Blue and Indian Red (10 to 1)

Orchid—White with equal parts of Crimson and Ultramarine Blue

Royal Purple — Cobalt Violet, with equal amounts of White and Ultramarine Blue added

Wistaria—White with Ultramarine Blue and Crimson (2 to 1)

GRAY

Dove Gray—White, with Raw Umber and Ivory Black (2 to 1)

Flint Gray—White with Raw Umber, Burnt Umber, Ivory Black (2, 1, 1)

French Gray—White with equal amounts Ultramarine Blue, Yellow Ochre, and Raw Umber

Gunmetal—White, half as much Ivory Black, some Burnt Umber

Pearl—White, Raw Umber, touch of Cobalt Blue

Slate—White, Lamp Black, Raw Umber, touch of Venetian Red

Steel—White, Ivory Black, Raw Umber

Taupe—White, Ivory Black, Burnt Umber

BROWN

Beaver—White, Burnt Umber, Raw Umber (8, 1, 1)

Beige (*also called Ecru*)—White, Yellow Ochre, touch of Raw Umber

Bronze—Yellow Ochre, White, Burnt Umber, Cobalt Blue

Buff—White, Yellow Ochre, Raw Sienna

Café au Lait—White, Yellow Ochre, Burnt Umber

Cedar—White, Venetian Red, Raw Umber

Chestnut—White, Burnt Sienna, Burnt Umber, touch of Indian Red

Chocolate—White with Burnt Umber, Burnt Sienna in equal parts

Cinnamon—White with Yellow Ochre, Raw Sienna and Burnt Umber

Coffee—White with equal parts of Raw Sienna, Burnt Sienna, Raw Umber and Burnt Umber

Fawn—White, Burnt Umber, Burnt Sienna, touch of Raw Umber

Mahogany—White, Burnt Umber, Burnt Sienna (For wood stain omit White)

Maple—White, Raw Sienna, Raw Umber (For wood stain omit White)

Sand—White, Burnt Umber, Burnt Sienna, Raw Umber

Sherry—Chrome Yellow, medium and deep, Raw Sienna (also Topaz)

Tobacco—Raw Sienna, White and Burnt Umber

Walnut—White, Yellow Ochre (3, 2), touch of Raw Umber (Stain: Use Raw Sienna, Raw Umber with Burnt Umber)

TINTS

Cream and Ivory come ready mixed or may be mixed as follows:

Cream—White with small amount of Yellow Ochre and Raw Sienna

Ivory—White with Chrome Yellow, medium and Burnt Umber

Putty—White, Yellow Ochre, Raw Umber

Straw—White, Chrome Yellow, Burnt Umber

Sulphur—White, Chrome Yellow, light, grayed with Cobalt Blue

TO MIX THE PAINT

You will find a large pail such as is used for floor mopping a handy mixing bucket when preparing wall paint. Place this pail on newspapers, spread so the paint won't splash on the floor. Add strong color as desired to the gallon can of paint used for the base. (This is either white or a pastel tint as mentioned in column one of the mixing chart.) Stir well with a long stick that goes way to the bottom of the pail. Since the strong color being added is heavier than the base color, it has a great tendency to sink to the bottom of the can. As you stir, the wooden stick will take on the color of the mix. Pick it up and study it from time to time. When you think it is the right color, paint a sample stick the size of a shingle and place it in the sun to dry.

When it is thoroughly dry, test to see whether it is the color desired by holding it up against the wall *in all parts of the room.* This is necessary because the same color will appear several shades lighter on the wall opposite the windows, and will seem grayer on the wall that has the windows. Many people prefer to take this fact into consideration, and mix the first color for the window wall. Then gray it slightly for the two side walls of the room, and still more for the wall across from the light. This makes the walls all seem to be of the same tone.

Study this color in the daylight. Study again by the light of the lamps in the evening.

If you still feel that it is right, start the final mixing.

Cover the large pail with cheesecloth firmly bound across the top of the pail. Pour the paint into the pail. Move the cheesecloth onto the gallon container, and then pour back from the pail. Repeat several times until you are sure that the whole is thoroughly mixed.

Be sure to mix enough paint to cover all the walls. It is harder to match when mixing a second time than it is to have a little left over. The left-over paint may be used for woodwork, either as it is or changed to a deeper or lighter tone; or it may be poured into a covered jar and preserved for "touch-up" jobs of the future.

TO PAINT THE WALLS

To paint the walls start in a corner. Use a stepladder to paint the top under the picture moulding. If the picture moulding is to be the same color as the wall, paint it at the same time. To prevent the paint splashing on the ceiling use a cardboard shield. Hold this in the left hand as you paint with the right. If the cardboard gets soiled along the edge so there is danger of it smearing the clean ceiling, make a fresh one.

After you have painted the upper section of the wall, using even up and down strokes, covering all the surface as far as you can comfortably reach, move the ladder out of

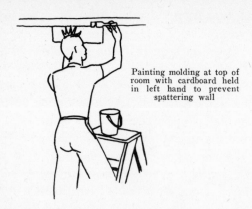

Painting molding at top of
room with cardboard held
in left hand to prevent
spattering wall

Have cardboard on floor and on wall when painting baseboard

the way, and paint the section directly below. Then paint the next convenient section, starting at the top again, finishing that and then doing the lower section. Make sure the strokes overlap; that no part of the underwall color shows between brush strokes. Do not go away and leave the job in the middle of the wall. Plan to complete the whole job at one time if possible, and choose a good day. Keep the windows open and the paint will dry faster.

Use as large a brush as you can conveniently handle, for the work will go faster that way; but if you choose too heavy a brush there will be unnecessary drag on your forearm muscles. Do not buy cheap brushes. The hairs fall out and are a nuisance. While good brushes may seem expensive, you can use them over and over again if you take care to remove all the paint from them after each job. Use turpentine to clean brushes that have been used for oil paint. Use clean water

to wash out brushes that have been used for water-color paint, or for plastic or resin base paints. All brushes benefit by a bath in soap suds after the first cleaning. The soap should be thoroughly rinsed out and the brushes dried before being wrapped in newspaper. To keep moths out add a few camphor crystals.

Use the cardboard shield to protect the woodwork around the doors and windows or the baseboard. Heavy paint spatters dry in blobs, which look bad showing through the smooth top coat added later. Use a clean rag to wipe off any splashes, and keep the floor protected with newspapers.

If moulding of contrasting color is to be put up to cover any joinings of wallboard, a good lazy-man's way is to paint it the right color first, then tack it in place with tiny nails and cover the nail holes with paint. If they do not dry smoothly so the nail is hidden, then the whole strip must be painted.

Sometimes wallpaper mouldings or narrow strips of wallpaper designs are pasted along these wallboard joinings. Consider carefully whether it will add to the decorative effect of the room before doing any of these things. The modern idea of wall decoration is *the simpler, the better.*

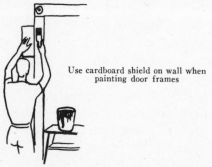

Use cardboard shield on wall when
painting door frames

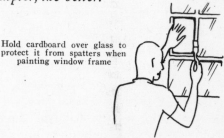

Hold cardboard over glass to
protect it from spatters when
painting window frame

HANGING WALLPAPER

Grandmother used to repaper her rooms every spring as a matter of course. She thought nothing of sending away to the mail-order house for enough new paper to cover the room, and would do it herself in one day. We are more out of practice perhaps, but should be able to do even a better job than grandma, because there have been so many wonderful new developments. Some of the wallpaper comes ready-pasted. It has a prepared back that only has to be soaked in water before the paper can be smoothed in place.

All of the papers are treated to resist fading and spotting, and can be wiped clean with a damp cloth. At the worst a really greasy spot may be removed with cleaning fluid or French chalk.

The new wallpapers are so attractive in design and color, and there is such a variety of them that it is smart to learn how to put them up yourself. Then you can redecorate your rooms whenever the spirit moves you, rather than being forced to wait until you can find a paperhanger.

When purchasing the paper give the dimensions of the room to the salesman. He will help you figure how many rolls of paper you will require. Most paper comes in double rolls, which are sixteen yards long. The single roll is eight yards long. Some firms permit the purchase of single rolls to complete the correct amount to cover the room. The width of the wallpaper is 18″. While a single roll would actually cover 36 square feet, because of the amount of waste necessary in matching the usual pattern it is wise to figure on the paper covering only 30 square feet.

To figure the correct amount, make a sketch of the walls to be covered. Measure the length of each wall and mark it down. Then measure the height of the area to be covered. Sometimes the wallpaper is only carried up 30″ from the floor to form a colorful dado. Sometimes it covers the upper part of the wall above dado panelling. Draw in the doors and windows. Mark their sizes, for no paper will be required for these areas, or for the fireplace opening. One roll of paper is saved by every door and window, or by

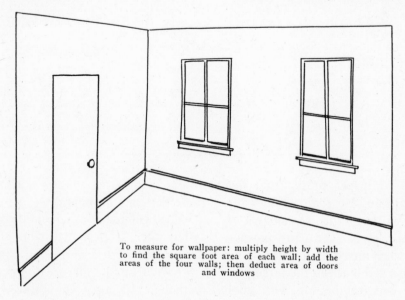

To measure for wallpaper: multiply height by width to find the square foot area of each wall; add the areas of the four walls; then deduct area of doors and windows

every two windows. Figure up the complete square footage of the wall area, deduct the door and window areas. Then divide the amount left by 60 feet, and you will have the number of double rolls required for the wall area to be papered.

CHART TO HELP IN ESTIMATING THE NUMBER OF SINGLE ROLLS OF WALLPAPER REQUIRED

SIZE OF ROOM (in feet)	SINGLE ROLLS ON WALL			BORDER BY THE YARD	SINGLE ROLLS FOR CEILING COVERAGE
	Ceiling Height				
	8 ft.	9 ft.	10 ft.		
4 by 8	6	7	8	9	2
4 by 12	8	9	10	12	2
6 by 12	9	10	11	13	3
8 by 14	11	12	14	16	4
10 by 16	13	15	16	19	6
12 by 16	14	15	16	20	7
12 by 18	15	17	19	22	8
14 by 22	18	20	22	26	10
15 by 16	15	17	19	23	8
15 by 18	16	18	20	24	9
15 by 23	19	21	23	28	11
16 by 18	17	17	21	25	10
16 by 22	19	21	23	28	11
17 by 25	21	23	26	31	13
17 by 35	26	29	32	37	18
18 by 25	21	24	27	31	14
20 by 26	23	28	28	33	17
20 by 34	27	30	33	39	21

Buy a large wallpaper brush from the paint supply store, and buy some wheat wallpaper paste. Two bags will be enough to cover a large size room. The paste powder seems to swell when mixed with water, so be careful not to put too much in the large pail to start with. Mix thoroughly with cool water, using an egg beater if necessary to be sure there are no lumps.

You will need a sharp knife and a metal edge ruler, a clean dry cloth and a clean damp cloth. For a professional job it is well to have a small roller to iron out the seams although this last is not absolutely necessary.

Have a large work table on which to place the paper while smearing the paste on the back. Professionals use large boards placed on trestles.

You can use the floor if you cover it with clean papers first, although it will be hard on your aching back. It is wise to have a team of two work at this job. Then you can cut and measure the panel strips, and smear them well with paste while Hubby smooths them into their proper place. It goes far more quickly this way. In any case you will both find that you will have to wash your hands between each strip. The fewer pasty finger marks left on the paper to be wiped off, the better the job.

For the first strip, start in one corner. Choose the longest wall, with the fewest doors and windows to interrupt the space. Cut off the selvage of the paper, the left hand one, turn face side down on the table, or floor, and smear well with the paste. Rub absolutely smooth, so there are no lumps. Fold the lower third over on the panel, with paste sides together. Do not crease the fold edge. This is only to facilitate handling, because a full length strip, when wet with paste, is rather awkward. Do not worry if the paper seems wilted and flabby. It should. Hand it to the person on the ladder who will place it evenly along the top edge, under the picture moulding, or flush up against the ceiling.

Before smoothing firmly in place it should be checked to be sure it is straight, that the left hand straight cut edge is along the corner of the room. After checking the placing, gradually smooth down from the top with the dry clean cloth, taking care to rub out as many air bubbles as possible. Some of these air bubbles will flatten out and disappear as the paper dries.

After smoothing out the upper third of the strip of wallpaper, unfold the lower two-

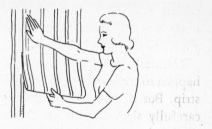

Smoothing wallpaper in place, matching edges

thirds that are turned together, and smooth down in place. Wipe off excess paste that squeezes out from underneath with the damp cloth.

Prepare the next strip by cutting off the left hand border. Measure down from the top of the first strip to find out just how far down the pattern matching mark occurs. You will see one of these on each selvage of the paper. When cutting the next strip make sure *that the matching mark is the same distance down from the top edge.* Plan on more length, rather than cutting any of the strips the exact length. It is easy to trim off any excess, but impossible to add a patch in the length of the paper without it showing.

Use a razor blade or a very sharp knife to trim off this excess. Put the metal edge ruler in place, and cut against this to be sure that you have a perfectly straight edge. Also always use the metal edge ruler when trimming off the selvage.

When you come to the short area above or below the window, or above the door, try first the short sections that have been trimmed off in matching patterns. Sometimes these will fit nicely, and will save cutting a special length of paper.

In order to fit wallpaper around wall brackets or lighting fixtures, or around radiator outlets, and electric switch plates, some special care is necessary. The switch plates may be unscrewed and removed, then replaced after the papering is complete. With lighting fixtures on the wall it is usually possible to release a screw or two, and slide the wall plate enough away from the wall so the paper may be fitted around it.

Naturally it is easier if these wall brackets happen to come right at the edge of the paper strip. But if they do not, the paper may be carefully slashed with an X and slid over the bracket. If it is impossible to fit it over a broad wall plate in this way, the neatest way is to slash in horizontally from the nearest edge of the paper. Then fit the paper around the bracket and lay the edges of the slash neatly together in such a way that the pattern matches.

Similar surgery will be necessary if radiator pipes go into the wall, and the procedure to be followed is the same. The paper is slashed from the near edge, and fitted around the pipe. It is difficult to fit the paper down in back of radiators, and as it is impossible to see through them, you will find it quite satisfactory if you carry the paper about four inches below the level of the top of the radiator.

PAINTING WOODWORK

The woodwork in a room consists of the baseboard and the picture moulding, the framing of the door, and the door itself and the framing of the window, and the sashes around the glass. This may be painted the same color as the walls but is often painted a different tone to add more emphasis to the decorative scheme. In fact, in some rooms the scheme may call for this woodwork to be painted in a distinct contrast. For instance, one very attractive room, which was painted as a background for fine old mahogany furniture, had lime green walls, with shiny navy blue for the doors and other woodwork. A small entrance hall, walled in a fine paper of dull rose and old gold, had doors and woodwork of dull black with the mouldings of the doors painted gold.

Mix the paint in the same way as described on page 39. Be sure to strain through the cheesecloth. If a shiny finish is desired, ask for gloss paint; if a dull surface, ask for flat paint. An expert can mix other liquids into flat paint to transform it into gloss, but it is better for the amateur not to do so. However, after the flat paint has been put on, if the dull finish is not satisfactory then the woodwork may be shellacked or varnished.

Use a smaller brush than used for the walls. For the baseboard a 3″ one will be right, while for the narrow window mullions you will find it easier with a 1″ brush. Cut cardboard shields to prevent the paint spattering on the already painted or papered walls. Use brush strokes that follow the direction of the moulding, and there will be less danger of splashing on the walls, or ceiling.

To paint the door another larger brush may be used for a flat flush door, such as is used in the more modern homes. If the door is divided in panels the most satisfactory manner of painting is to paint across the top horizontal, then paint the set-in panels, then the perpendicular framing, and so on moving down the door, and finishing off along the bottom. Be sure there is a layer of newspapers along the floor under the door, so the floor will not be spattered.

If the framing of the panels is to be painted a different color, follow the same directions as given on page 47 for painting a stripe. Place the masking tape in the same way, waiting until the paint is dry before removing it.

Sometimes for a small formal hallway it is very attractive to marbleize all the woodwork. This may be done by following the directions for marbleizing on page 46 after the woodwork has been first painted with a background color and allowed to dry thoroughly. The lower dado section (30″) from the floor may also be marbleized, then topped by a two-inch wide grooved moulding for a very rich effect.

PAINTING FLOORS

Unless you have purchased an old house that you are modernizing, you will usually find your floors ready-finished waiting for final waxing. Hardwood floors are most popular, and come in the majority of houses. Most people, when they build, plan on hardwood floors as a matter of course. Although linoleum floors throughout the house are growing in popularity, the original cost is higher than wood floors, and thus they are not so universal.

If a hardwood floor is in bad condition it is wise to hire a man with a floor-scraping machine to come in and scrape off the old surface before it is refinished. Then it can be varnished or shellacked and waxed to a high polish.

If you want the light wood finish use clear-varnish. Start in the corner farthest from the door, and paint along the length of the wood strips. Do one section about three feet wide all the length of the wood. Brush the varnish well into the wood across the grain first, then with the grain. Do the next strip, making sure that the varnish overlaps, and no blank spaces are left. Finish the last strip in such a way that you can step out of the room, and shut it up *until the floor is absolutely dry.*

There are quick drying varnishes now available that take only a few hours to dry in good sunshiny weather. Again we say, never paint on a rainy or damp day.

If there are spots in a floor which has had a great deal of traffic and is badly worn, they should be double varnished. If you have not gone to the trouble and expense of having the floor scraped, and are planning to do it yourself, first be sure it is thoroughly clean. Scrub it well with a brush and strong soapsuds. Rinse well and wipe with a dry cloth. After it is thoroughly dry, varnish the worn spots and let dry. Sandpaper at the edges, so there is no hard line around the edge of the patch. Then varnish the whole floor as directed above.

Bleached Floors

The vogue for "pickled pine" and other bleached woods has made these very light-colored floors popular. The old finish must first be completely removed. Then the floor may be treated in either of two ways. 1. Use a commercial bleach. Wipe this generously onto the floor, and allow to remain until it sinks in thoroughly. You may find that two treatments or more are necessary to accomplish the effect you desire. After the right tone has been reached, varnish with colorless varnish or cover with shellac. 2. Scrub the floor with a strong solution of scouring soap, generously applied. Rinse and dry. Paint with white lead paint, doing a fairly small section at a time. Do not allow it to dry, but wipe off with a rag. Remove the paint from the surface of the wood grain, but leave it in the deep pores, which were prepared for it by the strong soaping. Complete the floor in this manner. Allow to dry, and then finish with shellac.

Stained Floors

A similar effect may be gained with hardwood floors and color added to the scheme at the same time. Floors treated with the second system may have either black, green or other colors rubbed into the grain and then shellacked. Or, a color stain may be diluted and applied to the floor before it is shellacked and waxed.

Painted Floors

If the wood is not hardwood, and if it is badly worn, you may prefer to cover the surface entirely with paint. In this case, buy a special floor paint, and proceed in the same manner as directed for varnishing, starting in the corner farthest away from the exit door, and working with the wood strips until the floor is all covered.

Spattered Floors

Many early American floors had very attractive and colorful painted floors achieved by scattering several different colors of paint in spatters all over the completed ground color. This is easy to do, and looks well in informal rooms. A butter yellow floor spattered in brick red and bright blue would look well in a peasant type room with painted furniture. In a breakfast corner dabs of salmon pink and acid green, spattered on white, would be gayly modern in effect. Or for baby's room blue spattered with pink and white would be attractive. Even worn bathroom linoleum takes kindly to such treatment. Although the paint spoils the resiliency of the surface of the linoleum, it provides a fresh finish.

After the floor has been painted and the ground color is thoroughly dry, mix the other colors in shallow dishes. Take small brushes, and dip lightly into the saucers of color. Aiming at the floor, flip the brushes against a ruler, or wooden stick or the back of the wrist sharply, so the color spatters down. You may find it wise to practice on newspaper for a bit until you know how far away to hold the brush, and how hard to hit it against your wrist. You do not want blobs of paint, but rather a scattering of small color dots. Allow the first color of spatterings to dry before spattering the other color, as you

do not want them to fuse, nor do you want to walk on the floor until all is completely dry.

When working along the edges of the floor, care must be taken not to spatter the wall. Pieces of wrapping paper or newspapers may be attached to the walls as protective shields if some sort of tape is used that will not mark the walls. Scotch tape, or rubber cement tape may be used for this purpose.

MARBLEIZING

For this an unsteady hand is required rather than a steady one, and the popular tool is a feather. Mix two colors of paint in saucers. Choose two that will contrast well with the already dry background color. For instance, if the background is soft, dull green have one saucer with black paint and one

Marbleizing

with white. If there is a pinky-tan background use deep green and yellowy-white. If there is a pale blue background use deep blue, either a dark navy blue, or royal blue with emerald green. It is not necessary to hold the colors to the colors that nature chose when she made marble, although you may if you wish. In this case you would streak pale gray with deeper gray and black. Or you would streak a soft amber with white and greenish-gray.

Dip the tip of the feather into one color, and trail the tip unevenly across the wall, the floor, or the woodwork, whatever is to be marbleized. You can also marbleize furniture or lamp shades with smart effect. Do not have the trailing marks even, nor yet parallel; vary them in thickness, in direction and in depth by bearing hard on the feather at times, and at other times lifting it so it barely touches.

After the first color of feather streakings have dried thoroughly, streak with the second color. You will find it helpful to have a sample of imitation marble, or perhaps a picture of marble from the encyclopedia to help you obtain a natural effect.

This treatment is excellent for uneven surfaces that are scarred or pitted. Somehow the pattern disguises the poor condition of the ground underneath.

PAINTING STRIPES ON FLOOR OR WALLS

Sometimes the decorative scheme calls for a painted stripe around the walls, or up and down, or around the border of the floor. Most amateurs are dismayed at the idea, for they feel they never could keep a smooth edge, that their brush would wobble outside of the line.

You can make the straightest, most even edge imaginable with the help of the same tape mentioned above. This is placed along the wall, or floor, on a chalked line, and smoothed into place. Another strip is placed the desired distance away. Then the area between is painted and the tape removed after the stripe of paint has dried.

This same system is used to protect the door or wall panels when painting the mould-

ing framing them. It may even be used to paint the most decorative swirls and shapes to frame an ordinary mirror or to frame a window, if you have the patience to cut and shape the tape to the desired design drawn with chalk on the wall.

Stick scotch tape around any shape to be painted

PUTTING UP WALLBOARD OR TILE BOARD

Sometimes you will want to add some of the attractive wood-veneered plywoods to one wall of your room, or to form a 30" dado around the lower part of the room. Inasmuch as these come in different sizes, as well as different finishes, it is well to save yourself as much sawing as possible by ordering the width that will fit. For instance, a narrow plywood panel, held horizontally will form a dado. The modern way is to attach this in place without either baseboard moulding, or top edge moulding, forming a smooth flush expanse of the wood.

The wider panels are used for the all-over wall treatments and are easy to fit together. One panel is nailed in place with the nails hidden in the edge, then the next is fitted in place by the groove at the edge, to hold it firmly locked. If the panel does not have edge tongue and groove—and not all do— then small-headed nails will be necessary at other places in the sheet of plywood. These may be covered with a bit of putty and plastic wood, then toned with a little oil color rubbed on with a cloth very carefully. Or, the panels may be framed in a two-inch flat moulding which covers the nails.

A striated wallboard that looks as though the hard pine had been grilled with sharp claws is attractive, and easy to use, as the nails that hold it in place hide in the uneven grooves of the wood. It may be used in natural tone, or treated with a gray or colored stain. Another very attractive way to finish it, is to paint with one color, then rub off before it is dry, thus allowing the color to show only in the grilling.

This plywood may be used perpendicularly, horizontally, or for unusual effects it may be cut on the diagonal to form a herringbone effect. It is inexpensive and may be used on both the exterior and the interior of the house. Other plywoods are to be had in plain pine, rift oak, quartered or flat cut oak, quartered or flat cut walnut, ribbon mahogany or flat cut mahogany, plain maple, white or red birch and in gumwood at varying costs.

Thin wood veneers have been mounted on cloth backing to form Flexwood. These come in the same woods as those just mentioned, as well as in curly maple, birdseye maple, satinwood, cypress, laurel and other woods. The sheets are eight or ten feet long, and 18″ or 24″ wide. These are attached to the wall with special adhesive, and warning is given that the Flexwood must *never be hung on wet plaster.* If you are a neat and efficient worker, you may find it possible to attach this attractive wall finish yourself. However, we recommend that you engage the services of a professional for this job. It is far more difficult than just attaching wallpaper.

TILE BOARD PANELLING

Tile board plywood, with shiny baked enamel surface tile in various colors, is pro-
curable in large panels. Plain shiny panels, not marked off like tile, but also in plyboard panels are also available. These are very attractive in the kitchen and bathroom, and come with full directions for their application. If these directions are carefully followed, they may be applied without difficulty. When the directions are ignored, trouble results. If you plan to put these panels up in your home consult the local supply house for the ones that are easiest to apply. Then be sure you also buy the special nails, and the right kind of edge moulding.

LINOLEUM

There are two kinds of linoleum. One is of floor thickness, the other, called Linowall, is of wall thickness. The wall linoleum is of similar thickness to the Flexwood described above, and makes a most attractive wall finish for a bathroom, a kitchen, or a child's playroom. The same rule holds for its application. It is wiser to have it applied to the walls by a professional.

The floor linoleum comes in a variety of thicknesses. There is the very heavy battleship linoleum, which comes in plain colors.

Laying floor tiles

This is often used on table tops, or counter tops for kitchen or workroom. It is strong and wears for a long time. Jaspé is two-toned with the coloring in striations. The marbleized has a spotty texture, which only faintly resembles marble, but makes an attractive floor, whether used in an all-over piece with a plain border, or used in contrasting color blocks. The inlaid linoleum is made up of several different colors of linoleum cut and fitted together in a pattern to be assembled on a backing. Special designs are available, worked out in made-to-order inlay. These are used in stores and restaurants, as well as in hallways, children's rooms, bathrooms and kitchens. Embossed linoleum may be an inlaid linoleum with grooves pressed at the joinings of the colors. This resembles tiles, and is not to be recommended for use on kitchen floors. Spilled food has a bad way of working into these grooves and is hard to wash up. All linoleum floors should be kept well waxed.

Linoleum may be laid by the amateur. The blocks are easier to handle than the large pieces, which must be cut to fit around pipes or obstructions. In any case you will need a strong and very sharp knife and a large can of the linoleum adhesive.

The floor must be absolutely smooth, as any bumps or uneven spots will cause undue wear. Apply the linoleum paste evenly on the level surface using a broad putty knife to spread it smoothly. Work on only a few square feet at a time. If you are applying the tile, set one tile at a time, with the adhesive spread beyond the edge of the tile. Smear more adhesive, set another tile, and so on, gradually working around the original tiles, and expanding into the room.

The linoleum must be placed firmly and smoothly. A heavy roller is best for this, as it removes the air bubbles better than standing on the linoleum will do. Edges or seams should be weighted down until they are thoroughly dry, so they won't roll up. But *before you do this be sure that none of the adhesive has worked up through the cracks.* Wipe this off while it is wet. Do not let it dry in ugly spots that will have to be scraped off with a dull knife.

You can make your own inlaid designs, although this is a difficult procedure. Draw the design on tracing paper, and transfer to the already laid floor. Use the linoleum knife to cut out the section. (See sketch.) Lift out and use this as a pattern to cut linoleum sections of a contrasting color. Spread fresh linoleum paste over the backs of these pieces and fit into the openings. It is wise to try for accurate fit before spreading on the adhesive. Then any edges that are not smooth and even may be adjusted before the pieces are pasted in place.

To patch worn linoleum use this same system to set in fresh pieces of matching material.

PAINTING KITCHENS OR BATHROOMS

Gloss paint is used on the walls of kitchens or bathrooms as the high shine makes it easier to keep clean, and the reflected light helps the illumination. This is applied in the same way as directed for other wall paint. The stock colors may be used. They come in the large gallon cans, and these pastel shades have a clean look that is most attractive. If, however, you wish to follow the color suggestions for kitchens and bathrooms which are found in Chapter VII, and balance the large white expanses of the fixtures with deeper color, these stronger colors may be mixed as directed on page 39.

APPLYING DECALCOMANIAS

Although attractive decalcomania designs are now available for other rooms such as playrooms or nurseries, many of the designs have particular application to kitchen or bathroom. They are colorful and gay, and may be easily put on to add a bit of pattern to an otherwise plain wall or cabinet. These decals cost only around ten or fifteen cents and come with full directions for application. You can have flowers or fruit, or provincial designs of peasant figures, hearts and ribbons. You can buy larruping cowboys or cuddley teddy bears.

STENCILS

Another method of adding gay color is to stencil the walls, the furniture, the draperies, or even the floor. You can buy a stencil pattern for one or two colors at the local paint store, or you can make your own.

To make your own stencil you will need to make a "mask" of strong paper or stencil board through which to apply the design. See sketch on page 47. Trace the desired design on this stiff paper and use a sharp knife or razor blade to cut it out. Be sure to leave a frame around each cut-out section, or the design will fall apart.

Lay this against the wall, or dry, painted surface to which it is to be applied, and attach with masking tape or Scotch tape. Prepare the color in a saucer. If it is to be applied to wall or floor, use regular wall paint or oil color. If it is to be applied to fabric, buy special textile paint for use on fabrics. It looks most attractive to stencil the same design around the edge of the curtains, and on the dish towels, and to repeat the design on the wall and cupboards of the kitchen.

Use a brush with short bristles. Plop up and down in the shallow paint in the saucer, then use the same up and down motion against the stencil. Cover every exposed section, then carefully remove the stencil without smudging the design.

If there is a second color to be used, there will be a separate mask prepared. Do not apply the stencil mask and the second color until the first is thoroughly dry, or you run the risk of smudging it.

PAINTING PORCH FLOORS OR CEMENT FLOORS

Special paint must be purchased for cement floors or for porch floors. The same directions for painting the floors follow as for painting wood floors. Start in the corner away from the door, paint all in one session and choose a fine bright day for the job. Two coats are usually required and make a better job than a single one. Allow the first coat to dry thoroughly before applying the second.

V

ARRANGING THE FURNITURE

THERE IS now a Home Planning Kit on sale, which makes the arrangement of furniture as much fun as any parlor game. This has a piece of wood marked off with grooves to permit cardboard walls to be fitted in the proper place. Rooms proportioned to the size of your own room may be set up, and you have the fun of moving the "furniture" around into different arrangements. Certainly it is far easier to do this in miniature than to do it in full size.

You can make your own "kit," and have fun playing house. You can plan the rooms over and over until you have the very best arrangement. Then when you buy the various pieces, as described in Chapters II and III, the delivery men can place them on the spot. Or if you own all the furniture, and are moving in complete, you can stand with the sketch in your hand, and tell the moving men where to place the piano, the couch and all the chairs.

If you don't want to go to the trouble of grooving wood to hold the walls, just rule off cardboard to the size of the room, or use the tracing paper as directed in Chapter II. You will do a better job at this room arrangement if you also make what decorators call "elevations." These are perpendicular sheets representing each wall, with the doors and windows marked off on them. If your imagination is good, you can visualize them and work from only the flat floor plan.

Because of the popularity of built-in furniture we believe that you will find it easier to plan if you do make the elevations. Draw these to the same half-inch scale as the floor plan. If your walls are 11' high you will require a strip 5½" deep, and as long as the scaled distance of the wall. If the room is 13' wide by 20' long, drawing them to the scale of ½" for each 1', will give you one strip for each short wall of 6½", and one strip for each long wall of 10".

Mark each door and window, paying particular attention to the door by which the room is entered. This is most important, for the room must not be so arranged that when someone comes into the room he is greeted by the backs of the people already assembled there.

ARRANGING THE LIVING ROOM

Let us start with the living room. As we have said before, this is really the most important room in the house, for it is where your family spend most of their waking hours, and it is the room that greets your

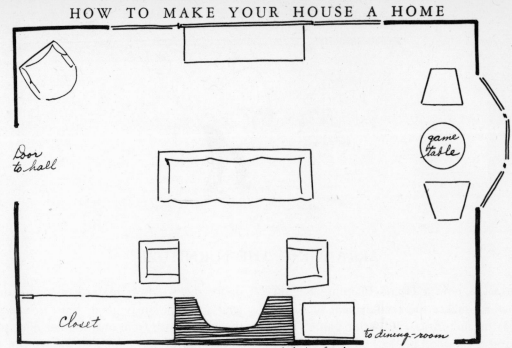

Traditional type room—couch facing fireplace

friends. In planning the room, therefore, it is necessary to take into consideration these two aspects.

One very attractive living room, planned for a young married couple by a leading decorator, put its best foot forward when the family were entertaining at evening parties. The room was lighted most attractively by pale pink candles in gilt wall sconces against a dull blue-green wall. But the sad bride soon discovered that she had no place where she could sew or read comfortably during the day. The room was therefore only partly successful.

There are two types of living rooms, generally speaking; those in traditional houses and those in modern houses. In the traditional houses there is usually a certain formality of balance. The traditional furniture groups itself naturally into such arrangements. The modern rooms are varied in arrangement. There may be a balanced arrangement, but there is far more likelihood of asymmetrical or uneven balance in the placing of the fireplace and the furniture.

Let's consider the traditional rooms. These are in homes of American Colonial, Cape Cod, English, Georgian or Southern Colonial character. Usually there is a fireplace centered in one wall. The windows may be on the same wall with the fireplace or on another wall. We hope they are well balanced, other-

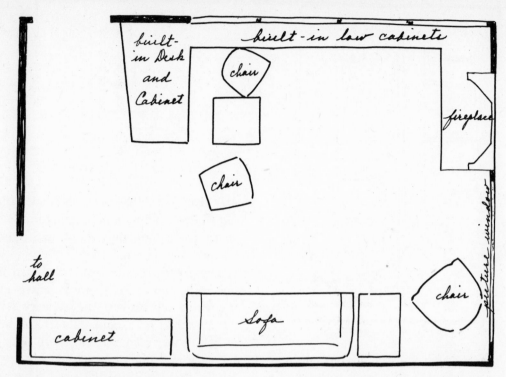

built-in Desk and Cabinet

built-in low cabinets

chair

chair

fireplace

to hall

chair

picture window

cabinet

Sofa

Modern living-room—furnished with great simplicity but with adequate seating and storage space

wise our decorating problem consists in arranging the furniture to suggest that they are.

Usually the room is oblong. This is easier to arrange than a square one. An oblong that is in good proportion is easier to arrange than one that is very long and narrow.

The center of interest in the room is the major grouping of furniture. This usually is grouped around the fireplace if there is one. The fascination of fire makes it a cozy part of the room in the winter, and in summer, with no fire on the hearth, the grouping may still be attractive, if well planned.

Balanced arrangement of two couches in front of fireplace

In a room such as the one sketched, the entrance door is opposite the fireplace. The windows alongside the fireplace mean that daylight falls attractively near enough to the chairs and couch so that reading or sewing are possible by day. By placing lamps on end tables, alongside the couch and between the two comfortable chairs, at night there is adequate light for these same pursuits, or for pleasant conversation. The late visitor entering upon guests sitting in front of the fireplace, having afternoon tea, will not come in the door to be greeted by backs of furniture or people.

If the door is at the short end of the room, then the arrangement in front of the fire should be changed. The larger comfortable sofa now faces the fire. The two large armchairs are at either side of the hearth, and the coffee table stands comfortably between. This arrangement requires tall, strong table lamps either alongside the couch, or balanced

Balanced arrangement of two chairs and coffee table in front of fireplace

alongside the chairs to provide an adequate amount of light for all seated in this group of furniture. (See sketch.)

In either case the rug used, if not of room size, would fit into the group, either being slightly larger all around than the coffee table, or large enough to extend under the chairs and couch to tie the whole group together. (See the sketches for detail.)

In any room arrangement there should be plans for seating at least six people. If the room is so small that you have had to eliminate a six-foot sofa and use a four-foot love seat instead, it will be necessary to have two comfortable chairs or large ottomans that may be used for seating extras. It is always handy to have at least two side chairs, or chairs without arms and with straight backs, in any room. They are useful for playing cards, and there are people who always prefer them to a low, soft comfortable chair. When buying the chairs it is wise to consider this fact. It is also wise to have the man of the house "try on" one chair for size, while you try on the other. His longer legs

may require a deeper seat, you may wish one not so deep. You are both going to use those chairs for a long time. Now is the time to be sure they fit you.

These extra chairs may be ranged along one wall, and make a nice balanced grouping with a tall bookcase or secretary desk, or with a table, or a radio cabinet. If there is a desk in the room, one chair will usually sit in place in front of it. If you are fond of games, perhaps you will wish to have two at one end of the room with a game table always ready between them. Then it makes a handy spot for quick meals. (See sketches.)

Balanced arrangement—using two chairs and a couch

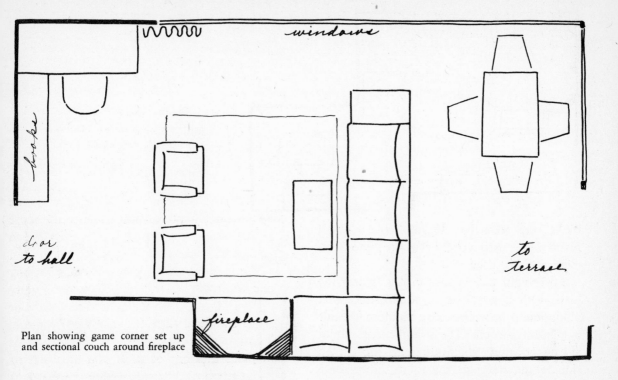

Plan showing game corner set up
and sectional couch around fireplace

Tall pieces of furniture are usually placed to balance either windows or doors. For instance, if there is only one window, which is placed off-center on a wall, using a secretary desk or bookcase the same distance from the other wall will create better balance. (See sketch.) This may be done in the same way to balance a door.

If a wall has no architectural feature, such as a door or a window, it is a good place to create an important grouping by placing a tall or large piece of furniture there, perhaps flanking it by other smaller pieces.

If a long low couch takes up a good deal of one long wall, it is attractive to use tall cabinets alongside, or use end tables with tall, important looking lamps to create the same effect.

Never have a monotonous arrangement of furniture, with all low pieces, or all tall pieces, along a wall.

Never place furniture catty-cornered in the room. Always place it parallel or at right angles to the wall. There is lately a great tendency to have a large desk set out into the room, with the end of the desk placed between two windows, and a large lamp placed against the wall on the desk. This

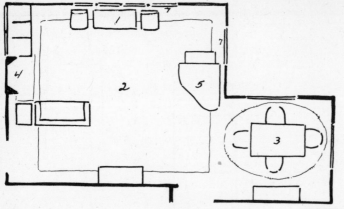

How to place pianos in the room

A With straight side along wall—light over shoulder
B With straight side along window wall

1 Table	5 Piano
2 Rug	6 Built-in cabinets
3 Dining	7 Windows
4 Fireplace	

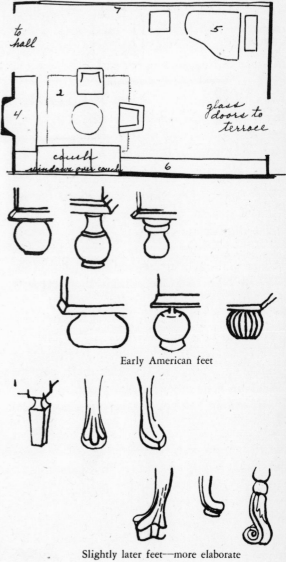

Early American feet

Slightly later feet—more elaborate

looks very attractive. If you have a small piano that is used a great deal the same treatment could be used.

An upright piano looks fitting against the wall, with a bookcase or a record cabinet alongside. A baby grand is a bit more difficult to place in a room. The straight side should always go along the wall, with the curved side setting out into the room. Since there should be light for reading the music and seeing the keyboard, it is advantageous to have the light from the window falling over your left shoulder as you sit on the piano bench. A floor lamp placed near the piano is better than table lamps placed on the piano, for they might jiggle in an annoying way when the musician is playing.

A piano is apt to make any room look crowded, so unless music is really a part of your life, don't let it hamper your efforts to make an attractive room. It used to be a "keeping up with the Joneses" necessity in grandma's day, but it is not today.

This brings up the matter of *scale*. Any very large furniture is apt to make a small room look crowded. A huge couch, or breakfront book case might dwarf any average size room. When you buy furniture take care not to get any one piece so large that it attracts undue attention in the room, or makes all the other furniture look lost.

Also in combining furniture of different

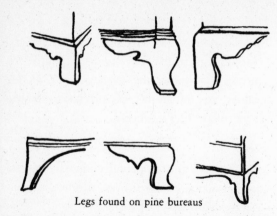

Legs found on pine bureaus

styles, whether antiques, or reproductions, care must be taken to see that they go well together. Because big, simple pieces were in style during some periods, with smaller daintier pieces used in other eras, not all furniture of all periods look well together. It is easy to combine furniture of the informal styles, grouping the so-called "peasant" pieces together. The eighteenth century furniture, whether of English, American or French origin, is comparable in line and proportion. They may be used together. The sleek formality of the Regency and Empire furniture make that style attractive, but only when used with its own, not combined with the more informal styles.

Modern furniture may be used with some period pieces, and in some period interiors. In fact, even if we are using the most simple Early American pine furniture, we would not relish the authentic benches on which our ancestors sat. So we substitute comfortable couches and upholstered chairs, taking care to see that they conform in general line and proportion. Carrying it one step forward permits large simple furniture—that is, out-and-out modern, to be used with large simple pieces in traditional styles. A matter of proportion makes it look well. The slim, Swedish modern pieces look well with the daintier proportioned pieces of other periods and styles. Again, only a matter of proportion. So

use your eyes, and study these pieces together. You will find that you can gain attractive effects with unusual combinations.

Exhibition rooms of department stores and interior decoration sections of magazines will help you gain knowledge of styles and periods. But here are the pieces that you can combine, grouped for your convenience.

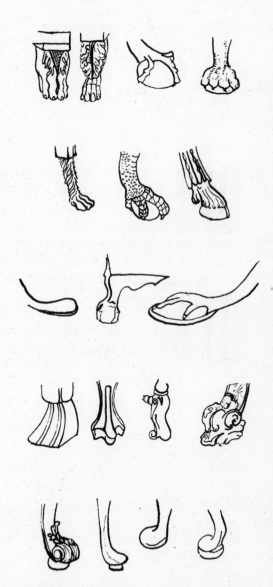

More formal legs found on mahogany furniture

IF YOUR HOUSE IS—
    Cape Cod Colonial
    Saltbox style
    Early American
    Cotswold Cottage
    English Timbered
    Whitewashed Brick, French Provincial

Then ask for painted peasant furniture—
    Dark Oak
    Natural Oak
    Bleached Oak
    Pine, Cherry
    Maple
    Unfinished Fruitwood or Walnut

These woods will be found in simple styles, and may have turned legs, whittled legs or curved-out legs.

Chair seats may be wood, shaped to fit, called saddle seats; or woven of rushes, splats, or cane. They may have tied-on seat pads or boxed cushions.

When you buy upholstered furniture ask for wing chairs, Lawson or club chairs, love seats or sofas.

Tables may have big slab tops above stretchers, turned legs, or may have wings supported by arms; you know, the gateleg table. Coffee tables are miniatures of old tavern tables, even of cobbler's benches.

Cabinets have simple panelled doors, drawers with wooden knobs or brass handles or open shelves for display of dishes.

Mirrors or simple pictures are wooden framed, sometimes with gilt trimming.

Rugs are hooked, woven on hand loom, Oriental or plain.

Fabrics: simple prints, homespuns, chintz, gingham and casual fabrics. Quilted materials popular.

Wallpaper: simple flower designs, plaids, stripes, peasant figures and scenes. Reproductions of old papers.

small wooden knob

"tear drop" brass drawer pull

turned legs

Hitchcock chair

Maple chest

Windsor chair

Boston rocker

IF YOUR HOUSE IS—
    Brick Colonial
    Clapboard or shingle Colonial
    Georgian
    Southern Colonial

Then ask for Colonial or eighteenth century or
Chippendale or Georgian furniture—
    Mahogany
    Walnut
    Cherry

These will be English or American in style with
Cabriole legs.

You may also use French furniture of walnut
or wood painted in light tones.

Veneered wood, fine cabinetmaking, nice proportions characterize these pieces.

Chair seats, flat pad, inserted in frame, or
shallow padding.

When you buy upholstered furniture for an informal effect choose Lawson or club chairs,
sofas or love seats. For more formal effect,
Chippendale sofa and open armchairs. Wing
chairs for all types.

Tables with leaf supported by swinging leg,
tilt tops, consoles, and card tables. Tables in
pairs, great variety of styles.

Cabinets, secretary desks, bookcases, with glass
or mirror or wood panel doors; drawers with
brass handles and escutcheon plate. High
and low chests of drawers, brass handles.

Mirrors framed in mahogany, or gilded carved
wood.

Pictures of landscapes, or portraits framed in
wood or gold frames.

Rugs, all over carpeting, room size plain rugs,
Orientals, textured or carved rugs. Large
hooked rugs.

Fabrics: brocade, damask, antique satin, chintz,
cretonne, printed linen, toile de Jouey,
quilted fabric.

Wallpapers: in flower designs, or reproductions of old paper, simple scenic designs,
stripes, quaint scenes.

brass drawer pull

IF YOUR HOME IS FORMAL COLONIAL OR GEORGIAN of brick, stone or clapboards either Southern or Northern style and you wish the more formal furniture of the late eighteenth century type, ask for Hepplewhite, Sheraton or Adam type furniture made of mahogany, satinwood, or painted wood; or French furniture of Louis XV or Louis XVI type made of satinwood, walnut, or painted wood.

You may also use Regency, Empire or Federal furniture.

These pieces are dainty and graceful, lighter in construction. They are more suitable for a home without children, that lives a calm, well-ordered existence.

Choose open-arm upholstered chairs, or French "bergères" or scoop back or armless upholstered chairs. For sofas ask for Chippendale, Sheraton, or Regency; or for Duncan Phyfe style. See all of these before choosing. Side chairs with shield shape. or oval backs, straight legs.

Tables veneered in mahogany or walnut marquetrie, with leaf or top edged with metal trim, brass feet on legs.

Cabinets, bookcases, chests of drawers with oval brass escutcheons and handles, straight or reeded legs. Graceful swell-front shapes. Light woods often combined with mahogany.

Mirrors framed in oval or oblong gilded frames, simple, lovely in proportion, often with flowers and swags, wreath and arrow decorations.

Pictures, fine color engravings, portraits, scenic color engravings, embroidered motifs, or flower groups.

Rugs all over carpeting, Chinese rugs. (Aubusson carpets, used in the period, may be used over rug pad.) All over carpeting in classic motifs, wreath, laurel leaf, Greek fret, etc. Soft flower patterns.

Fabrics: damask, brocade, satin, taffeta, chintz, toile de Jouey in simple, small patterned classic designs.

Wallpapers: reproduced from period papers showing small scenes, or classical spots, figures, flowers.

IF YOUR HOME IS MODERN choose whether you wish the style to be informal, with big, bold effects, or more formal, with smaller scale and highly polished woods.

For Informal Modern emphasize natural textures of wood, fabric, flooring and wall surfaces by the way they contrast.

Choose furniture of bleached oak, redwood or cedar, of painted or lacquered wood, or of wrought iron.

These pieces will be well constructed, large and simple. They will be upholstered in homespun, textured cotton and rayon, linen, sailcloth, mohair, block-printed cotton, plaids, checks, woven stripes. Draperies will pull across window wall and be of any of the above fabrics.

Rugs woven of shaggy textures, or of plain carpeting, used in such a way that much linoleum or wood floor is shown. Rush, grass or other fiber rugs.

For Formal Modern emphasize the pale blond wood tones of birch and maple, or of oak, lacquer, black painted furniture with classical lines from Empire or Regency influence. Laminated wood may be used, but leave plywood moulded into shape for more informal interiors.

These pieces will be upholstered in similar fabrics to above, or in fabrics with smoother surfaces, such as antique satin, velveteen, corduroy.

Carpets with designs or textured patterns in classical motifs. Plain broadloom, Chinese rugs. Shag or flat woven cotton rugs.

IF YOUR HOME IS SOUTHERN PATIO STYLE with low rooms of spacious size, tiled floors, or broad wood planks

Then ask for dark walnut or old oak furniture of Spanish or Italian influence; or choose the French Provincial or Italian cottage furniture in the simpler heavy styles. Or use Jacobean or Elizabethan furniture. They are right in simplicity of structure and proportion. Some of the Early American pine and oak pieces look well. Reproductions of any of these are satisfactory.

Use the simpler modern pieces, the ones bold in proportion. The natural cedar and redwood, the bleached oak, and gray tinted woods.

For upholstered furniture, large club chairs and sofas look better than the more delicate styles.

Built-in furniture looks well with striated wood finishes.

For fabrics choose homespun, hand-blocked looking linens, naive chintz, bold toile, woven stripes or bold textured effects. Use vivid jewel colors, strong clean contrasts.

Painted walls, or textured walls, rather than wallpaper.

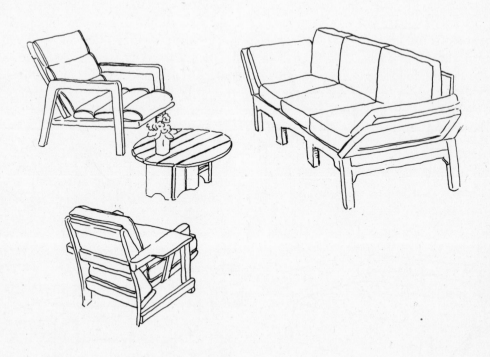

PROBLEM ROOMS

If the room is not in good proportion to start with, the furniture that you choose, or the way you arrange that furniture, will help make it appear so. In small rooms the furniture should group around the wall. Any furniture that sets out into the center of the room will impede "traffic," and lead to barked shins. One famous teacher of Interior Decoration recommended planning the living room for "parking space" and "through traffic." This is especially necessary if other rooms open off the living-room, and there is apt to be passing back and forth.

If the room is rather square, by placing the larger pieces along two opposite walls, they may seem to come closer together. Then the addition of a mirror at the end or ends of the room will make these walls seem to go further away, and will make the room appear oblong instead of square.

If the room is too long and narrow, center mirrors in the long walls, "pushing them back" for better proportions. Or paint these walls a different color, or use pattern on the narrow end walls. (See sketch.)

Placing the furniture at right angles to the

Center mirror on long wall

long wall helps to "cut" this length and makes the room seem of better proportion. Color is useful in creating different proportions in a room. If the ceiling is high, by painting it a dark or a vivid color, or by papering it with bold patterned wallpaper, you can make it look lower. Another way to make a room look lower is to decorate the lower half in a different color. A dado of marbleized paper, or wallpaper carried only 30″ up from the floor will make the room appear lower.

Unfortunately most of us wish to make rooms appear higher, rather than lower. This may be done by sweeping the draperies way to the floor, and having them contrast strongly in color with the wall. Or you can use painted stripes; or there are wallpaper pilasters or columns that may be pasted at intervals to achieve a formal colonnade effect.

By painting a portion of the wall, and papering a small section, an effect of emphasis is achieved, and height is added to the room. Long panels of mirror placed between the windows add an effect of height and also of spaciousness.

Large, heavy furniture crowds a small room so, if the room is not large, choose daintier pieces. Open armchairs are comfortable and look less clumsy than huge roll over-arms. If the room is huge, choose large pieces, but avoid having too many of them or they will seem ponderous, and the room will look cluttered.

You can combine various periods or styles of furniture as the charts show. You can also combine various woods. But do keep a sense of formality and informality, for it is as important as a sense of proportion.

BEDROOM ARRANGEMENTS

The primary consideration for the bedroom is that it should be a comfortable place to sleep, to dress, and to have privacy away from the rest of the family. One of the most successful modern homes had the master bedroom so arranged that the unit divided in four sections: the sleeping section, the bathroom, the dressing-room, and a small sitting room arrangement of fireplace, chaise-longue and couch.

This is perhaps more luxurious an arrangement than most of us can afford, both from

point of view of space consumed and furniture used. It is ideal, and the planning of even the most modest bedroom should take into consideration these features.

Besides the bed or beds, there should be a comfortable chair and a small side chair, a bench or stool for the dressing-table, and adequate storage space for clothes. The sleeping beds or couches should be well placed so they have adequate ventilation without a draft sweeping across the bed, and so the early morning light won't awaken you. If the headboard is placed against an outside wall this is easily achieved. (See diagram.) If placed on an inside wall, the window should be far enough away so that the light does not hit the bed.

Curtains may be drawn across the window, but they shut out the air as well as the light. Blinds that are closed are apt to clank in the breeze and awaken the sleeper. So it is wise to plan so these will not be necessary.

Placing the beds in a corner, or head to head, keeps them away from the light. (See sketches on page 12.) In most cases a more conventional placing of the single bed, or the

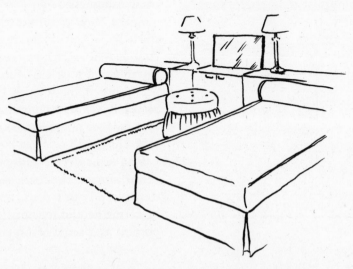

Rug between beds—repeats the shape by being oblong

double bed, is with the head against the wall and a table or small chest at each side holding a lamp. When twin beds are used they may be placed close together, either using the same spread as shown in the sketch on page 12, or with different spreads. Then they will also require a lamp cabinet at each side for balance. If the twin beds are placed apart a single cabinet can carry one lamp between the beds.

If a dressing-table is used, it should be placed next, for it requires good light. The mirror may hang on a wall between two windows so there will be good light. Or, the table may be placed in the corner window, or it may be placed right in one window. (See sketches.) With the bench in front of the

dressing table, this makes a complete unit, and forms a secondary "center of interest" less important than the sleeping "center." To complete the dressing unit it will be necessary either to have chests of drawers in the room or to have built-in units set in the closets. Some prefer this latter method, and it does give a sleek look to the bedroom, with everything shut away behind doors. If you prefer this, and your closets are large enough, it will be wise to have such units set in while the house is being built. They are

apt to cost less if they are a part of the original contract, and the carpenter can make them while he is still in the house.

Some of the lumber mills feature units that may be bought and set in. These are planned for either men or women. Do buy one that has the right size for his clothes, and does not have drawers that are too deep. Read closet section at end of this chapter.

As noted in the chapter on buying, if you wish to have a complete set of bedroom furniture, it is now possible for you to buy this on the open-stock plan, gradually accumulating the pieces. This may necessitate rearrangement of the pieces. You will find it smarter to make the complete plan before you start acquiring the furniture, having them set in the place for which they are intended as soon as they are purchased.

Work out several arrangements of furniture of the scaled floor plan before deciding. The size of the room will pretty well determine the type and number of pieces you will use. A double bed requires an area 50″ wide by 75″ long plus the area needed to move around it comfortably when the bed is made. Twin beds close together will require an area of 72″ by 75″ and must be easy to move about, so they may be swung apart for making them up. If they are placed with a small chest in between they should have 20″ allowed, plus the area for moving around their perimeter for making them. Make your decision which type of beds you will use in your room after taking measurements of available space.

DINING-ROOM ARRANGEMENTS

The usual dining room once had a table placed in the very center with the required number of chairs surrounding it. Times have shown more change in the style of furniture arrangement in this room than any other in the house. Now it is unusual to see the table placed in the center of a separate dining-room. A small table may be placed in the center of an alcove off the living-room that serves as a dining-room. A bench may be built in one corner of the living-room, and a large table placed in front of it. A long narrow table may sit against a wall, with a few people able to sit at it while it is left in place. When there are extra guests the table is moved out from the wall, and guests are seated along with the family all round the table.

Or, a small table may be kept set up with the two or four chairs that are usually used by the family, with extra chairs flanking a serving table or console along the wall. These are pressed into service when the extra leaf is added to the table, or when it is extended. This unit may be part of the living-room, it may be in a corner of the dining-room, or in a large bay window. It has the advantage of being a nice spot to sew, read, play games and do all the other things that require a table, when it is not in use at meal time.

Economy of space means that the dining-room is doing double duty these days. If

Laminated maple and birch furniture

decorated sensibly it may serve as a kind of hobby room, and it will be an extremely comfortable gathering spot for the family and friends. If this is your plan, consider buying chairs with rather more seat and back upholstery than the ordinary dining chair. If we are sitting up at the table, carving a steak, maybe we want a rather prim, sit-up chair. If we are spending the evening playing bridge, that same chair may get a wee bit hard in the seat, or cut in odd spots on the back.

So try out the chairs carefully before you buy, if such is your intention. There is no reason in the world why two of these chairs should not be armchairs. Men especially seem to enjoy the comfort of an armchair in restaurants; why not give them one at home. You may like them, too, and you may find, if you are "cook and waitress," too, that an armless chair is easier to slide out of when necessary.

If you are picking up old furniture, you may find it much easier to obtain two arm-chairs and two side chairs that look well together, even if they aren't the same family, than it is to find four or six matching side chairs.

The handiest pieces of modern furniture are the storage chests that are planned for dining-room linens and silver. Instead of having a few deep drawers, they have many shallow ones. This means that you can store only a few linens in each drawer; thus they will not wrinkle each other, and you will not forever find that the very one you want to use is buried at the bottom of a deep pile. Do investigate these. If they don't seem to fit with your idea of dining-room furniture, you might find a place for them in the serving pantry, or even in the kitchen.

ARRANGEMENT OF PICTURES

Many people avoid the use of pictures, and the enjoyment they give, simply because they are afraid of improperly presenting them. There are styles of picture hanging, just as there are other styles in decoration. In our grandmothers' day there were the steel engravings that hung above the haircloth sofa. These were usually of morbid subjects. Then the myriad of small oil paintings, each in its own gilt frame began to cover the walls. The most fashionable parlors were those that showed barely an inch between the pictures; the walls were literally spattered from dado to ceiling.

Today we no longer want the entirely bare walls that were a reaction from too many paintings. We do want a few well-chosen pictures, nice in color, with sufficient interest so we can really enjoy them. For those of us who have not inherited family portraits, or lovely originals of engravings or old prints, there are many beautiful reproductions available. One group of artists have been banded together under a very clever organization to produce original lithographs and etchings at a price the average homemaker can afford. These can be purchased from this gallery directly by mail or may be found in local stores.

This same firm makes lovely color reproductions of water-color and oil paintings that so accurately reproduce the original that only the most skilled expert knows the difference. Some of the larger museums have made accurate color prints of their treasures. The Metropolitan Museum of Art in New York has reproductions in a variety of sizes, framed or unframed. These are reasonably priced, and may be purchased at the museum or by mail. The Brooklyn Museum has a similar service, and carries it a step further with small reproductions of animal sculpture, admirable for gifts as well as for decoration.

For those who are using modern furniture there are lovely reproductions of famous paintings to be had at the Museum of Mod-

Have a group of four flower prints, uniformly framed, above a bed or cabinet to repeat straight line

One large picture looks well alone

ern Art, New York City. These may be had either framed or unframed. So whether you are a devotee of Picasso or Van Gogh you can have what you want at a modest price.

No doubt other museums in your locality have a similar service. Many people like to visit their museums, study the cherished objects there, then have a special reproduction made for them. Although this is more expensive it has the advantage of being more personal. One lady who was very fond of a famous marble bas-relief of a madonna obtained permission to have it photographed. The print was finished in soft gray tones and set into moulding on the wall above her mantel, thus making an attractive permanent decoration.

Photographs of ship models or of fire engines could be enlarged for a boy's room, or period dolls and costume figures for a girl's room. There are also many attractive prints taken from old books. They range from old maps to ships, fighters, riders to hounds, huntsmen, costume prints and flowers. The more decorative of the old ones are usually expensive, but many of them have been well reproduced. One of the better magazines recently printed a portfolio of beautiful flower prints. A famous print-maker reprinted the Audubon Birds in the large size of the original plates. Currier and Ives prints are also available in reproductions.

The latter are more suitable to informal interiors of cottage style, in which maple or pine furniture has been used, with casual fabrics such as chintz or cretonne. The birds and flower prints seem to fit well into any interior.

The eighteenth century decoration, that of Colonial or Georgian furniture made of mahogany or walnut, looks particularly well with pictures such as those originally used with it in period interiors. You can get hints or ideas from the rooms you see in your local museum, or in art reference books. Usually these pictures were portraits of starchy looking gentlemen in uniform, or dainty ladies dressed in satin or velvet. There were also engravings showing a gentleman in knee breeches trying to kiss a lady in full panniered skirt. Landscapes also were fashionable. These pictures were usually rather large, but smaller reproductions are available. Hunting pictures, coaches, other scenes of life of the period all look well.

Also used with this period furniture are all the Chinese decorative art objects. Charming enamels, painted wall panels, screens and decorative carvings.

For the more formal classical style, scenes of Greek temples, reproductions of statues of gods or goddesses, pictures of Napoleonic soldiers and ladies, also hunting and coaching scenes may be used. Belonging also to

Hang family pictures or heirloom silhouettes in "all-alike" frames inside the window casing

this style are flower groupings spilling from an urn, or groups of musical instruments.

In arranging the pictures, size is of the greatest importance. If the picture is large it is usually used by itself to complete an attractive grouping of furniture. (See sketch.) Some of the larger prints may be used with smaller ones grouped beside or around them.

If the prints are small they should be used in a group. They look better if they are all framed, or matted and framed alike. If the group they are to complete needs a horizontal effect, then they are placed in a straight row above the furniture, with as many being used as desired to gain the effect. (See sketch.) If the effect to be gained is height they may be hung in a perpendicular group, either grouped in a square as shown in the sketch. If only three are available, two should be placed across the lower line, with one placed above them. You may find it helps to make your decision if you cut out pieces of wrapping paper the size and shape of the pictures, and use Scotch tape to attach them to the wall while you are making up your mind as to the correct placing.

All pictures should hang as nearly as possible on the eye level. This is usually around five feet from the floor, but if all the family is tall, lift this by a few inches.

The old method of having wires hang from a picture moulding is way out of style, and rightly so. The wires are always unsightly especially when decorated further by cords and tassels. The new and far more attractive way is to use a strong angled nail and hook, especially designed in various sizes

Group of prints framed alike add unity to furniture arrangement

to hold different weight pictures. This is nailed directly to the wall. Because this is so, it is necessary to determine exactly where the picture is to go before fixing it in place, as you do not want your wall marred by unsightly nail holes. If a bad mistake has been made the hole may be filled with plastic wood or plaster patching compound, sandpapered flat, then colored carefully with water color or oil paints so it blends in with the surrounding walls. If you do not have such paints you can even use one of sonny's wax crayons to give the wall a touch-up.

Families collect many pictures of loved ones, and these should be hung on the wall, rather than add to the clutter of table tops. They may all be framed alike, or matted alike, or they may be framed in a variety of frames. Then they may be arranged in a group above a desk, around the mirror, above a bureau, or may fill in an otherwise uninteresting corner in living room or bedroom. One attractive way is to hang them inside the window frames if the frames are deep enough to carry them. (See sketch.) If the window is really deep set, you might make a regular family portrait gallery of it.

THE USE OF MIRRORS

Mirrors are so helpful in decoration that it is unfortunate people have the idea they are so expensive. Bought from an average store they usually are, for you will obtain

only the best and heaviest of mirror plate glass. If your budget does not permit this, by shopping in the neighborhood you can often locate a small mirror shop. This specialist can put a large wall mirror in place for you at less than the usual charge of the store mirror uninstalled.

Mirrors add size, light and sparkle to any room. A large one filling the wall above the mantel, or set on the wall between the windows will repay you in enjoyment. We all know how necessary a full-length mirror is to be sure the slip is not showing and the skirt hangs evenly. These may be installed on the inside of a closet door, but have far more decorative value and are more serviceable if they are placed at the end of the hall.

Smaller mirrors may be set in wall panels or may be used to top small tables. These mirrors may be obtained from the local dealer, or may be cut to fit, if you give him an accurately cut paper pattern. It is easy to see how much more charming a mirror top is on the dressing-table than one of ordinary glass.

There is on the market now a mirror glass scored off in small squares, mounted on a felt backing. This is not a very expensive product and may be made into table place-mats, or purchased ready-made in that form. It may also be added in a panel above a console table in the hall, or used to cover a curved wall section in the dining room, for it has the advantage of being flexible.

Housewives have discovered that mirror strips on the window sills cut down dusting time, that mirror plaques under house plants are more decorative than ordinary coasters and are just as practical.

Framed mirrors may be had in a variety of styles to fit into any type of interior. In the maple type of decoration use wood frames of similar wood, perhaps with a top-shaped cresting as is shown in the mirror on page ... For the other styles consult other mirrors sketched on these pages. In modern interiors most of the mirrors are unframed, and are set flat to the wall.

KITCHEN ARRANGEMENT

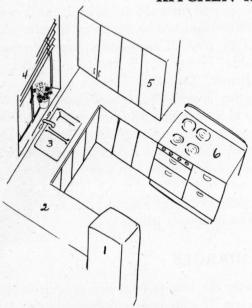

U-shaped kitchen arrangement

1 Refrigerator
2 Work counters—storage space above and below
3 Sink
4 Window
5 Storage cupboards
6 Range

Actually there is little furniture that needs arranging in the kitchen. Usually when you move into the house, the kitchen is pretty thoroughly planned, with the sink all in place. Maybe the cabinets, refrigerator and range are not yet in place. Maybe you are the person planning that house, and have a real "say" about the arrangement.

The most satisfactory arrangement for a kitchen is the U-plan. This saves you the most steps, for the sink is in the center, under the windows, and the range on one side, with the refrigerator on the other. Counter and storage space fill the area between, thus providing room for foodstuffs and for pots and pans. All those lovely shining new ones may look very attractive hanging out "in public" when they are very new, but later you will be glad to have them kept under cover. Hanging

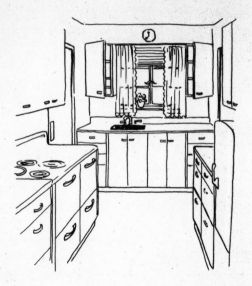

You will find that trays and platters are easier to store if another cabinet has shallow shelves just for them, while rotating shelves in the deep corner cupboard make it easier to reach things. (See sketches.)

If you have a differently shaped kitchen from the one shown (page 74), you may find that the L-shaped plan is more satisfactory. Here again, the range and refrigerator flank the sink, and provide room for drainboards on both sides if desired. If the doors are placed at either end of your kitchen, it will be necessary to leave "traffic space" through the center. If you arrange the units as shown in the sketch, there will be room for a dining alcove alongside the windows. By placing a tall cabinet of shelves to separate the kitchen section from the alcove, easily accessible storage space for frequently used dishes is provided.

them in a cupboard alongside the stove means that you can take your pick at a moment's notice. (See sketch.)

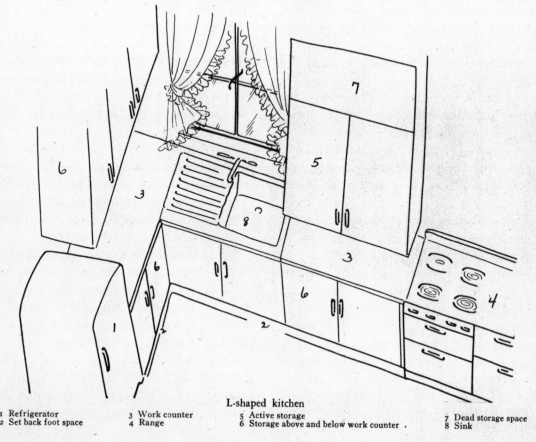

L-shaped kitchen

| 1 Refrigerator | 3 Work counter | 5 Active storage | 7 Dead storage space |
| 2 Set back foot space | 4 Range | 6 Storage above and below work counter | 8 Sink |

VI

RUGS THAT FIT THE ROOM

THERE IS no doubt that buying the rugs for the home offers one of the largest problems to the homemaker. There is a large money investment involved if the floors are to be properly covered with good grade rugs that will wear well. It takes an expert to know what a good rug is, and most new homemakers have not had time to become rug experts.

The first decision that must be made is the type of rug to be used in each room. Once prevailing styles practically dictated what one must use. Our mothers all wanted Oriental rugs for their best rooms; our grandmothers demanded wall-to-wall carpeting. Today we can pretty well choose what we like, without worrying whether our neighbors will be unpleasantly critical, or whether the best rooms will not follow the prevailing style.

There is just no such thing today as a prevailing style in rugs. Some people demand wall-to-wall carpeting in either patterned or plain weaves. They like the feeling of luxury it gives, and claim it is easier to keep clean. They know, too, that it covers floors of mediocre wood, or of flat, smooth cement, thus saving the cost of a fine hardwood floor.

Others like a large rug, and ask for a broadloom in "room size," allowing it to show a border around the room of polished hardwood. Others have had Orientals given to them, and use them with pride as a feature of a lovely room.

Some people prefer the cotton rugs, either those with flat woven texture, or the shaggy one with deep twisted pile. They have discovered that these seem to shed dust quickly and are easy to wash at home. They look well on polished wood floors, and come in gay, bright colors.

Still others have always liked hooked rugs such as our forebears made, and find they go astonishingly well with modern furniture. They also like the economy and sturdy wearing qualities of other "rag rugs," the braided ovals, or the loom-woven oblongs.

There is no doubt that among all these you will be able to find the rug that you want for each room of your home. Some you may buy as temporary expedients, saving the larger investment until later. So here is information to aid you in deciding.

Carpeting comes in 27" breadths. These you will see standing in rolls in the rug department of your store. They vary in price according to the weave, and according to the thickness of the pile. You can sometimes find very good buys in this carpeting, and have it seamed together, then bound or fringed on the ends. The seams are not obtrusive, particularly if you have chosen a patterned carpeting, and if the matching of the pattern is carefully done. This carpeting is also used for halls and stairways. On the latter it should be well padded, and held firmly in place at each corner of the step with carpet tacks. One very smart young bride discovered a sale of carpeting samples, and put them on her stairs herself, a different color for each step. A gay effect, economical and unusual at the same time.

An amusing effect could be obtained by choosing three lengths of different color carpeting to repeat the other room colors, in draperies, wall and upholstery, and have them seamed together for a "room size" rug.

Broadloom is the name for the carpeting that is woven on a broader loom than the 27" carpet, *no matter what the type of the weave.* Thus when someone says they have a broadloom rug, all that is certain is that it is not sewn-together carpeting. The widths start at 3′, and are also 6′, 9′, 12′ or 18′ wide. This makes it possible to have a "room size" rug or all-over carpeting without sewn seams for almost any size room. In most cases the 9′ by 12′ rug is chosen, as that fits the average size living-room.

The weaves are, in the order of their cost, Tapestry, Velvet, Axminster, woolen Wilton, worsted Wilton, and Chenille. The most inexpensive, the Tapestry weave, is formed by uncut surface of yarn loops. These resemble hooked rugs, and ensure unusual wear, particularly if a thick rug is chosen, or if the thinner grades are used with a rug pad. These rugs lack the resilience and sound absorption found in the cut pile rugs. There have lately been some attractive tapestry rugs made with high and low pile of the same color yarn forming an attractive all-over design. Other tapestry rugs may be bought in large ovals and oblongs with designs that resemble the hand-hooked rugs in their use of flower patterns, but are rather more strongly colored. (See diagram for enlargement of the weave construction.)

Velvet rugs have a cut pile, rather short in length, and can be used where the "traffic" is light, or where budget limitations demand an inexpensive rug. It will not wear as long as the thicker Wiltons although it is similar in construction. *Always* use a rug pad under a

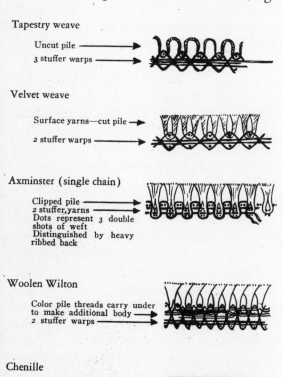

Tapestry weave

Uncut pile
3 stuffer warps

Velvet weave

Surface yarns—cut pile
2 stuffer warps

Axminster (single chain)

Clipped pile
2 stuffer yarns
Dots represent 3 double shots of weft
Distinguished by heavy ribbed back

Woolen Wilton

Color pile threads carry under to make additional body
2 stuffer warps

Chenille

Clipped pile
Catcher thread
Dots represent weft
4 stuffer warps

Velvet rug. (See diagram for enlargement of weave construction.)

More Axminster carpets are produced than any other type. They are woven in a wide range of qualities and pattern or color combinations. Excellent for sound absorption and for a sense of luxury, they do not compete in wearing quality with either the Wiltons or Chenille. The better grades provide deep pile, and closeness of weave. (See diagram for the way in which the double row of weft and binding yarns are held in place by needle thrust weaving.) This rug comes in a variety of designs.

Woolen Wilton is heavier and coarser than worsted Wilton, is compact in surface yarn, deep in pile, and woven on a strong foundation. It is excellent for a long-wearing carpet. See construction detail diagram. These rugs are made in plain and patterned designs, as well as in textured carpets with "carved" pile shaped to catch the light.

Worsted Wilton is recognized as a luxury rug. The finer and more expensive worsted yarn provides fine detail in the Jacquard patterns woven in color or textured pattern. It has a sturdy structure, due to the surface yarn being carried under between pattern tufts and woven into the rug backing. Because of this firm tying in of the surface yarn it does not shed, and thus is particularly recommended for dining-rooms where the fuzz of a shedding carpet would be objectionable.

While all these rugs are woven on a backing of strong jute, Chenille carpeting has, in some cases, a backing of wool. It is characterized by a deep pile of great density, and comes in widths up to 30'. Sometimes it is woven in plain colors, other times in bold modern designs, and in other cases it is woven to resemble a hand-made Oriental rug closely. These Chenille rugs are expensive, and luxurious in character. (See diagram for detail of weaving.)

Although most homemakers have chosen the all-over-one-color broadloom carpeting, there is an increasing tendency to ask for pattern woven designs. These may be made up of cut and uncut pile; or of high and low pile. In some cases the pile is carefully carved to form a contour design. This demands a deep pile to start with and is therefore usually found only in the more luxurious grades of carpeting.

Texture patterned rugs do not show soil and spots as readily as do the plain rugs. Patterned rugs, with a variety of colors in the design, show soil even more slowly and so are recommended for dining-room rugs. Here small grease spots, caused by falling food, do not show as quickly as they would on a plain carpet.

All these broadloom rugs are advertised and sold at so much a square foot or so much a square yard. The advertisement usually quotes the price of that popular size, 9' by 12'. Perhaps some of them seem to be much more expensive than others, and you have wondered why. The price depends entirely on the quality of material and workmanship that have gone into the rug, and *here is a case where you get what you pay for.* You pay for good wool that will not fuzz off in embarrassing tufts and whirls when people walk on it. Most new rugs will do this for a little while, but you certainly don't want it to keep up. You pay for the good dye that made the rug yarn uniform in color, not streaky or mottled. You pay for strong, firm backing and the depth and closeness of the pile which stands up from that backing.

There are too many tricks that make it possible for unsuspecting householders to be gypped when buying rugs. So here is the time when you must be sure either to buy a trademarked brand you recognize, so you know the manufacturer stands behind the rug; or buy from a store you can trust.

Room size rug

Second-hand rugs are seldom a good investment. The first good wear has been taken out of them by somebody else, and they can only be a stop-gap at best. It is not often that you can find a really good buy at an auction gallery or at a used furniture store.

So if it's a nice living-room rug that you want, save up for it, and buy only when you are sure that you have the right one.

The size of the rug is easy to determine. There should not be more than a foot and a half of bare floor, *at the very most*, showing around the border of the rug. A wider border would not give the rug a chance to hold all the furniture together in cozy style. (See sketch.)

If such a plan is beyond your pocketbook try an oval rug, with a border of fringe stitched all around to make it look even larger. Or place a smaller oblong rug with one furniture grouping, and another with the other grouping. This is done many times with hooked rugs, or Orientals, or with shaggy cotton rugs.

COTTON RUGS

Constantly growing in popularity are the colorful cotton rugs. These are made by the finer manufacturers, and are produced in a variety of types. Some of the "string" type have colored cords pulled through and knotted on an unbleached muslin or canvas ground. Others have the tuftings woven into a backing, in much the same manner as the wool rugs. Others have a braided or a flat woven texture and are reversible. By visiting the stores you will see what a variety of these are obtainable.

Some of the larger cotton rugs are as expensive as wool rugs. The smaller sizes cost less, and some smart homemakers find it economical to buy several and sew them together at home.

One of the advantages of cotton rugs is that they come in very bright gay colors which often add a great deal of spice to a color scheme. You may prefer these bright colors to the more conservative tones of wool rugs. As previously mentioned they are easy to wash out in the home washing machine, *if they are not too large in size*. Many housewives also find them easier to shake out, or sweep clean of the daily accumulating dust.

HOOKED RUGS

The hooked rugs made by our forebears used up the rags that collect around any household, making good use of worn underwear, stockings, overalls or housedresses. Because there is often a need for a small colorful rug, many gaily patterned ones have been brought to the cities from farm and mountain communities. Some of them are inexpensive, and they are usually rather loosely hooked, with large tufts, on a burlap or canvas background. The finer ones cost more, and also wear longer.

Recently one of the large rug companies have supplied interesting designs in attractive color schemes to a mountain community of North Carolina. This group is producing some very attractive rugs in sizes up to 9' by 12'. Because of the simplicity of the designs, and the softness of the colorings, these rugs look well in all interiors, whether traditional

or modern in style. They are good investments and wear well.

The clever homemaker will find it interesting also to hook her own rugs. Printed burlap, with the design ready for hooking, may be bought in the needlework department of the stores. These may be hooked with wool yarn, purchased at the same time as the burlap backing, or with rags cut into narrow strips and dyed in the colors desired. There is a patent hooker that is threaded with the yarn or rags; when thrust into the burlap this makes loops of uniform length, which may later be cut or left in the looped pile as wished.

There are also canvas sections printed for cross-stitch rugs to be worked in wool yarn. Small occasional rugs may be crocheted, braided or knitted, or made of string hooked through a canvas backing. The latter are better for bathroom or nursery than for the other rooms.

WOVEN RAG RUGS

The same firm that makes hooked rugs makes woven rugs of yarn and cord which resemble homespun. These rugs may be made on home looms as well. In some communities there is an older woman who has such a loom, and will weave a rug for you, using your own collection of rags. Such rugs look well in hallways, or as stair carpets. They are limited in width by the size of the loom, and limited in length by the length of cord that can be used for stringing. If so desired, several can be pieced together to form a room-size rug, but long wear is apt to make them pull apart at the seams.

There are machine-made parallels to all these types of rugs. In some cases they may be preferable, stronger, better in coloring and design. In most cases, however, a fine, hand-made rug has a more attractive quality. Particularly this is so if it has been made with loving care at home, or has been made to fit a certain color scheme treasured by the homemaker.

ORIENTAL RUGS

The oldest type of hand-made rug is, of course, the Oriental rug. Many of these have been brought to this country. They vary greatly in size and in the quality of workmanship. Some are as fine as the most exquisite velvet, and are woven with silver and gold threads, run between the tiny hand-tied knots. These are on the walls of our museums, and are far too fine to place on the floor.

When their popularity was at its peak in this country, the large stores sent rug buyers through Persia, India, Turkey and Afghanistan to buy all the available rugs. These buyers frequently chose certain designs and colors, and the Oriental weavers worked with those in mind. So the Oriental rug became commercialized, and rather less varied in design. Although some of them have backgrounds of dull blue and blue-green, most of the rugs

Oval rug at foot of stairs

are in tones of rust red, amber, tan and brown. Some of them have a border that repeats the same motif around a central panel which represents a Persian garden full of trees, flowers, birds and animals.

An expert may be able to look at the rug, and tell just where it came from. This is all right for the expert, but you are far more interested in the wearing qualities of the rug and how it fits into your home. These rugs are hand-tied of wool that has been raised especially for them. It is therefore a strong wool, and is dyed in special dyes. The older ones were dyed in vegetable colors, which held their brilliancy well. Modern ones are dyed with a variety of dyes, some of them vegetable, and some of analine pigments.

The number of knots to an inch, the depth and thickness of the pile is next to be considered. Most of these knots are the Ghiordes knot, a strong looped twist that holds well in the warp and woof of the back weave.

If you are buying an old Oriental, it may be in better condition than one that is newer. Always examine the rug to see if it is worn in spots. Hold it up to the light to discover if there are any weaknesses or breaks. This will often reveal a patch. Sometimes a rug has been skilfully patched, and will last as long as one that has not. This means that the patch has been well woven in at the edges, and that the pile and design match the general colorings and design of the rug, and do not show. A square piece cut out of another rug, laid on with the edges joined, will always look bad, and will not wear well. Having a rug patched properly is expensive, so don't buy a worn rug with this idea in mind, until you have estimates from a really good workman.

CHINESE RUGS

Chinese rugs are not usually included in the groupings of Oriental rugs, simply because of the difference in the designs and colorings. The Ghiordes or the Senna knot is used, but the pile is looser and longer. The main body of the rug is plain, in soft gold, beige, gray or other pleasant background tones, with slightly raised designs of Chinese symbols. These are sometimes in the form of dragons, but more usually are geometric in character.

ORIENTAL RUG REPRODUCTIONS

There are machine-made rugs that closely approximate the hand-made Oriental rugs. These are woven on Jacquard looms, and reproduce all the fine colorings of the original Orientals. Because the polish or sheen of the old rugs was obtained from use, many of these modern rugs are washed in a chemical solution to give more luster. These are sometimes called Domestic Orientals, or American Orientals.

Each of these rugs should be laid over a rug pad, as it will thus have its life greatly extended.

Small Oriental rugs may be used on bare floors, or may be laid on all-over carpeting to correlate small groupings of furniture. They should always be laid parallel to the wall; never catty-cornered. Since there is great danger of small rugs slipping, they should never be placed at the foot of a stairway; it is wise to have small suction cups or bits of rubber attached at the corners to prevent slipping.

CARE OF RUGS

Fine rugs should be well cared for. They should be gone over daily with a carpet sweeper, and have a weekly cleaning with a vacuum cleaner. Twice a year they should be cleaned professionally, no matter how careful the home care has been. Many people like to take the rugs up during the summer, feeling that the bare polished floors make the rooms seem cooler, and are easier to care for. In this case the rug should be cleaned before putting it away. If possible it should be stored at the cleaners; or, if it is returned to the home it should be rolled in a large sheet of treated paper sold for this purpose. This will serve to keep moths out. If there is no paper like this to be had, roll the clean rug carefully, dusting on moth crystals as you roll. Then wrap the outside with paper, and tie firmly with string. Stick paper tape over seams of the paper to hold the moth crystal scent in and keep moths out.

If spots get on the rug they should be removed immediately. Use a clean cloth on liquids, and a cloth wet in cold water to wipe up soft drinks or anything with sugar in it. Ink spots may be removed with powdered talc if taken care of promptly, while carbon tetrachloride is recommended for grease spots or stains. It is wise to keep the Government bulletin on Spot and Stain Removal handy for any household emergency. Room-size carpets and rugs in "traffic lanes" should be turned from time to time so the wear will not always come in the same spots.

Dyeing rugs has not proved satisfactory in most instances and is not to be recommended. If, however, a rug is of a thoroughly unsuccessful color, and it is on hand, it may be attempted. An Oriental that had been specially ordered and made after the usual delay was delivered in the wrong colors. The shades were too light and yellow to suit the dining-room for which it had been planned. In this case dyeing was attempted and was brought to a successful conclusion. The rug became a soft blue-green, while the reddish design simply appeared deep brown. The natural streakiness of the color in an Oriental is not amiss in such a rug, but certainly would

be more unpleasant were it to appear in a broadloom.

SUMMER RUGS

Many of the so-called summer rugs of sisal fiber, rush or grasses have grown popular for modern interiors. Their simplicity, their frank display of interesting texture and complete lack of pretense have made them most popular. The one most likely to be seen comes in large foot-square blocks, sewn together to make a rug of the size desired. Sometimes this covers the whole floor, sometimes only a section of the floor of polished hardwood or linoleum.

Most of these rugs are in the natural soft tan of the grass or rush. Some of them have blocks or strips of the dyed fiber worked in for contrast.

These rugs have the great advantage of costing less than other rugs and wearing very well. An oval rug of braided rush costs about $30 in a size approximately 9′ by 12′. The other rugs cost according to the number of squares and sell by the square foot, sewn together.

SEWN TOGETHER MODERN

Another development that is attractive and easy to use in rooms that are hard-to-fit is a rug that comes in large squares. The center of each square is flat woven, with the border deep-tufted of cotton. These come in any color or combination of colors desired, and sell for about $4 a square yard. They can be ordered so they fit a jog in a hallway, have an extra set-out section for an alcove, or have a cut-out section for the hearth. This is a great advantage. Other rugs must be cut to fit, and you lose the price of the material wasted. These rugs hide the seamings in the deep tufted edges, too.

LINOLEUM FLOORS

There has been a great deal of interest in well-polished linoleum floors for living-rooms, hallways, dining-rooms and bedrooms as well as kitchens and hallways. The original cost is slightly higher than hardwood floors, but they are easy to care for, and fewer rugs must be purchased when the house is furnished. They are warmer than wood floors to the touch, and the cork of their construction offers some insulation.

Many of the plain color or marbleized linoleums make very attractive and liveable room backgrounds, and fit in well with color schemes. There are also the inlaid linoleum floors, mentioned in the chapter on Preparing the Rooms. These you yourself may do at home, although they are difficult to do. If the design is at all complicated, it is wise to have a professional carry it through to a successful conclusion rather than fuss with it yourself.

Linoleum tiles are obtainable, and rubber or composition tiles, too, which can be laid by yourself. These make attractive floors for small rooms. Cork blocks and other composition floorings are appearing in the stores. In making over an old house they can be used to renew the floor, *providing* there is an absolutely smooth even floor foundation.

Another inexpensive floor, reputed to be attractive, is made of large panels of ply-wood or Prestwood, laid on a smooth sub-floor and kept well waxed and polished to prevent wear. This is still in the experimental stage, but the idea is well worth watching.

THE COLOR OF YOUR FLOOR

The color of the floor, and of the floor covering, are discussed in the chapter on color schemes. Since there are rugs in a wide range of colors and hard floor sur-facings in color, too, there is practically no limit to what you can do with this part of your color scheme.

Most of the large or small rugs purchased are one color, with perhaps texture variations of that color. It is easier to fit this single color into the scheme than it is to fit it in a patterned rug. All-over patterned carpeting, with large flower groupings, for instance, makes a strong pattern over a large area. This means that flower printed draperies would be too much—would make the room look too spotty. Nor would you enjoy a printed wallpaper, unless it was something very simple, like a soft stripe or line plaid.

Chinese rugs have simpler patterns. Their large areas of background make it possible to use patterned drapery or slip-cover material. Be sure to try *large fabric samples* hung near the rug before making a decision.

Oriental rugs usually have an all-over design of many small figures or motifs. These are usually soft enough to form a background and not so strong that they obtrude themselves as a pattern. Therefore, in most cases, you will be able to use other patterned fabrics in the room, providing they are suitable in color and character. You would not choose an informal peasant print; but you would like a soft hand-blocked linen, or a chintz adapted from a rare old bit of fabric. You would like rich velvet or brocade or damask far better than boldly plaided canvas or casual gingham.

Whatever your rug purchase, be very sure it is the right thing for your room. It is a larger investment than draperies or slipcover, and one that you will want to "live with" for many years. Do not hesitate to ask for as much professional advice as you can obtain before making this purchase. But after obtaining the advice be very sure it is what you and your husband and family will enjoy.

If yours is a casual family that troops in

and out all day, you will need a sturdier rug than some families who live more formally. This does not mean a lugubrious color. Many of the strong colors stay clean looking as long as the dark colors, and are far more cheerful to live with. With present-day inventions for keeping rugs clean even light-colored rugs are far less impractical than they were a few years ago. So tell the expert what the use will be, and let him help you with that consideration in mind.

VII

LET'S PLAN THE COLOR SCHEMES

ONE OF the most important parts of your home is the color scheme. You want to have pleasant color combinations, color schemes that will make you feel happy and gay, or that will be soothing and restful for the man of the house when he comes home from a hard day's work.

Doctors and psychologists have proved that color has a tremendous effect on our lives. They tell us that some colors depress people and some vivid shades irritate the nerves to such an extent that they can cause meal-time squabbles if used on the dining-room walls. They even tell us that "favorite" colors are such because they cause a pleasant reaction; we like them at once, and respond to them.

Maybe clear red is your favorite color. You like it because it is gay and vivid. It is a very good decorating color, but only when used in small areas. Any room perks up and smiles when it has a gay bowl of vivid red tulips on the table, or when one small chair

has a vivid lacquer-red seat. Chintz draperies or upholstery with red roses, or other gay flowers, are always attractive and help to bring summer warmth into a cool, quiet room.

On the other hand too much red would be dreadful in your room. If you were old enough to remember the best parlor in Grandma's house, you would remember that it had deep red wallpaper made in shiny and dull surfaces to imitate patterned brocade. This was on all the walls, with rosewood or mahogany furniture upholstered in shiny black haircloth in front of it. It is no wonder that these parlors were kept closed most of the time. So much red on the wall would have encouraged Grandma to talk back in an unladylike manner when Grandpa told her she was spending too much on the household budget.

The sitting-room was walled in quite different colors. Though not versed in the art of decoration, the woman of the house knew what she wanted, and blue covered the wall here.

This ever-popular color is a wonderful background. It is as popular today for walls as it was then, perhaps more so, for it is a color that makes rooms appear larger. In today's small houses we need to use every subterfuge to add an appearance of size. According to color authorities all cool colors recede. This means that all cool colors have this happy faculty of making rooms appear larger.

Let's see what these cool colors are. They are blue and all the colors that have blue mixed in them. They are:

Blue-purple   Blue-green
Blue   Green
        Yellow-green

Probably no one would want walls painted in the most vivid shades of these colors. While there is nothing more gorgeous than the deep blue-green of the sea, you would soon grow tired of it on your walls. While you love the green of grass and leaves on the trees, the reason you like it so well is that it is combined with the blue of the sky and the brown of the tree trunks.

But there are so many wonderful shades of these colors. There are the pale shades with lots of white in them that are called pastel tints because of their chalky qualities. There are the "dusty" shades of these colors which are lighter, and at the same time slightly subdued in tone, slightly dull in character. Then there are the dulled tones of the colors; these are fashionable now, and are fun to use in rooms that do not need the illusion of size. *The darker the color, the smaller the room*

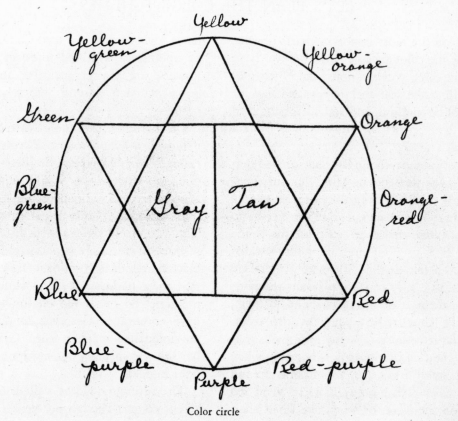

Color circle

COOL COLORS

Color	Pastel Tints	Dusty Shades	Dulled Tones	Strong Colors
Blue-purple	Hydrangea Hyacinth Heather Chalk	Delphinium Amethyst Heliotrope French blue	Egg plant Wedgwood Plum	Cornflower
Blue	Baby blue Sky blue Ciel Forget-me-not	Alice blue Delft Sapphire	Navy blue Midnight blue Inky blue	Azure Cobalt Ultramarine Flag Royal
Blue-green	Aquamarine Robin's egg Pottery blue Persian blue Turquoise		Myrtle	Electric Peacock Jade Turquoise Ivy
Green	Apple Lettuce	Jasper Evergreen Moss	Bottle green Hunter's green	Emerald Leaf
Yellow-green	Chartreuse Lime green Citrine Almond Pistachio	Pea green Sage Olive Mustard	Reseda green	Parrot green Paris green Poison green

will seem. Let's visualize these colors. See how many of them are favorites of yours.

Because these colors are "cool" they are better used on rooms that have heaps of sunlight, or that face south, or rooms of homes built in warm climates. Naturally they are most satisfactory for the predominant note of the complete scheme if the home is to be used only in the summer. Or, if you plan to have one color scheme for the summer slipcovers and draperies, with another related change for the winter, you could plan a cool harmony for the first, and a warm harmony for the second.

Now, let's consider the warm colors. These are red or any colors with red in them:

Red   Red-orange
Red-purple   Orange
        Yellow-orange

You will notice that clear yellow does not appear on either list, for it is not a warm color unless it has red in it, thus making it an orange tone; nor is it a cool color unless it has green in it, when it tends toward the lime-green or lemon-yellow shades. This is only in a literal sense. For convenience in classifying tints, dusty tones and dulled

WARM COLORS

Color	Pastel Tints	Dusty Shades	Dulled Tones	Strong Colors
Red	Pink Watermelon Strawberry Rose Carnation	Dusty pink Dusty rose Bois-de-rose Old rose	Maroon Seal brown Mahogany	Scarlet Fire red Ruby Crimson Cardinal American Beauty
Red-purple	Orchid Mauve Lilac	Raspberry Mulberry	Wine red Burgundy Bordeaux Garnet Claret Plum	Fuchsia Cerise Magenta Shocking pink Cherry
Red-orange	Flesh (some) Peach (some) Persimmon Camellia Coral Salmon Shell pink	Terra-cotta Pompeian red	Henna Brick Russet Auburn Hickory brown	Vermilion Chinese red Lacquer Geranium Poppy
Orange	Paprika Flesh (some) Peach (some)	Nasturtium shades Burnt orange	Chocolate Chestnut Autumn leaf	Orange Tangerine
Orange-yellow	Apricot Chamois Champagne Putty Straw Maize Cream	Amber Ecru Honey beige Sandalwood French beige Buff Flax Natural		
Yellow	Daffodil Butter yellow Jasmine	Sulphur Saffron Old gold Snuff	Tobacco brown	Sunflower yellow Sunshine yellow Canary Gold

shades, let's take the liberty of putting it alongside the warm colors. It's a "sunshine" color, and thus comes nearer the warm shades in its true strong intensity.

See chart of colors on page 88.

Lucky you, with all these colors to work with. They are produced in fabrics, draperies and rugs, or you can mix them yourselves in wall paints. So many colors are produced, not to confuse you, but to provide you with the tools you need to make a lovely home. If you are timid about your ability to match or harmonize colors, if you are afraid you are "color blind," then your local store has one of those color-correlating plans just for you.

These have been especially designed by manufacturers with folks like you in mind. The hard work of matching and relating rugs, drapery and upholstery fabrics and wallpapers has already been done for you. You can ask for the BHF plan, or for Quantacolor, or for Wishmaker. In many stores there is also a trained decorator who will help you with specialized advice. This is a store service and costs you nothing, so inquire about it if you need help and don't want to do this matching all by yourself.

There are several easy ways to plan color harmony. Choose the "favorite" color first. This is the color that you wish to predominate in each room, or to set the theme for the whole house. A related theme for the entire house is most satisfactory. One smart homemaker discovered a lovely piece of wall paper to use on her living-room walls. It had soft tones of blue and pinky tan. She had the rug for the living-room repeat the pinky-tan tone. The upholstery was either blue or tan striped in blue. The draperies were plain dull blue with a textured weave.

The hall just outside the living-room had plain walls of the soft blue in a deep delphinium shade, with polished linoleum floor in a deeper pinky tan than the living-room

rug. The accessories of this room picked up some deep coral tones from the wall paper, and the mahogany furniture blended in well.

Another charming small home had the theme of terra-cotta and gray. This theme was carried throughout the house. The living-room was paneled in bleached, or pickled, pine plywood around the lower part of the room, with pale gray and silver striped wall paper above. Draperies were of rayon and cotton in a novelty weave, while the upholstery of the large couch and two comfortable chairs was in flower-printed chintz, with a background of paler pinky peach than the terra-cotta draperies.

To carry this relation into the other rooms was very simple. One bedroom had a flower printed chintz with a white background for its soft shades of peach-pink and blue hung against peach and white striped wallpaper. The other bedroom used a flowered wall paper with a tiny design. Highly glazed chintz curtains of white were ruffled in deep flounces of dusty rose-apricot to match the bedspreads.

Planning a color harmony for the entire house this way produces a more harmonious whole, and thus a happier place to live. There are no sudden shocks when one leaves one room to go into another as there would be if purple keyed one room, yellow a second and green a third. So do plan your color scheme by considering each room as a whole; then consider its relation to the adjoining room. In the foregoing schemes one was based on the cool color blue. This scheme is therefore predominantly cool, and should be used if the living-room of the home faces south, or has sunlight for part of the day at least. The other house scheme was based on the warm color terra-cotta, or the grayed shade of red-orange. This was balanced by the cool gray, just as the other scheme was balanced by the warm pinky tan. The latter scheme is best in a room facing north, or one that needs the illusion of warm color.

City homes are sometimes so swamped by tall buildings that little sunshine reaches into them. They require color schemes that create an illusion of sunshine. Study the schemes that follow for suggestions to suit your rooms, and choose the one that uses your favorite color or solves the room problem of your home.

COLOR RECIPES FOR LIVING-ROOMS

To Bring Sunshine into the Room

Walls: Sunshine yellow

Draperies: Red and white stripes

Slipcovers: Red and yellow gingham

Furniture: Dull maple or mahogany

Rugs: Rag-woven, brown, tan, yellow, red shades mixed

For a Room That Has Sunshine Part of the Day

Walls: Suntan beige

Draperies: Blue-green printed with bold leaf pattern

Upholstery: Texture - woven orange and brown-turquoise velveteen

Furniture: Bleached oak or mahogany, or painted black

Rug: Deep blue-green, floor size

For a Room with Large Windows and Lots of Sunshine

Walls: Deep delphinium blue

Draperies: Textured cotton woven with sparkle threads of metal or plastic

Slipcovers: Bold printed linen - like cotton natural ground, design of ink blue and deep rust brown

Furniture: Bleached oak, or mahogany

Rug: Ink blue, or deep rust brown

(The choice of the warm rust rug or the cool blue rug depends on whether the room is to be kept really cool, or warmed up a bit.)

For a Room with an Adjoining Alcove (Create a theme, then modify)

Walls: Striated textured wallboard tinted soft gray

Draperies: Bold patterned print of horizontal stripes using red, yellow, black, green, and white

Slipcovers: Plain mohair, or texture-woven cotton of red, yellow and black

Furniture: "Outdoor" cedar, finished in deep blue-gray

Floor: Polished black linoleum with yellow cotton rugs, or bare wood in broad planks, with green rugs

The subordinate theme:

Walls: Painted pale butter yellow

(Note that with gray walls more colors may be used.)

Upholstery: Green on black painted chairs

For a Summer Home with Lots of Sunshine

Walls: Aquamarine wall paper, printed in white and yellow

Draperies: Glazed chintz, printed in blue flowers, green leaves

Slipcovers: Lemon yellow chintz, bound with turquoise

Furniture: Painted white, or bleached wood, or dull black lacquer

Floors: Polished wood, left bare, with cotton string rugs of deep blue-green

Winter Color Scheme for a Cozy Living-Room (To save fuel)

Walls: Dusty rose

Draperies: Bold printed roses, with big blue-green leaves

Upholstery: Velveteen in blue-green, printed linen in large roses, on pale cream

Furniture: Walnut, mahogany, or bleached oak

Floors: Carpeted wall to wall in textured blue-green carpeting

These rooms are schemed to be restful. This is desirable for your living-room. You spend a good many hours there. You and your husband entertain your friends there; the children bring in their clutter. You do want a room that is easy to get along with, rather than one which is so stimulating that after a while it becomes boring. Dining-rooms are a different story. They should be gay and bright. A small dining-alcove off a living-room or a kitchen should share the color scheme of the more important room; but a dining-room all by itself can be considered as a separate entity.

Contrast sets the key here. Instead of trying to harmonize closely balanced colors, try combining colors on opposite sides of the "color circle." The color circle is a wheel of colors, name-placed according to their order as we learned them in our rainbow-days. Yellow is placed at the top, with the parade of warm colors descending gradually along the right side, and the cool colors similarly placed on the left side. Study the diagram on page 86, for that will show you the placing of the colors and their relation one to the other.

It is easy to see that orange is directly opposite blue; that red is directly opposite green, that purple is directly opposite yellow and placed at the lowest point on the circle. These colors are complementary to one another. They are the kind of contrasts you use when you want to achieve an exciting costume. They work the same way in room decoration.

The contrasts of the hyphenated colors, yellow-orange to blue-purple, red-orange to blue-green, and yellow-green to red-purple, are complementary, too. They are more muted than the clear colors mentioned above, because of the very fact that they are obtained by mixing two clear colors together. Thus they are never quite as strong in contrast as the clear colors.

Do bear in mind, *when using contrasting or complementary colors together that one of the colors should predominate.* One may be in larger areas, or it may be stronger than the other.

COLOR RECIPES FOR DINING-ROOMS

Small Dining-Room for a Country Home

Walls: Feathered pine boards tinted dull yellow-orange

Draperies: Deep blue print on white linen, blue chintz valance

Upholstery: Blue chintz bound in orange

Furniture: Pine or maple

Rugs: Hooked rugs, tones of tan, brown, green and blue

Table Linen: Dull blue hand-woven linen

China: White with blue design

Small Dining-Room for a City Apartment

Walls: Painted stark white with purple and gray wall paper border

Draperies: Yellow antique satin edged with purple fringe

Upholstery: Chair seats purple velvet

Furniture: Painted black with gold trim

Rug: Old gold Chinese carpet

Table Linen: Yellow linen, purple monograms

China: Pale gray china

Dining-Room with Wall Paper

Walls: Chinese wallpaper printed in green and coral on dark gray ground. White woodwork

Draperies: Lime green rough cotton, white blinds, with green tapes

Upholstery: Deep coral

Furniture: Mahogany, or bleached oak, or white painted French style

Floor: Polished wood with deep coral cotton rug

Sunshine-Filled Dining-Room

Walls: Pale gray, spattered with turquoise, blue-purple and green paint in small spatter-dash design

Draperies: Printed cotton carrying colors of spatter

Chair Seats: Blue-purple mohair, binding on draperies of same

Furniture: Walnut, or mahogany, or "outdoor finished" red cedar

Floors: "Pickled" hardwood in pale gray tone. Deep blue-green oval carpet

Table Linen: White, edged with color, or gray, or blue-purple linen

China: Pale gray with wreath of blue-green leaves

Dining-Room with Oriental Rug (Perhaps you inherited one)

Walls: Pale terra-cotta pink

Draperies: Hand-blocked flower and bird print on natural color linen

Chair Seats: Needlepoint in dull shades found in rug, or velvet of one of the dull blue-green shades

Furniture: Mahogany, walnut, or bleached woods

Linens: Natural color, with embroidered monograms of deep rust

Rugs: Oriental rugs in tones of rust, brown, orange-yellow, and blue-green

China: Patterned in soft all-over flower design in very soft colors, or plain pinky-tan china

You can make up your own gay color schemes, working each step out carefully, using contrasts as described in the complementary color schemes, gradually evolving a complete relation of walls, draperies, rugs and accessories. When you plan the color harmony have a large sample of the fabric, the wall paper or the planned wall color in the room for about two weeks before you make up your mind that it is just what you want. You will be surprised to discover that you will often change your mind. As you live with a color, you either like it more and more every day or it is the wrong color for a room and you soon dislike it.

When the color goes on the wall at first it may seem stronger than the color you desire. This should be, for when all the other things are placed in the room, when the draperies are hung, it will seem softer, less strong and vivid. So don't be timid with colors, particularly when you are planning a room where you spend so little time as the dining-room. Stimulate sparkling conversation and home-time gayety by a sparkling color scheme. But don't have it so garish that you will have to keep a bottle of digestive tablets handy. Just strike a happy medium.

Now for the bedrooms in the house. What do you want in your own private chamber? Do you want dark walls so the light won't wake you early? Do you want a bedroom that is partly study, parlor, sitting-room and bedroom. This style of room has increased in popularity. Many homes have had all the bedrooms furnished like personal sitting rooms, with huge comfy couches that convert to beds at night.

Have you a suppressed desire for a very frilly, feminine dressing-table, a fragile fabric for the spread on your bed, and a truly feminine color scheme? Don't forget there's a man in your life now; give a thought to his wishes as well as your own. Most of them prefer something crisp and clear-cut. It can be dainty as well, particularly if you choose a fabric that launders easily, and see that it makes frequent trips to the washing-machine.

COLOR RECIPES FOR BEDROOMS

Dainty Bedroom with Washable Fabrics

Walls: Painted pale turquoise blue

Draperies: Printed yellow rosebuds with green leaves

Slipcovers, dressing-table and spreads: Yellow, bound in deep turquoise. "Dust ruffles" of print on beds

Furniture: Honey maple, or birch, or bleached wood

Rugs: Cotton string, deep turquoise

Bedroom with Few Windows, No Sunshine

Walls: Painted pinky white, wall paper border of deep pink flowers placed 30" from floor

Draperies: Cherry pink ruffled in white, or hung over ruffled organdie tie-back curtains

Slipcovers, dressing-table: Cherry-pink flowers on dotted ground of green and white. *Bedspreads:* Quilted white cotton over flounces of printed fabric

Furniture: Painted white with narrow stripe of cherry red

Rugs: Scatter ovals of soft green, or deep cherry

Small Room, To Make It Look Larger

Walls: Plaid paper in blue and white. White painted doors and woodwork

Draperies: None

Slipcovers, dressing-table: White glazed chintz bound in blue. *Bedspreads:* White top, with side ruffles of blue and white stripe

Furniture: Mahogany, walnut, or maple

Rugs: Blue and white stripe woven rag rugs

Room with Too Much Light, Large in Size

Walls: Dull heliotrope lavender

Draperies: None

Bedspreads: Cotton dyed to match walls. *Dressing-table, slipcovers:* Bold patterned flowers, predominating deep rose shades

Furniture: Dark lacquer, mahogany, or walnut

Rug: Oval carpet in deep plum on polished hardwood floor

Bedroom with Dormer Windows

Walls: Papered with small flower printed paper, painted inside dormers to match deep blue in paper

Draperies: Sheer net, ruffled and tied back, over roller shades of striped chintz in blue and white

Slipcovers: Blue and white striped chintz. *Bedspread:* Plain deep blue, with striped flounce. *Dressing-table:* Sheer net, flounced over plain blue

Furniture: French Provincial type fruitwood, or honey maple, birch or cherry

Rug: Rose and blue braided rag rug on polished wood, or polished dark blue linoleum

Bedroom-Sitting Room Combination (Ideal for part-time guest room)

Walls: Striped gray and white paper, dark gray woodwork

Draperies: Toile print in wine red on white background, trimmed with wine red ball fringe

Slipcovers and Tailored Couch Cover: Wine red, rough-woven rayon and cotton, with sofa pillows of jade green, pale gray, bright blue

Furniture: Red cedar, bleached oak, walnut or dark maple

Rug: Large gray woven cotton, or dark gray textured broadloom

Bedroom-Playroom for Growing Children

Walls: Covered with polished plywood, colored Linowall, or plastic-coated wallpaper that can be wiped clean; color, light tan

Draperies: Loosely woven white cotton that launders easily, hung from under painted red valance board

Slipcovers: Sailcloth in blue.
Bedspreads: Red and white checked gingham

Furniture: Maple, or painted white or deep blue

Rug: Washable cotton in blue

Nursery for Baby (A scheme that avoids the conventional blue and pink)

Walls: Pale butter yellow. Turquoise woodwork

Draperies: Turquoise glazed chintz, sheer glass curtains

Slipcovers: Deep yellow, rough textured cotton, cotton fringe dyed turquoise for trim. Appliquéd crib spread in white with pastel colors

Furniture: Painted white, or honey maple

Rug: Squares of cotton bath mats in yellow and turquoise, sewn together checkerboard style

Such utility rooms as kitchens and bathrooms have a good part of their color scheme already dictated by the fittings such as sink, range, refrigerator, tub and lavatory. In most modern homes these are gleaming white. While some bathroom fixtures have been made in pastel colors, they have not been successful in interesting the homemaker, or they cost more than the budget permits. Therefore, in most cases the color scheme planned for the room must take into consideration large areas of white. This means that the other color used should be stronger. This is no place for anemic, timid use of either color or pattern.

Some new homemakers have definitely requested kitchens that look less like experimental laboratories, and are cozy and comfortable for the long hours the homemaker must spend in them. Many of these kitchens have dining alcoves as a part of the kitchen, and they offer a chance for gay color and for the use of the new wipe-clean, plastic-coated fabrics.

COLOR RECIPES FOR KITCHENS

Kitchen with Dining Alcove

Walls: Paper in bold plaid of red and green, except for area around stove. This painted gloss white, with peasant decals

Cupboard Doors: Decorated with peasant decals

Furniture: Stained green pine bench and table

Window Curtains: Red film plastic with white starched cotton ruffle

Floor: Green linoleum

Kitchen with Small Windows

Walls: Flesh pink shiny paint

Floor: Black and white block linoleum

Draperies: Flower print percale used as valance across top of window and to ruffle sheer cotton sash curtains

Furniture: Apple green with seat pads of flowered cotton

Kitchen with Broad Windows (Country style)

Walls: Prim scenic paper, coated with transparent varnish or wax around stove area

Draperies: Bold plaid homespun or gingham

Furniture: Pine or maple with seat pads of plaid

Floor: Broad waxed boards, or linoleum in natural wood color. Linoleum in warm red-brown color tile pattern

Kitchen, Planned for Party Entertaining

Walls: Painted, with guest signatures added and painted on

Draperies: Guatemalan cotton, horizontal stripes, gay colors

Furniture: Painted black, each guest stool a different color

Floor: Polished red linoleum

Small Kitchenette, in City Apartment

Walls: Painted gloss white to give impression of more size and to add light. Wallpaper border with flower design pasted on cupboard doors just inside moulding, with corners carefully mitered. (If doors are of glass paste wallpaper inside, using colorless rubber cement to attach in place)

Draperies: Flowered plastic coated fabric, pleated to stay back so no light will be shut out

Furniture: Painted deep rose to match flowers

Floor: Deep green linoleum, or black and white tiles

COLOR RECIPES FOR BATHROOMS

If the bathroom is attached to a bedroom, the color scheme should be dictated by that room. The predominant color may be the same, or the subordinate color may be made predominant. For example:

Bathroom to Go with Bedroom-Sitting Room in Gray and Wine Red

Walls: Pearl gray

Bathroom Fittings: White

Drapery and Shower Curtain: Wine red. *Towels:* Wine red with gray monogram

Floor: Marbleized dark gray linoleum with wine-red border inserted

Bathroom to Go with Dormer Window Bedroom

Walls: Pale blue of same color, but lighter than used for dormers

Shower Curtain and Window Curtain: Striped blue and white washable chintz as used in bedroom

Floor: Dark blue or soft gray linoleum, blue woven rag rug

Bathroom Facing North

Walls: Deep rose

Shower Curtain and Window Curtain: Transparent white with silver, gray and turquoise stripes

Floor: Gray and black blocks; rose cotton rug

Bathroom Facing South, with Sunshine

Walls: Green tile or tile board

Fittings: White

Curtains: Blue and lavender flowers printed, green leaves. *Towels:* White, large green monograms

Floor: White tile, green string rug

Small Bathroom, in City Apartment

Walls: Gloss yellow to suggest sunshine

Shower and Window Curtain: Springtime green transparent plastic with pinked edge ruffles. *Towels:* Light green with dark green monograms, or yellow with black monograms

Floor: Green and white marbleized linoleum, yellow string rug

Perhaps there are other rooms planned for your house. Then make your own scheme, taking into consideration the type of room it is to be. Game rooms are used for entertaining. They can be as gay as a child's playroom. A room that is used for the enjoyment or study of music, or for home work of a busy professional man, should have a restful color scheme. If you plan to entertain friends frequently, plan your living-room with a game or card corner. This might be decorated in a different scheme from the main room, but one that uses some of the same colors.

An interesting trend is to have one wall of a room papered, with three walls painted. Or, in some cases one wall is covered with plywood paneling, and the other walls are in color. Or, patterned wall paper is used just around a single grouping of furniture, to lend it importance and add interest. Don't forget to consider each separate element when planning the color scheme. Consider the color of the wood of the furniture, and include that in your scheme for it cannot be ignored.

One very clever decorator found she added interest to her color schemes by adding one small note of discord. She planned the scheme carefully so it was perfectly balanced, then, like a good cook, she added a bit of spice in the way of a vermilion bowl, or a vase of pottery blue, or a mounted print of a vivid tropical bird. That takes artistry, but it is a taste that can be acquired. So plan your color scheme carefully. Then don't forget to add a bit of spice.

Lamps and lamp-tables in window

VIII

FABRICS AND WALLPAPER

TEXTURE, PATTERN AND DESIGN

TWO OF THE most important tools of decoration are the fabrics used for draperies and slipcovers, and the wall paper applied to the wall. In all the preceding color schemes there has been mention of patterned fabrics used with plain walls, or plain materials used with patterned walls. This is an easy rule to follow if you want to be on the safe side in your decorating.

There is also the very handy "Rule of Three" used by many famous decorators. This permits the combination of three, one printed with a definite design such as flowers, scenery, etc; one plain, with perhaps a surface texture formed by the weave; and one with a geometric pattern such as a check, plaid or stripe. This latter may be one of the rough-woven textured cottons, or it may be a bold print. You will enjoy forming such combinations, using your own good taste to decide which designs go well together.

Never make your decision from a small sample. Buy or borrow at least a yard-square size to use in the room, laying it against the chair it is to cover, or against the wall it is to paper. It is amazing what a different effect is obtained when all the wall is papered. You liked the design in the sample book because of its clear-cut boldness; but you forgot that the room was large and there would be a lot of it used on all four walls. Or perhaps your husband asked that his favorite large chair be covered in green. When you bought the green you chose a vivid colored cotton. After the chair was covered, you realized a darker shade would make the chair less obtrusive, seem smaller and fit in with the general room scheme more satisfactorily. So be sure to try large pieces of the color or pattern before making your decision. Use your imagination to picture it in the size area it will cover and prevent any costly mistakes. Because there are so many yards necessary to cover the chair, sofa, or make draperies, because a papered wall requires lots of paper and is not very easy to do over, you may have to live with some mistakes for a while. So do think carefully and plan the fabric scheme along

99

"Rule of 3" in fabric against plain painted wall—couch covered in flower
print to match draperies; comfortable chair slipcovered in stripe; armchair
upholstered in texture

with the color scheme. When you buy the material let it be just right.

If your town does not give you a large variety of materials try the mail-order stores which offer an attractive choice of style and color. Many of the large metropolitan department stores will send you material and wall papers. Some of them have no means of sending you samples, while others will send you samples of "decorator size" if you are willing to pay for them. Return them when you order, and have that amount credited on the further payments.

Home-decorator magazines carry advertisements of fabric manufacturers and wall paper firms who put out booklets of their designs. Many will also send you decorators' samples or smaller swatches of the fabric, if you write them your request.

One fabric manufacturer has invented the "sister prints" to help you with your deco-

rating. One fabric is printed with large bouquets or flower patterns. Another print has the same flower, perhaps in smaller size, used in another arrangement. This may be in a striped grouping, either trailing down the length of the fabric or across it. Or, it may be spotted in the center of diamond-spaced ribbons. This manufacturer also plans a plain fabric to repeat one of the predominant colors, carrying this out in a textured weave or in a smooth sateen. He may also provide a stripe, or a polka-dot fabric to assist you with a geometric.

If you buy these materials your shopping problem is very much easier than going from store to store and trying for color matching. This same firm also makes wall papers and rugs, ensembling some groups in this more complete way.

Some of the fabric manufacturers work with wall paper manufacturers. The material is printed with the same design as the paper. Thus, if you wish, you can cover the wall with the same design as that you use for the draperies. Or you can have the wall opposite the windows papered with a paper printed just like the draperies. This would be more effective if the other three walls of the room were painted or papered in a plain harmonizing color.

In using the "Rule of Three," remember that it applies only to the average size room. If the room is quite small you will want only two materials, preferably one plain with one patterned. For instance, in Sonny's room a pen-line striped wall paper makes a nice background for circus printed chintz. In that tiny guest room black and white checked gingham makes a nice splash against a coral pink painted wall. In a small study, walls papered with a scenic wall paper look best as a background for homespun textured deep green cotton draperies.

In a small room all the designs should be kept in proportion. Keep the large patterned leaf print, the bold stripes and huge plaids for the larger room. In the smaller room choose daintier patterns, less predominant textures. Large pieces of furniture are less apt to "stick out" into the room if they are covered with fabric that matches the wall behind or blends into the coloring. This is a principle of camouflage. On the other hand, if you have one treasure—a chest of drawers you have inherited, or a lovely secretary—you can add attention to it and make it form a center of interest by silhouetting it against a painted or patterned panel of color that contrasts with the rest of the wall.

You will gain many ideas of fabric and pattern use from home-decoration magazines, or from exhibition rooms in department stores. Many times you will be able to find ideas that you can copy exactly for your home. Sometimes these simply stimulate you to an ingenious idea that is all your own. One smart homemaker realized that her summer slipcovers took a lot of wear from her four small sons, so she bought sailcloth to upholster the side chairs and make covers for the upholstered furniture. Another realized that cheesecloth would fit into her budget better than the other glass curtain fabrics, so she dyed it a sunny yellow and used it for the windows and to drape an heirloom four-poster bed. Many of the artists at a famous summer colony dye unbleached muslin into lovely colors, and use them in varying combinations for their home decoration.

If you can't find the fabric that you want in the upholstery department of your store, try the dress fabric department. Many of these are inexpensive. The ones of lighter weight will do for bedroom draperies, and the heavier, stronger ones may be used for slipcovers. Slipcover material must be strong and firm in order not to pull out at the seams and in order to stand the hard wear and tear.

Many of the dress fabrics may be used for bedspreads and dressing-table skirts, too, for these do not require such strong material. It should be something that will not wrinkle and crush when taken off and put back on the bed daily.

Some of the new materials that are treated with surface finish are very practical for household use. A wipe with a damp cloth cleans them, or they rinse out in the washing machine to good-as-new state. There are nylons, glass cloth, for the materials that are so woven they are easy to care for, or there are Koroseal, Beutanol and other surface-treated cloths. These coatings may be applied to chintz or to sheer fabrics. The material may be plain or printed. The fabric is crisp in appearance, with a surface sheen that stays on throughout laundering. They are excellent for use in dirty cities, or at the seaside where dampness seems to make most fabrics go limp in a short while.

Some of these plastics are also available in "unsupported film." This means that they form a sheet similar to a shower curtain, without being applied to a woven fabric. These films may be had in very thin weight or in a heavy weight which is commercially used for upholstery. To date the heavy weight is not available for the homemaker to use to upholster furniture. But ready-made furniture comes already upholstered in a wide variety of attractive colors. This material will not scratch, mar or take spots or stains. It is therefore most practical for rooms where children and pets are to have free reign.

These plastic coatings are also being applied to wall paper and to other wall surfacings. One plastic wall finish comes in rolls like wall paper and may be applied over a nicked or badly surfaced wall. It resembles the striated surface of Weldwood, the striated plywood, and may be painted any color. Its natural tone is a soft putty tan. Another texture of the same plastic surfacing material resembles a weave similar to a heavy corded burlap. These are more expensive than ordinary wall paper, but their advantage is that once applied they will wear forever.

MATERIALS SUITABLE FOR GLASS CURTAINS

Soft materials suitable for tailored panels rather than ruffled ones:

Gauze—This indicates a loose open weave, whether the inexpensive linen gauze popularly called "theatrical" gauze, or the more expensive silk or rayon gauze used for fine curtains. Variety of fabrics with a figure woven in to make a pattern, or plain.

Glass Fabrics—These are made plain, with a figure woven in, with contrasting color stripe or with a printed design. They are difficult to stitch, but hang attractively and launder well. They are woven from fine spun glass threads, thus do not absorb dirt and dust, and are not affected by climate.

Lace—Lace panels may be purchased ready-made, or may be bought by the yard in a variety of patterns. (May also be had for bedspreads or tablecloths.)

Lawn—Fine fabric used for baby garments; suitable for bedroom curtains. May be had plain or printed in dainty patterns.

Madras—Woven fabric, soft and sheer, taking its name from the part of India where it was first manufactured. Often used for casement cloth, in pale gray, tan or white.

Marquisette—Sometimes ruffled, but this soft gauze-like, square-meshed fabric looks far better in tailored panels. May have "cushion dots," puffy chenille spots, or other pattern woven in. May have color designs woven on or printed. Often used for "cottage sets" for the kitchen.

Muslin—Plain-woven cotton fabric, light in weight, plain, printed, or with dots woven in, or embroidered on the surface. May be ruffled. Mousseline de soie, luxury version of muslin in silk, used for very rich rooms and fragile effects.

Net—A variety of weaves, from the small-sized octagonal mesh, through large open-weave mesh designs. These may be purchased by the yard or in ready-made panels. Fishnet, hand or machine knotted linen or cotton twine, often dyed in color for casual effects in summer homes.

Ninon—Luxury fabric of rayon, similar to voile; most satisfactory for glass curtains because of softness of folds together with firm, even weave.

Nylon—Luxury fabric, woven of nylon yarn in weave similar to ninon.

Scrim—Coarse gauze with stiffened finish; somewhat similar in effect to marquisette.

Voile—Plain weave, sheer fabric, obtainable in fine weave or in a coarse weave.

If your window is too small to look modern you can seam together several widths of fabric for a "window wall drapery." Loop part of it back with a long strap tieback.

A straight length of fabric lined with plain sateen is looped over arm brackets for the drapery. The dust ruffles of the bed and the pillow frills in the same Beauty Rose glosheen contrast with quilted spreads.

One large room becomes living-room and bedroom when chests are placed to form a low partition. Twin beds are placed head against these chests after fabric slipcovers hide the unfinished plywood backs. Plain fabric drapery across the window, plaid wall covering, and striped bedspread fabric go well together.

Even a small room looks well with a large patterned fabric. The couch slipcover and draperies are patterned in yellow, green, and gray roses to contrast effectively with the warm golden-tan shades of the waxed knotty pine panelling.

Deeply flounced slipcovers are easy to fit. Often they do not need any back placket to slide on and off. Notice the method of fitting short slipcover around the wooden chair arm.

Courtesy R. H. Macy and Co.
A wallpaper reproduced from a "document print" is just right with Early American pine and maple furniture.

Courtesy F. Schumacher and Co.
Boldly patterned rose wallpaper is rich for one wall of either a living-room or bedroom. It should be used on the wall opposite the draperies if they are patterned, or may be used on the window wall if plain fabric curtains are used.

Suitable for use in either a modern or a traditional room are these two papers. The striped repeat may be used perpendicularly to make the wall seem higher, or horizontally to make the ceiling appear lower.

Courtesy Catherine Blondin Associates
Some of the newest wallpapers are designed for modern type homes. These show bold stripes, bamboo woven print, or woven plaid effects. Others are textured like tweed, or printed to resemble looped fringe.

Courtesy Catherine Blondin Associates

Courtesy Catherine Blondin Associates

Courtesy Catherine Blondin Associates

Courtesy Catherine Blondin Associates

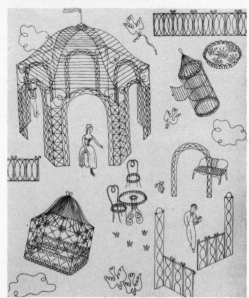

Courtesy Catherine Blondin Associates

At left:

Modern in feeling "Outline" comes in an off-white background, with a tracery of color forming the design. This is particularly suitable for a rather small room with draperies and slipcovers of plain fabric to match the tracery.

Crisp materials suitable for ruffled glass curtains:

Dimity—Plain or printed crisp cotton muslin.

Dotted Swiss—Plain muslin fabric, with woven-in dots in contrasting weight thread or contrasting color. The real dotted Swiss is an imported cotton, coming from Switzerland, as the name implies. There are many similar fabrics domestically woven.

Film—Fabrics of unsupported plastic film similar to shower curtain material may be made into attractive ruffled curtains. Film-coated scrim, marquisette, ninon, nylon, or organdie may also be used.

Organdie—Plain or printed sheer stiffened muslin woven of fine twist cotton. Particularly attractive with ruffles, the permanently finished organdie holds its crispness through many launderings.

MATERIALS SUITABLE FOR OVER-DRAPERIES

Brocade—Luxury fabric used for formal rooms, particularly traditional rooms of Colonial or French and English eighteenth century styles of furniture. The fabric has a woven pattern that looks as though it had been embroidered. Sometimes the background has a twill weave and sometimes a satin weave. Brocatelle has the surface designs of heavier yarns to resemble hand embroidery. Sometimes these are of metal thread, linen or cotton.

Calico—Originally printed in India with "tree of life" patterns, these rather thin cottons were extensively used in the eighteenth century. Simple adaptations of calico designs have flowers, fruit, birds, and other rather small designs. Fabric may be quilted as well as plain.

Chintz—Similar in weight to calico, chintz may be had in plain colors, or printed designs of wide variety. Glazed chintz has a treated surface glaze; some permanently glazed to last through repeated launderings.

Cretonne—Similar to chintz and calico, but made with heavier yarn of cotton. Comes in plain or printed designs of great variety. May be used for slipcovers, too.

Crewel—Natural colored linen embroidered in gay colored wools by hand during the late seventeenth century and early eighteenth century was very popular for draperies and upholstery. Modern machine-made reproductions used for homes furnished with furniture of this style.

Damask—Drapery fabric of one color thread woven in pattern design by a combination of plain and twill weave. Effect is somewhat similar to brocade, but more like fine linen tablecloths, which are really linen damask. This makes luxurious hangings, particularly suited to use with fine mahogany furniture. Made with linings of sateen these should wear for many years and repay the cost of the original investment.

Faille—This is a ribbed material formed by lighter weight threads being woven over a coarser filling thread. The heavier weights are called bengaline and ottoman. Other rib-weave fabrics are grosgrain, poplin, and rep. Moiré is a faille with a watered design pressed into the ribs under extreme heat. These fabrics are usually of rayon, but may be of cotton or silk.

Gabardine—Twill-woven cotton, with diagonal raised rib, may be had dyed in plain colors or printed. Excellent for slipcovers.

Gingham—Plain weave cotton dyed in various colors before weaving; or plaid cotton woven of yarn dyed threads. Originally a dress fabric, now widely used for curtains and slipcovers for country houses, informal rooms and for children's rooms.

Glosheen—Mercerized cotton with a reversed satin weave that produces a permanent sheen. May be had in plain colors or printed in lovely designs. Excellent for draperies or slipcovers.

Jaspe—Mottled-looking woven fabric, made by using uneven strands of contrasting colored warp and woof threads.

Mohair—Variety of plain or printed fabrics woven from hair of Angora goats. Excellent for long wear, but more expensive than fabrics of cotton or rayon.

Moiré—(See definition under faille.)

Percale—Flat-woven cotton fabric, plain or printed. Originally intended for house dresses and aprons, often used for informal draperies and slipcovers.

Piqué—Heavy cotton with a corde, or "waffle," textured surface formed by heavier filling threads woven in with lighter weight warp and woof threads. Originally a dress fabric, also used for draperies and bedspreads, dressing-table and other slipcovers.

Pongee—Uneven weave of light and heavy weight threads, originally of pure silk, imported from India and China; now made also of rayon and cotton.

Poplin—Fine light-weight fabric with a ridged weave similar to faille. Drapes attractively and wears well. Though originally a fabric for men's shirts, is now used extensively for bedspreads and slipcovers as well as draperies. May be of cotton, silk, rayon or other synthetic fiber.

Rep—Surface texture of heavier cross threads, either plain or figured. May be of cotton, wool, mohair, rayon or silk.

Satin—High lustrous surface is caused by longer "floating" surface thread carried across two or more under threads. In rayon or satin this makes fine luxury draperies. They should be lined with sateen for sufficient body.

Sateen—Cotton fabric with satin weave. Used for linings of draperies, or dyed and printed for draperies or slipcovers.

Shantung—Similar to pongee, but with heavier "slub" yarn. This is a yarn that has thicker spots at uneven intervals. Since the wild silk taken from "undomesticated" silkworms is uneven in texture, fabric woven from it is sometimes called raw silk or wild silk.

Taffeta—Another luxury fabric with a smooth, crisp weave, showing a delicate surface sheen caused by the contrast of color between the warp and woof threads. This may be "changeable taffeta," so woven that it changes color in surfaces and shadows of the fabric. May be used in cotton, rayon or other synthetic fibers or silk. Should be lined for best effect. Excellent for ruffled flounces.

Velvet—Luxury fabric more often used for draperies in our mothers' or grandmothers' day. Sometimes used in formal rooms. Should be made with sateen lining.

MATERIALS SUITABLE FOR SLIPCOVERS

Chintz—(See definition on preceding chart.)
Cretonne—"   "   "   "   "
Denim—Cotton fabric, strongly woven of firm threads. Material should be bought with preshrinkage guaranteed, or should be preshrunk by laundering before cutting slipcover.
Faille—   (See definition on preceding chart.)
Gabardine—"   "   "   "   "
Gingham—"   "   "   "   "
Glosheen—"   "   "   "   "
Mohair—"   "   "   "   "
Percale—"   "   "   "   "
Piqué—"   "   "   "   "
Poplin—"   "   "   "   "
Rep—"   "   "   "   "

Sailcloth—Lightweight canvas used for slipcovers that have to be sturdy, or for upholstery on out-of-door furniture.

Sheeting—Material similar to percale or to heavy-weight muslin; may be used for slipcovers during shortage of other materials. May be dyed in attractive colors.

Ticking—Woven material originated for mattresses; may be used for sturdy summer slipcovers. Should be shrunk before making as some ticking has a great deal of "filling." When this is washed out the ticking is likely to shrink a great deal.

MATERIALS SUITABLE FOR UPHOLSTERY

Brocade and Brocatelle—(See Drapery Chart for definitions.)

Corduroy—Rib-woven cotton velvet; very durable and practical.

Cretonne—(See Drapery Chart for definition.)

Crewel—   "   "   "   "   "

Damask—   "   "   "   "   "

Faille—   "   "   "   "   "

Frisé—Fabric with a surface pile of uncut loops, strong, long wearing of mohair, cotton wool, or rayon. Velvet is made of cut loops, in similar weave to frisé.

Gabardine—(See Drapery Chart for definition.)

Genoese Velours—Plain or twill weave background with raised velvet or frisé tufts forming a design. Often found in large pieces of upholstered furniture.

Mohair—(See Drapery Chart for definition.)

Moiré—(See Drapery Chart under faille.)

Plush—Deep or shallow pile velvet woven with mohair. Used on many modern furniture pieces to offer contrast to sleek finish of wood. Very fuzzy type called kinkimo.

Rep—(See Drapery Chart for definition.)

Tapestry—Machine-woven patterned fabric, strong and heavy; adapted from ribbed fabrics originally hand-woven.

Velvet—Additional threads woven into the warp and woof of the background to form a loop pile, which is sheared into tufts of even height. A luxury fabric suitable for the most formal rooms, with either silk or rayon pile on a cotton or rayon ground.

Velveteen—Cotton pile on a cotton ground. This fabric is stronger than velvet and more suitable for upholstery. Lint and dust show, particularly on the dark colors. Occasionally used for slipcovers for winter use.

WALL PAPER

Some wall paper is washable, the material and the color of the printed design being so treated that any soil or spots may be washed off with a damp cloth. Naturally these are the best papers to buy and, in most cases, are no more expensive than papers that are not washable. The prices of the paper varies according to whether it has been printed by hand or by machine. Naturally the former costs from four to five times as much as the latter. There are even very lovely hand-painted panels, if you are feeling extravagant enough to want to pay around forty dollars for one panel to set in the wall.

Some of the papers come in a single roll; some in a double roll. The single roll is 18" wide by 8 yards long. Some imported papers are wider and come in a longer roll. Figure that a single roll will cover approximately 30 square feet of wall surface, for usually there is a wastage of about 6 square feet in matching the pattern.

Before you buy the paper for a room, make a diagram of the wall surfaces to be covered; deduct the door and window sizes to arrive at the right amount. Usually the doors are 3' wide by 7' high, with window area 3' wide by 6' high. Mark these off on the graph of the walls; measure the room height, width and length. Then do the figuring. Find out the number of square feet of wall surfaces in the room, divide by 30 and you will find the number of single rolls that are necessary. If the number comes out even, add a single roll so you will be sure to have enough. If the amount left over nearly approaches a single roll, add a double roll for insurance against having to run downtown for more in the middle of the job.

If the room is to be papered only part way up, approximately 30" from the floor to form a decorative dado, measure the running feet and multiply by 2½' to find the number of square feet required.

If you are papering the inside of a closet, figure the wall surfaces in a similar manner.

If you are using a wall-paper border, take the measurement of the wall surfaces where the border is to appear; then buy the number of rolls of wall-paper border required. Many rooms look attractive with a painted wall, trimmed with an attractive wall-paper border placed around the top of the room under the picture molding or just below the ceiling.

If the room has dormers, you will find it difficult to match a definite pattern at the edge of this angled wall or ceiling. The inside of the dormer may be papered in a plain contrasting color, or painted; or a paper with an all-over, rather indefinite pattern chosen for the entire room.

Many traditional papers have been accurately reproduced, so that you have old French, English or American papers to choose from at a fraction of the cost that the hand-blocked originals cost. These look well when used with traditional furniture, whether they are original antiques or reproductions.

The firm that sells you the paper will be able to suggest designs which will suit the interior you plan. In many cases they are named in such a way as to indicate their origin.

Here are a few suggestions:

For a Country Home with a French Provincial or Early American or Pennsylvania Dutch atmosphere, choose papers with quaint motifs, chintz designs, scenes of country activities, flower bouquets, wreaths or garlands in rather small size and prim in character. Choose designs that look as though they had been taken from Delft pottery, or which look as though stenciled or block-printed by hand.

For a Georgian or Colonial Home with eighteenth-century antiques or reproductions in mahogany or walnut or maple, choose papers with larger designs, sometimes alternating flower group with scene. Many of these are geometrically repeated, having an oval, or square, or diamond effect controlling the pattern. Or, use the scenic painted panels for formal rooms such as hall, living-room, dining-room. These panels may continue around the room or be spotted attractively in one wall, or in the center of wood paneling. Or use paper that has a Chinese flavor, for the eighteenth century was the time when sailing ships brought treasures back to the homes of England, France and America. Wall-paper or painted panels were among the most prized importations. For the bedrooms use larger flower patterns, or stripes with flowers, or garlands with ribbons. Use designs that look like chintz or lovely hand-blocked linen or damask.

For a More Formal Home of Regency style, or Southern Colonial, with furniture that is classical in design, Hepplewhite, Sheraton, or Federal in style, choose wall paper that repeats the classical motifs. This may have striped paper, contrasting a dull and satin finish, or columns, or a laurel wreath, an urn, or the anthemian, or some such classical motif. If flowers are used, the bouquet is more formalized. If scenery is used, it has a Grecian or Pompeian treatment.

For a Modern Home there are new papers with weave effects, or plaid, or soft stripes, the heavy textured papers before mentioned, or papers simulating wood veneers. For formal modern there are papers that simulate marble, or others which use a classical column design.

For the Home That Combines Modern with Traditional good taste and judgment are necessary in choosing the paper. For it may come under any of the above headings, or none. You may choose a paper to suit the color scheme or to offer contrast in texture or pattern. Be sure to try an adequate size sample before buying the paper for the complete room.

WALL PAPER IN THE BATH-ROOM OR KITCHEN

Wall paper is often used in the bathroom or kitchen to add gaiety and charm to what might otherwise be a rather dull colorless room. The wall paper is usually one with a treated or glazed surface to shed soil, grease or soot, and to withstand steam. However, any paper will stand up well in these rooms, so if you do not find the design you wish in a treated paper, do not hesitate to try another one. If you wish to use wall paper right close to the stove, and also wish it to be protected from grease and soot, it may be varnished with a colorless transparent varnish, or coated with white shellac, or waxed with special wall-paper wax.

Wall paper in the nursery is also surface treated to protect it, or you can buy one of the coated wall papers as mentioned on page 105.

Wall papers for playrooms are often amusing in character and bright in color. Here also, if they are to be subjected to hard wear,

if balls are likely to bounce against them, you may wish to coat them with a protective finish.

A small powder-room may have a gay paper, more spectacular in style than one you would use were the area to be covered more extensive. It is fun to have one with a gold or silver background, even printed on black or on vivid lacquer red.

Often the wall paper will set the color scheme for the whole room, as in the room that had walls covered with a lovely soot gray paper, printed in a Chinese design of lacquer red, jade green, and oyster white. These colors set the scheme for the rest of the room. Dull white finished furniture was upholstered in jade green, and string rugs of lacquer red were on the black polished floor. The draperies combined the two colors, with alternate colors hanging at the sides of the window and crisscrossing above to form the swag valance. Obviously with such a wall paper the draperies had to be textured plain color rather than a pattern. Even a damask or brocade would have been too much.

IX

BUYING LAMPS, CHINA AND GLASSWARE

IN ANY room the lamps or lighting is of the utmost importance to the beauty of the room and to the physical health of the occupants. Many oculists assert that we would not require glasses if there had been no shadows or glare to strain our eyes. Yet many rooms are so arranged that few of the occupants can see to read or sew or study.

Some rooms are planned selfishly. They have one comfortable seating spot, with a well-arranged lamp beside a comfortable chair. The first person there is well cared for. The rest suffer. In planning a room, any room of the house, due consideration must be given to the uses planned for that room. In your living-room you will wish to read, sew, study, play games. These require one kind of light, a light that has definite direction. You will also wish to have another kind of light, softer in character, available when talking with guests or listening to favorite radio programs.

Light therefore should be adaptable to those different needs. In the bedrooms there will be a need for adaptable light also. One kind of light is necessary for dressing, to be sure the slip doesn't show, that the rouge is evenly applied. Still another kind of light is needed for reading in bed or for relaxing with a bit of sewing or knitting on a chaise-longue. Even dining-rooms can use changes in lighting. One type of lighting can be used for the usual family meal. For entertaining, candles may form part of the table decoration. In that case a softer light would be used in other parts of the room.

Hallways should always be lighted clearly enough so there is no possibility of accidents, but glare is less attractive here than a soft, warm glow. On the other hand the "work-rooms" of the house—the bathroom, kitchen and laundry need strong shadowless illumination.

Perhaps your house has part of this lighting already installed. If you have bought a ready-built home, or had one built for you, the lighting fixtures have been installed as part of the building contract. These may consist of ceiling lights or of wall lights. In many of the new homes, however, there is a tendency to provide socket outlets and have the light provided by lamps. This may be done in every room, or only in the major rooms, leaving a ceiling fixture and wall brackets to take care of the hallways, kitchen and bathroom.

If these are well designed, they may become an attractive part of the decorative scheme.

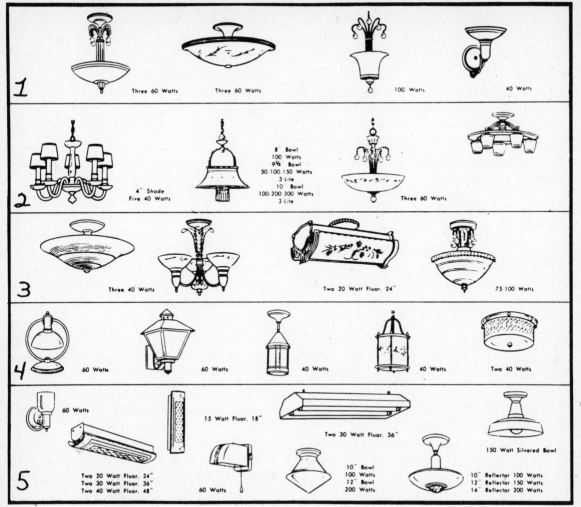

1
Three 60 Watts Three 60 Watts 100 Watts 40 Watts

2
4" Shade Five 40 Watts
8" Bowl 100 Watts 9½" Bowl 50-100-150 Watts 3-Lite 10" Bowl 100-200-300 Watts 3-Lite
Three 60 Watts

3
Three 40 Watts Two 20 Watt Fluor. 24" 75-100 Watts

4
60 Watts 60 Watts 40 Watts 40 Watts Two 40 Watts

5
60 Watts
Two 20 Watt Fluor. 24" Two 30 Watt Fluor. 36" Two 40 Watt Fluor. 48"
15 Watt Fluor. 18"
60 Watts
Two 30 Watt Fluor. 36"
10" Bowl 100 Watts 12" Bowl 200 Watts
150 Watt Silvered Bowl
10" Reflector 100 Watts 12" Reflector 150 Watts 14" Reflector 200 Watts

Lights adapted for use in various rooms: (Courtesy Westinghouse)

1 Living-room
2 Dining-room
5 Kitchen and laundry
3 Bedroom
4 Entrance and hall

Unfortunately, many of them look as though they had been designed by someone who was overfond of swirls. They lack the beauty of simplicity. If you have one of these ceiling fixtures, you may handle it in several ways. The fixture may be removed, and a metal plate used to cover the ceiling opening. This is then painted to match the ceiling and is most unobtrusive.

Or the fixture may be removed and a more attractively designed one substituted. This cost is well justified. For about $10 an attractive new ceiling fixture may be purchased, or for about half that sum you will be able to pick up an attractive old one in a small shop. Antique ceiling fixtures may cost around four or five times as much, but many of them are so attractive that the expense will be justified in the long run.

The new fluorescent ceiling fixtures are attractive and simply designed. These can be installed by an experienced electrician, and although the original cost is more, the upkeep is less than an incandescent lighting fixture, for they consume less electricity.

An inexpensive "dodge" is to buy a drum

shade of paper and suspend it under the lamp fixture in such a way that the whole thing is covered. This was effectively done by a decorator who had to live in a hotel room temporarily. She covered a square drum shade with a striped wall paper, carrying the paper across the bottom as well as on the sides. The same striped paper was used for shades of the standing lamps, and thus an attractive ensemble was created.

If the wall fixtures are unattractive, similar treatments can be used, or the whole fixture may be removed, the wires turned in, the hole patched with cardboard and the wallpaper carried right across. It is surprising how many old homes or apartments have the wall space ruined by panel framing of molding strips, with a wall bracket right in the center. These spaces are far more attractive without the lighting fixtures, and without the molding, too, if your landlord will permit its removal.

Since wiring short-circuits cause some of the most serious home fires, it is wise to consult an expert before making any alterations in the wiring, or before changing or removing lighting fixtures.

The other form of lighting most used is lamps. These may be floor lamps or table lamps, and the number of them used depends in great part upon the number of outlets available. When planning a new home it is of the greatest importance to plan for adequate sockets for lamps, radio, telephone, and for other electrical requirements of to-day. Housekeeping is infinitely easier if you do not have to disconnect lamps and radio in order to use the vacuum cleaner.

One of the cleverest of the modern inventions is a baseboard strip incorporating socket outlets every few feet. This is properly insulated, and may be added to a home that has insufficient outlets. It is far safer than overloading a single outlet by adding a multiple plug, from which a number of cords radiate in all directions.

By sketching a floor-plan arrangement of furniture on tracing paper and laying it over the architect's blueprint, you can plan exactly where outlets for lamps will be most convenient. If these are hidden behind furniture they will look far more attractive than if a long strip of light cord trails across the floor; and it will also be safer than having your family exposed to possible sprained ankles.

Lamps are found in a great number of styles and with decorative features to attract any taste. The shades may be simple and tailored, or fussy and fancy, all trimmed with ruffles or fringe. The style of the lamp should be suited to the room in each case. If the room is frilly and feminine, then by all means choose a lamp with a frilly, feminine shade. If it is casual in style, with a country-house atmosphere, choose a simple pottery or brass base, and top with a plaid shade of fabric or a parchment shade. If the room is formal in style, then the shade may be of fabric or it may be trimmed with upholstery braid or fringe. If the style of the furniture is adapted from the classical, then the lamp should be classical in style. See sketches for a variety of styles that are useful in these various interiors.

Adequate light near chaise longue for reading or sewing

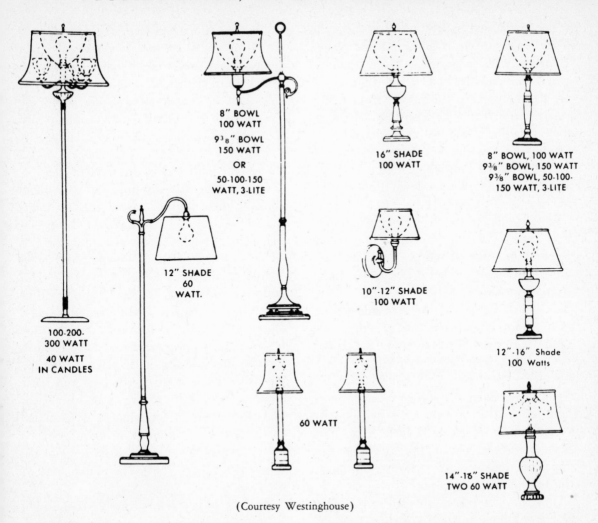

8" BOWL
100 WATT

9³⁄₈" BOWL
150 WATT

OR

50-100-150
WATT, 3-LITE

16" SHADE
100 WATT

8" BOWL, 100 WATT
9³⁄₈" BOWL, 150 WATT
9³⁄₈" BOWL, 50-100-
150 WATT, 3-LITE

12" SHADE
60 WATT.

10"-12" SHADE
100 WATT

12"-16" Shade
100 Watts

100-200-
300 WATT

40 WATT
IN CANDLES

60 WATT

14"-16" SHADE
TWO 60 WATT

(Courtesy Westinghouse)

Modern interiors demand modern lamps, and there are many attractive ones with bases of metal, glass, wood or pottery. In most cases the shades are of the greatest simplicity, and are made of paper or of homespun-like fabrics. (See sketches on page 115.)

The size and scale of the lamps are of the greatest importance. Floor lamps come in great variety from the usual swing arm type of wrought iron, brass or wood to tall torcheres of bridge lamps with an inverted bowl. Many of these are planned for the three-way light and have a switch that makes it possible to adjust the light to the needs of the users. With these bulbs light may be obtained of 300, 200 or 100 watt brilliance. This naturally provides great light, and requires a larger room, or a darker wall or ceiling, or fewer fixtures. In a smaller room it is possible that a three-way bulb providing 50, 100 or 150 watt brilliance would be sufficient. These are usually used for a slightly smaller bowl than the other bulbs. (See accompanying chart for details.)

In groupings with wing chairs, or other "tall" furniture, floor lamps of the 5' height look better. With the modern low-slung furniture lower-scaled lamps look better. If you are combining modern furniture with traditional in one room, choosing the height of the floor lamp will be determined by the scale of the furniture it is to stand alongside. Placing a taller lamp in a corner provides extra illumination because of wall reflections, and also helps keep the height from being overpowering. Tall floor lamps are necessary alongside a piano, and the inverted bowl type is extremely popular for game groupings. The light cast on the ceiling reflects back on the cards far better than a down-thrown light from the same strength bulb.

Table lamps are varied in style. There has lately been a vogue for taller ones, and placed on top of a 30" table a 24" lamp certainly lends more authority and provides a better light than a shorter one. For these a shade should be 16" to 18" across. Some of the most attractive lamps are 30" high and are shown in pairs. These are more expensive than small lamps, but don't forget, when they are lit they form a "center of interest" accent. Don't skimp on your investment here. Lamps of smaller size than the two dimensions given above give too little light, and cause eye strain. The money saved on the lamp may go to doctors for glasses, so splurge a bit on this decorative spot.

Three-way lights are provided in many of the larger lamps, and some of them have an inside china bowl to reflect the light onto the ceiling in a manner similar to the floor lamps. These usually require the 50 to 100 to 150 watt bulbs. For other lamps a 60 watt or a 100 watt will be sufficient, depending on the use to which the lamp is to be put and the opacity of the shade. Many of the new shades are of dark fabric or paper. These shed light above and below, but not through the shade. They therefore need stronger light bulbs than a lighter shade.

Some of the modern lamps are appearing with fluorescent bulbs. These are made in several different tones, and may also have a tube of transparent color slid over the bulb

to change the natural tone. For concentrated study or sewing or for art work a daylight fluorescent is preferred by some. This gives a cool blue light that is far less flattering than that with a warmer glow. Some lamps use the circular fluorescent bulb, a round tube that lies under the shade of the lamp. The fixture may combine an incandescent and a fluorescent bulb within the same shade.

In planning the lighting for your room consider these things. Are the reading lights placed so that the light falls on the paper, magazine or book without glaring in the eyes of the reader? This means that the lamp should be placed at the left side of the chair and toward the rear. Thus no shadow will be cast on the paper. Sewing requires good strong light, and should come from over the left shoulder if the sewer is right-handed. Reverse this rule for the left-handed person. Unshaded bulbs glare in the eyes and cause strain. High-placed fixtures cast insufficient light for reading or studying. A wide-angled shade casts more light than a drum-shaped one. A warm-toned shade casts a more becoming and more restful light than one of cool color.

Reading in bed is comfortable if the light is properly placed. Unfortunately, most bedside lamps are chosen for decorative value, not for practical use. Some are only 15" or 16" high. This is not sufficient to cast adequate light on a book. With the variety of head-lights for beds it is difficult to give a

Pin-up lamp for good lighting when reading in bed

hard and fast rule for the lamp height. It should be 30″ above the mattress to prevent your slumping while reading. For this reason wall pin-up lamps are growing in popularity. Since some of these are now more attractively designed than formerly it is wise to consider them in the bedroom scheme.

Dressing-table lamps are often more decorative than useful. Any woman would love a lighted-all-around dressing mirror like a stage star. Lacking that she is apt to borrow the bathroom mirror for make-up, much to her husband's annoyance, for he hates interruption while shaving. The up-and-down fluorescent lights in the bathroom cast clear light on her face. She can see without shadows far more easily than if she peers into a mirror with the light cast from a 9″ shade of a "pretty" lamp. Actually a 100 watt lamp is really necessary when applying make-up; yet seldom is the bedroom lamp large enough to accommodate one such powerful bulb, let alone two of them to show both sides of the face.

Built-in lighting is growing in popularity, and the above is only one of the arguments in its favor. Almost any room reacts well to the soft glow of a row of fluorescent lights set inside a molding at the top of the room. They reflect on the ceiling to provide light not unlike that cast into the room during the daytime.

In a house built to display the lighting of the future, other interesting built-in lighting arrangements were displayed. A bedroom had a bed set in a shallow niche. Beside the bed headboard at each side were perpendicu-

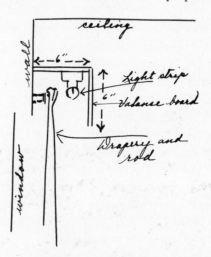

Lighting in valance board

lar columns of fluorescent light, covered with a panel of frosted glass. These 36″ fluorescent tubes were of 30 watts each, and other tubes of 20 watts were used at the side of wall niches to show off a collection of bric-a-brac.

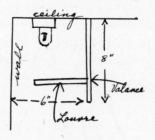

Room lighting with set-in fluorescent wall fixtures

Another bedroom had 36″ 30 watt fluorescent tubes set inside the valance boards to shed light down on the window draperies. In the entrance hall valance-board fluores-

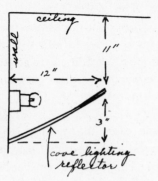

Method of making cove to reflect light on ceiling
(Adapted from Westinghouse specifications for Wanamaker "House of Vision")

cents were used on one side, balanced by others set under an 8″ board along the other wall. This board takes the place of a molding at the top of the wall, and projects from the wall 6″. The line of 36″ fluorescent tubes casts a soft glow down on the attractive wall paper. In another home an upstairs hallway had each corner filled with an angle of frosted glass concealing a perpendicular column of fluorescent bulbs.

In another case a hall was lighted by a line of bulbs set behind a chest so that the light shone on a mirrored wall. Lights may be placed inside the door frame of a tall cabinet, using the Slimline bulbs of 20 watts. Tall columns of grilled wood topped with ground glass cast light upward for attractive effect. You can make an indirect lighting fixture by drilling a hole for a cord through an opaque urn, placing a lamp within and putting a frosted glass circle over the top.

A fireplace molding can conceal a line of built-in lights that cast a glow either down on the hearth or up on the painting hung above the mantel. If you have a valuable old picture of which you are very proud, you can set a small spotlight behind a bowl of green branches in such a way that it shines up on the picture.

Making your own lamps or having them made from a treasure you have picked up is fun, and provides a more personal lamp. A bit of old carved wood, a decoy duck, a lovely small figurine or a beautiful old vase, all have their uses as lamps. A sense of proportion in planning the mounting and in choosing the shade is of the greatest importance. In some hardware or electrical stores ready-made lamp mountings are available. These have a weighted shaft which fits into a jar or a pot with the cord trailing out from the lamp mounting or the bulb socket. Some of these have a strong wire extension upright which shapes around the bulb to hold the shade, while others of smaller size require that the lamp shade have a wire support to fit tightly to the bulb.

There are also shops in large cities and in some smaller towns that specialize in mounting lamps. These have metal bases on which a vase, figure or china accessory may be placed. A metal shaft, which carries the electrical cord, bends up behind and over the decorative piece, and ends in a bulb socket with shade support of brass. These are satisfactory for small bedroom lamps if the accessory is of small size. In the case of larger sculptured figures, statues or bronzes, this treatment will make an attractive living-room or hall lamp.

These same shops mount vases or glass jars, old crocks or brass or copper jugs by boring a hole through which the light cord may pass. The shape may then be mounted on a wooden or composition base, and in some cases is filled to add sufficient weight to balance the top. Some very attractive lamps are made by filling glass jars with colored water in the manner of old-time apothecary jars.

In some cases the opaque jars are filled with clay to hold the light attachment firmly imbedded. This makes them very heavy, and may cause difficulty if the cord breaks. Some suggestions for making your own lamps follow, with ideas for shade materials accompanying them.

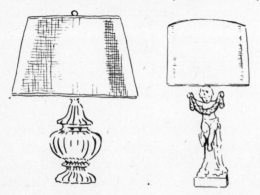

Informal Lamps to be used for Country Homes, Early American Houses, English half-timbered or Cotswold cottage style, in Ranch Houses or other homes with informal decoration:

Bases	*Shades*
Peasant pottery	Paper
Pottery figures or animals	Parchment
Pewter, brass or copper jugs	Waxed butcher paper
Candlesticks of brass, pewter, tin or	Homespun
wrought iron	Linen, gingham
Stoneware crocks or jugs	Stripes, checks, polka-dots,
Pressed glass bottles or jugs	plaid
Plain glass bottles, large	Peasant prints, toiles
Wooden utensils	Mounted maps, costume prints,
California pottery	bird or flower prints
Wood blocks	
Decoy ducks, carved wood in simple	
figures	

More Formal Lamps to be used with eighteenth-century furniture or in Colonial or Georgian homes:

Bases	*Shades*
Brass candlesticks	Waxed parchment
Crystal vases	Fine silk, China silk
Waterford glass	Shantung, pongee
China or porcelain vases	Brocade or figured damask
Chinese vases, jars or jugs	Taffeta, satin
Chinese pottery or porcelain figures	Patterned chintz to match slip
Dainty French or English china figures	covers or draperies
Silver candlesticks or vases	Trimmings of self-binding or
(Candlesticks with hurricane shades)	fringe, silk or rayon or gilt
Lustre ware	braid
Bohemian glass	

Painted tôle (tin) shade on metal base. This type of lamp looks best with Federal or Regency furniture

Lamps to Be Used with Classical Styles, Adam, Hepplewhite, Sheraton, Regency, Empire, or with Federal-type homes, more formal in character than above:

Bases	*Shades*
Pottery urns	Shade materials as above
Sheffield silver urns, candlesticks	Metallic paper
Fine glass candlesticks with hurricane shades	Marbleized paper
Empire style tôle lamps (painted tin)	Painted tôle
China and glassware as above	Lucite or opaque plastic

Corded taffeta ruffle tops a fabric shade—pottery base

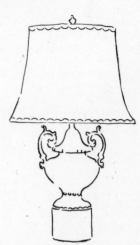

Silver base—stretched fabric shade

Modern Lamps to be used in modern or traditional homes:

Bases	Shades
Pottery shafts, jars or jugs	Paper
Wooden columns, glass or brass	Parchment
Spun brass or aluminum shafts	Heavy fabrics
Glass or wood blocks	Bold prints on fabric or paper
Lucite	Simple bindings
Carved figures, modern or extremely primitive	

UTILITY LIGHTING

Lights for the bathroom, kitchen and laundry are not really a part of home decoration, but they are distinctly important to the looks of the room and to the functions performed there. Johnny will never get his neck clean if the bathroom light is so bad he can't tell which is shadow and which dirt. Your husband will snag his disposition every time he nicks his face while shaving, because he can't see properly. So by all means plan on good lighting for your new bathroom, or tear out the bad lighting in your old bathroom. New fixtures may give you the long tube fluorescents or the bulb incandescent. A look at the accompanying watt chart for lights burned in them will easily remind you that less watts are required in the fluorescent fixture. Thus there is economy in the long run. Also many of the new fluorescent fixtures are more attractively designed than the old-time fixtures for incandescent bulbs.

For thorough lighting of the bathroom use two bulbs at each side of the bathroom mirror, and have another one near the tub, or so placed above the shower rod that there is plenty of light. Many families with small children also install a small lamp near the baseboard, or in it, to burn all night and thus cut down possible accidents. These lights require only a very small bulb, and use so little electricity that they are excellent investments against accidents.

For the kitchen or the utility room lots of light is a valuable help in the work. There should be one large fixture in the center of the ceiling, with another strong light above the sink and another above the stove. Since some ranges come equipped with lights, this may perhaps be eliminated in the room planning, but will be necessary for good meal preparation. Lighting engineers have many good suggestions to make as to the placing of other lights. They suggest that a line of fluorescent tubes, placed underneath the front edge of the wall cabinets, will cast clear light down on all the work counters. They suggest a swinging light be arranged to hang above the ironing board or above the meal-planning corner.

Any woman who has peered into dim cupboards trying to locate a favorite pot or cooking utensil will also welcome their suggestion of small lights that click on when the door is opened, in a manner similar to the lights in refrigerators. These would be valuable in any storage room.

BUYING DECORATIVE ACCESSORIES

After a room is finished with the furniture and rugs in place, the lamps plugged in and lighted, there is still another step necessary to make the room look homey and lived-in. That is to add the personal accessories. A few large ash trays attractively scattered through the room where the smokers may use them conveniently, a bowl of flowers, a green growing plant, a bit of fine porcelain—all these are the personal accessories that a family collects over a period of years.

Don't worry if there aren't many to start with. There will be a few which may have been wedding presents. Others you can pick up on trips and bring home to remind you of happy hours spent together. It is amazing what a conglomeration of different things will "go together" happily in one room. There is a bond between them all because of the fact that you have liked them; because they are chosen with one person's taste and ideas there is a certain correlation there.

Do beware of having a cluttered room. Our grandmothers may have had time to dust their bric-a-brac, but in our speedy day we prefer fewer knickknacks around. In modern rooms, with their sleek surfaced woods, very few accessories are necessary.

Here are a few groupings of accessories as shown in one very attractive room. They will give you an idea that odd things do go well together. On a small end table there is a glass decanter with wine, handy for casual drop-in guests. There are four charming wineglasses beside it. Nearby is a large majolica plate used as an ash tray. On the desk are two enamel ash trays, a French silver box to hold stamps and a lustre pitcher. On top of the cabinet that holds records is a large flower bowl with flowers, another majolica plate, and three decanters. A charming terra-cotta figurine is a center of interest for this larger grouping. On the coffee table are an iron-stone tureen filled with green magnolia leaves, an old jewel box that holds cigarettes, and a large pottery dish which is used as an ash tray.

For a hall cabinet, or table, a large jug of green leaves or a growing plant looks attractive. If they are not to be had, try to pick up an attractive Chinese figure or a group of pottery or china figures. To add life and color to a hallway, mirrored shelves with attractive glassware may be used.

Bedside tables too often show a clutter of useless objects. If ash trays are necessary, use a dish with a top that may be put on to prevent the stale smell of the cigarette butts from permeating the room. Have a covered china or glass or silver box for cigarettes, and a carafe or a decanter for water. If the bedside table is also a chest of drawers, Kleenex and other serviceable objects may easily be kept out of sight. Since these bedside things sometimes spill, it is a nice idea to top these cabinets with either plate glass or mirror glass. These add to the glow of the room, and are easy to keep dusted clean. They are just as practical as the glass topping your dressing-table.

For dressing-table accessories, eliminate the clutter of perfume bottles, and have instead a few well-chosen bits of china or glass in the way of a powder jar or a perfume jar. Old jewel boxes or unusual pieces are attractive here. So collect interesting, stimulating items, rather than have something just like everybody else has.

DINING-ROOM ACCESSORIES
China, Silver and Glassware

Many beginning homemakers wander distractedly through the maze of things offered in the china, silver and glassware departments, wondering what they should choose for attractive table settings. They really have two problems. They have all the day-by-day meals to consider as well as special occasions when they wish to entertain attractively.

Just as a wardrobe is planned to have best dresses for parties and sturdy cottons for work clothes, so the china and pottery chosen for your home will fill two needs. If you have had a lovely set of exquisite china given you for a wedding present, treasure it in a dustproof cupboard. Place rounds of cotton flannel between each plate or stand them on rubber-padded plate racks; even cover them with dustproof bags if you wish. Take them out for parties, and treat your family to their use at least once a week. They will appreciate the little celebration and you will keep the china in use.

For other occasions buy a less expensive set of pottery or earthenware. Modern pottery is far stronger than the older types, but even so, it tends to chip easily, or to crackle when washed in warm water. This term covers the vases, jugs and similar pieces made from baked clay as well as the heavy, informal tableware associated with peasant decoration. Early types were majolica, faïence or quimper. The former came from Italy or Spain originally, later from France. The latter two are more closely associated with France, particularly the quimper, which is made in the town of Quimper, France. Much of it has been imported to this country and is easy to recognize by the peasant figures in the center of each plate, with a free brush stroke border of green leaves around the edge. Pennsylvania Dutch designs also appear on much of our attractive American pottery, and others are decorated with fruits and flowers.

Pottery is gay, fresh, informal and attractive when used in casual homes, provincial type homes, country houses or modern interiors.

California Pottery is appearing in the stores with many attractive colorations, some handglazed, with the colors fused in attractive ways. These are especially popular for modern interiors.

Earthenware is not as bulky or heavy as pottery, but is opaque when held to the light, with a porous body baked under high temperature, and a glassy coat covering the clay. If cracked or chipped, this underbody is exposed, and will discolor with food or grease, thus spoiling the appearance and hygienic qualities of the earthenware.

English Earthenware is a finer, more costly grade, with more highly vitrified surface glazing. Finest grades are semi-vitreous, more durable and less prone to chipping. Comes in a variety of designs—casual, formal or sophisticated.

China is the best dinnerware you can buy, and is recognizable by its translucence when held up to the light. When tapped with a pencil it rings with a fine, clear note. It is made

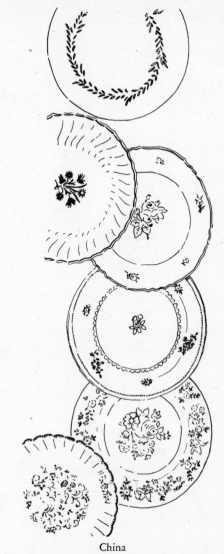

China

Simple styles for modern or for simple decorative schemes
More elaborate styles for 18th century or elaborate decorative schemes

with kaolin, a refined clay, which fuses completely or vitrifies at high temperature. Body under the glaze is hard, smooth, non-porous and non-absorbent. It will not crackle or craze, or absorb moisture if chipped.

Brilliant Colored Chinaware and unusual shapes are possible because high firing temperature permits use of pigments and clay not used for other materials.

Bone China has bone ash added to its clays, to give clear whiteness not shown in other ware.

Billingsley Rose is particularly effective when used with a lace table covering and accessories that carry out the delicacy of design.

Each piece of this pattern is adorned by a spray of roses, richly hand painted in natural colors by the finest china painters. It is called the Billingsley Rose for the itinerant painter, William Billingsley, who painted it originally for Spode in the early 1800's.

Gloucester is a reserved and dignified pattern that may be used harmoniously with all good Sheraton, Chippendale, or other 18th century backgrounds.

In America, shortly after the revolution many families in the South and East owned dinner services imported from China on the famous clippers. In England, too, fine homes were still filled with Chinese ware. Replacements for these old sets could be obtained but it required several years for a ship to make the round trip and bring them back.

Fitzhugh is particularly fitting for the dignity of 18th century dining-room.

The center of this design is the Chinese symbol of good luck surrounded by the four seasons. This pattern was originally shipped to America and England from the Chinese port of Foochow. A New England sea captain's wife, unable to understand the name, called it Fitzhugh. Replacements for the original Chinese sets were made by Spode of his famous Lowestoft body in the early 1800's.

Indian Tree is suitable for such period settings as Modern, Chippendale, Sheraton, Duncan Phyfe, or any good American or English 18th century background.

This charming old orange lustre Indian Tree was taken from the early Spode pattern books. According to the story, this was the tree the Indian magicians materialized and made disappear into the air before their rapt and astonished audiences.

Porcelain is the most delicate of china, so highly vitrified that body and glaze are fused into one. Elegant translucence and fragile quality make it impractical for all except rare use.

Earthenware, Pottery, or China may be purchased in sets or in open-stock. Invariably the sets seem more attractive in price and the temptation is to forget the day when casualties will have reduced it to a state impossible of use. Therefore it is best to decide on an open-stock pattern. Then for a time, within reason, replacements may be made as pieces are broken. It is well to remember that some firms do not keep a pattern going forever. So, as the budget permits, additions may be made in anticipation of needs of a growing family.

For the beginning you will need:

1 dozen dinner plates (10″ size)
1 dozen luncheon plates
1 dozen bread and butter plates
1 dozen salad plates (may be glass instead of matching china)
1 dozen dessert plates
1 dozen soup plates
1 dozen cups and saucers
1 dozen dishes for cereal, fruit, etc.
1 meat platter
3 vegetable dishes or bowls

To add later:

After-dinner coffee cups and saucers
Larger platter
Teapot, sugar bowl and creamer (unless you have them in silver)

WHAT YOU SHOULD KNOW ABOUT DINNERWARE BEFORE BUYING

Most everyone chooses dinnerware according to the design, the decoration and the color, because these are pleasant and appeal to the individual taste. The more you know about this decoration the better you will be able to choose china that lasts long and looks well.

Underglaze decoration is the term covering decoration applied to the "biscuit" or dull surface china before it is glazed. Overglaze decoration is applied to the ware after it is glazed. Glaze means that the china is surface coated with a "glass" mixture. This is applied by spray or by hand-dipping the china into the solution before it is fired.

The decoration may be applied by decalcomania, print, hand-painting, hand-filling, stencil, slip, lustre, embossing, banding or by a new process called engobing.

Decalcomania, or decals, are printed decorations made by lithographic process on paper coated with a special solution. These may use as many as twenty colors. They are cut from the large sheet in which the lithographic company delivers them, and applied face down to the dinnerware. Then the ware is put in water. The paper peels off, leaving the design on the dish. This is a quick method used on both overglaze and underglaze china. It can often be distinguished by the tiny dots or circles shown on close examination in an area that seems to be a shaded color.

In printing, the designs are engraved on copper plates, then transferred to special paper. The paper patterns are laid on the ware and rubbed with a soft flannel until they adhere firmly and evenly. This is more often used as an underglaze decoration.

A filled-in print consists of an outline or part of the design printed with a second color, or other additional colors added by hand. Sometimes this hand-filling consists merely of gold swirls or bands added to enhance the original printed underglaze design. These gold overglaze decorations must be treated with care, protected from hot water and strong soap.

Hand-painting was very expensive at one time, but now is done by a mass-production method in many factories in this country. This consists of each worker painting in only one portion of the design, or one color, before passing the dish on to the next worker.

Banding is usually done by hand, with a small machine to guide the worker's arm so he makes the bands exact in width. If the border is wide, either one of two methods may be used. The band may be applied with oil, and the color dusted on. This adheres to the oily surface until fired into a permanent decoration. Or the border color may be sprayed on by hand or machine.

Gold decoration is used on finer wares, and may be applied by hand, by stencil method or by printing. It is always an overglaze decoration, as it melts and runs under intense heat. Gold may be stamped onto the ware; liquid gold, less expensive and less permanent, is used for this process.

Slip decoration is the favorite method for decorating peasant-type wares; but it is used for many of the most attractive modern dinnerware as well. A thin clay mixture, called "slip," is applied to the ware, then cut into the desired design. This allows the body of the ware to show through. The underbody may be of a contrasting color to the "slip" which forms the glaze.

Lustre pitchers, jugs, and other decorative items are highly prized by collectors. Certain minerals are added to the glaze. When subjected to special firing, iridescent colors are brought to the surface. Antique lustre ware was in silver, gold or copper colors. Commercial lustre is made by painting a prepared liquid over the glaze, then firing in the decorating kiln.

Embossed ware has a raised decoration. This may be formed by the design being cut out of the wall of the mold, or it may be applied separately. The latter is the more expensive process, for it calls for delicate handwork.

In the engobe process, the clay is colored, then sprayed on to the baked ware (before glazing). This ware is then fired, so that the engobe is fused into the body while it is passing through the kiln.

The price of the china you buy will depend on the amount of handwork necessary in making it as well as the value of the materials that have gone into its making and the beauty of the design.

GLASSWARE

Glassware has become an increasingly important part of fine table settings. It adds a great deal to the joy of entertaining to have enough attractive glasses for the proper service of the beverages. What you will buy for your entertaining needs depends entirely on the requirements of your family. So check off the list below before you do your shopping.

1 dozen water goblets or tumblers
1 dozen smaller glasses for fruit juice
1 dozen tall glasses for iced tea, coffee, or highballs

1 dozen cocktail glasses
1 dozen old-fashioned glasses
1 dozen wineglasses
1 dozen champagne glasses
1 dozen liqueur glasses
1 dozen finger bowls
1 dozen glass salad plates (see China list)
1 dozen sherbet glasses

For a small family, or for lack of storage space, buy a half dozen of each if you are sure others can be added later as breakage occurs.

To judge the quality of a piece of glass hold it to the light, looking at it in profile.

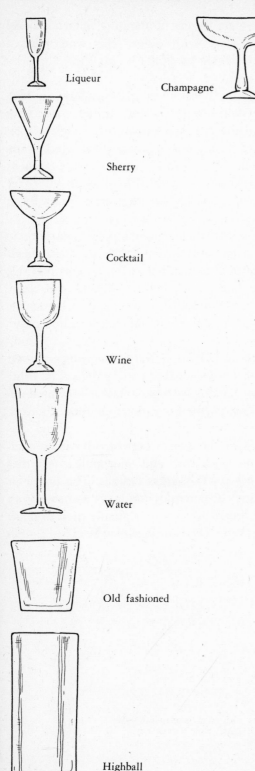

Liqueur

Champagne

Sherry

Cocktail

Wine

Water

Old fashioned

Highball

This will show any bubbles or imperfections in the glass. Good crystal glass, the more expensive, should be absolutely transparent and colorless and free of imperfections. Sometimes it is impossible to avoid small bubbles, but too many of these mar the beauty of the glass.

Study engraved or etched decorated pieces carefully to be sure the decoration does not cover bad workmanship or flaws in the glass.

Tap crystal on the edge with the fingernail. Good crystal rings with a clear note for some time after the glass is struck.

Study the joining and form of the stem on stemware. Many epicures prefer smooth round stems, so the glass may be twirled easily. Look for a firm joining of stem with base and bowl.

Clear, uncolored glass is preferred for fine wine and liqueurs.

Guaranteed chip-proof edges are a splendid modern invention, for there is nothing more unpleasant than to drink from a chipped glass. Rounded edges show the glass is hand-made. Machine-made glasses have a more sharp angular edge because they are ground.

Monogrammed glassware is fashionable and looks well on the table. Use the plainer glass with heavier base for these and choose a simple monogram.

WHAT YOU SHOULD KNOW ABOUT GLASSWARE BEFORE BUYING.

The cost of glassware depends on the material used, the method of making and the type of decoration. Glass may be made by hand or by machine. The hand-workers are highly skilled, their jobs often being handed down from father to son, generation to generation. Many of them are descendants of glassmakers of Europe, who came to this country long ago to continue their work in our famous factories.

Heavy simple goblet—
early styles

In hand-making there is the offhand method, where only the blowpipe is used; or blowing of the original shape, then placing it in a mold for the finished shape; or hand-pressing where both the outside and inside of the piece are shaped in the mold. In this latter method a solid iron "puntil" is used to collect the molten glass. The presser shears off the exact amount to drop into a mold as the plunger is pulled down to force the glass into every part of the mold.

In machine-making the glass is melted in a huge tank with an outlet near the blowing or pressing machine. The molds revolve on a conveyor belt with the exact amount of liquid glass cut off and dropped into the mold as the belt turns. For pressed ware an automatic plunger then presses the glass into every corner of the mold. For blown ware air is forced in by machine to shape the piece. No hand touches the ware until it has been annealed and the completely finished glass is presented, still on the conveyor belt, for careful "flaw inspection." Some of these machines make as many as 75,000 tumblers in a twenty-four-hour period.

Glass decoration consists of four major types: cutting and engraving, etching, pressing and firing of applied decorations.

Cutting glass is essentially a hand job, but machines simplify speed-up production. The design to be cut is marked out on the glass to act as a guide to the cutter. He then holds the glass against a spinning abrasive wheel kept moist with water. This work takes a high degree of skill for just the right pressure.

Less expensive cut glass is gray-cut, with the dull surface of the cuttings contrasting with the polished surface of the glass. Polished cutting uses felt or cork wheels and fine pumice as a finish polish, or the glass is dipped into an acid bath which dissolves off the rough surface of the cuttings. This finish may also be called "rock crystal cutting."

Copper-wheel engraving is done entirely by hand and is costly, for the artist needs great skill to manipulate the variety of wheels like fine dentist drills. These designs have great depth and shading, the drawing of the design often resembling fine pen-line drawings.

Several of the cuttings have names of their own. The Waterford cutting derives its name from famous Irish glass, but as now used describes diagonal or criss-cross lines or mitres. These may have fine dots or diamond cuttings in the spaces between the lines. Diamond and dot, and pineapple are other names for criss-cross designs. The puntil or puntie cut is round, and takes its name from the round iron knob originally used to mark the shape. Oval cuttings may be called thumb

Glass with stem in classical style
designed from Greek lyre

print, or egg shape. The egg and dart combines sharp spear-shaped lines with ovals. The edge cut is wider on one side, and is used when marking leaves. A mitre cut is a long, narrow, pointed oval. Fluting is an oval cut with rounded ends and straighter sides.

Etched glass has great delicacy of effect and usually is rather expensive. Plate etching is a complicated hand method requiring as many as fifteen operations to complete the design. First the design is etched on a steel plate, which is inked with a wax-like ink, and wiped off so only the design remains. Specially prepared tissue then is pressed on the plate to pick up the pattern, trimmed to fit and the pieces carefully fitted to the glass. Firm pressing transfers the design to the glass, and the paper is washed off with alcohol. The glass is coated with acid-resistant wax except for the pattern to be etched. The glass is dipped in an acid bath to etch the design into the glass. Careful rinsing to remove the wax "resist," and a final polishing-drying in sawdust completes the process.

Needle etching is less involved and more mechanical. Steel cutting needles mounted on machine arms scratch the design in the wax-coated glass. A dip into an acid bath etches the design.

Frosting is the simplest form of etching. All parts of the glass not to be etched are covered with "resist." The glass is dipped in the acid bath and the exposed *surface* is frosted. This method is often used for modern glassware.

Sand carving or sand blasting obtains similar effects. The glass is covered with "resist," with the portions of the glass not to be decorated covered with hard paper. By means of steam or compressed air, sand is blown against the glass until it gradually cuts it away to the desired design.

The pressing of glass by hand or machine has been previously described. Much popular-priced glassware is made this way, with some of the designs simulating antique pressed glass. Some of these are hobnail, waffle, fruit, honeycomb, and lace Sandwich. Sometimes the glass has a substance added to make it opaque like milk glass, or robin's-egg blue, or pink or "vaseline" yellow. Fine pressed glass is distinguished by its high lustre obtained by heating the glass after the pressing.

Fired decoration includes painting with enamel colors, banding in platinum or gold or silver, color banding, frosting, decals or screen-printed designs. These are all found in the more popular-priced glassware. The bandings are painted on by hand or machine. Frosting is obtained by dipping the glass in acid or by sand spraying.

There is a great variety of designs and shapes to suit every taste and to go with every table setting. As a general rule the pressed glass and simpler shapes look best with peasant pottery or in dining rooms of "cottage type." The cut or blown glass goes well with Georgian rooms and fine dinnerware. The modern blown or sand-blasted glass looks best in modern homes. For Federal or other formal interiors there are many classical glasses, with laurel wreath design etched in the glass or a column stem.

SILVER

Here again may be something that has been given to you, or that you have inherited. If not, you may acquire it gradually, using the check list as a guide. Sterling silver may be purchased in a complete set with the price based on the number of pieces in the set, or by the dozen of each item, or by the "place setting." This latter method makes it pos-

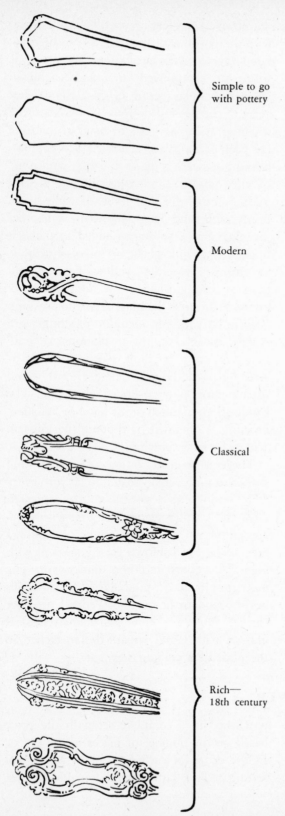

Simple to go
with pottery

Modern

Classical

Rich—
18th century

sible to buy enough for two people in the beginning, gradually adding to it on gift days until a complete set is acquired.

Plated silver is usually sold by the set or by the dozen since the investment is less. Plated silver may be obtained in any number of grades, from the very inexpensive, thinly plated "silver" to that heavily plated, with extra reinforcement at the points of wear. The best producers use nickel alloy as a base to provide the desired hardness and durability. The thicker the plating, the longer the wear and the better the investment.

Sterling silver is made of $92\frac{1}{2}\%$ silver with a small amount of other metal added to increase strength and wear. The same metal is used throughout, rather than one used over the other as plating. Very old sterling silver did not have an alloy added, and the forks and spoons are so soft they bend out of shape easily.

Here Is Your Check List for the Silver

You personally must decide whether you wish to have a full dozen for place settings, or whether you will only need six or eight of each. The list herewith chooses the medium pathway, and suggests eight of each.

Dinner Forks (8)   Serving Spoons (4)
Salad Forks (8)   Butter Spreaders (8)
Soup Spoons (8)   Gravy Ladle
Teaspoons (16)   Carving Set (large)
Dessert Spoons (8)   Cold Meat Fork
Stainless Steel Blade Knives (8)

To add later:

  After-dinner Coffee Spoons (8)
  Small Carving Set
  Dessert Knives (8)
  Dessert Forks (8)

For other serving pieces that may be of china, glass or silver (preferably the latter) we suggest:

Well and Tree Platter
Vegetable Dishes (2 in different sizes)
Salt and Pepper Shakers (4) or
Open Salt Dishes and Spoons (2)
Candlesticks
Water Pitcher
Small Serving Dishes for jelly, nuts, etc.
Gravy Dish and Tray

HOUSEHOLD LINENS

An important part of attractive table service is the linens used day by day, or for special occasions. Every homemaker takes pride in dainty table settings, and can make many of these linens herself. Often only a few hours and a bit of handwork on good material are necessary to reproduce really expensive pieces seen in fine stores.

Any table linen should be chosen with the color scheme of the dining-room and of the china in mind. If the china is gaily patterned with flowers, birds or scenery trailing all across the plates, then the table linen should be of the simplest. Use plain linen in soft colors to complement the china, or white linen damask. If you have chosen simple peasant pottery then the cloth should be of heavy linen, or homespun, or some fabric that is simple rather than dressy. You can use gingham in bold plaid, or printed dress cotton with a deep plain-colored border, or hand-woven plaids, or embroidered cross-stitch designs. If the china is white it looks better against colored cloths. If it has a strong color, then you can use gleaming white for a dinner cloth.

Many of the cloths shown in the finest shops use materials that would not have been considered a few years ago. For the finest cloths for special parties, organdie with organdie cut out and appliquéd in attractive designs are suggested. Such appliqués in rayon satin or metal cloth for extra-special

affairs are shown. Rayon woven in damask designs or spun rayon cloths resembling coarse linen are available for formal use. You can also use lace or formal white damask. For other dinners place-mats are proper. These are used with an oblong mat at each place setting. The napkin matches or contrasts in color. These may be trimmed with embroidery or with a large monogram.

Place-mats also are used for luncheons, or smaller cloths may be used if you prefer the wood of the table covered. For breakfast use gay informal cloths of cotton, linen, or rayon, or use the wipe-clean table mats that protect the surface of the table and save so much laundry time.

Here Is Your Dining-Room Linen Check List

1 large Dinner Cloth and 12 Napkins
1 Dinner Set—8 Mats, 8 Napkins and Centerpiece
1 Dinner Set—4 Mats, 4 Napkins and Centerpiece
1 Lunch Set—Cloth and 4 Napkins
1 Lunch Set, Mats and Napkins
3 Bridge Sets
1 dozen Fingerbowl Doilies
1 dozen Tea Napkins
1 dozen Cocktail Napkins
6 Tray Cloths (various sizes)
Pads for hot dishes
6 Wipe-clean Place Mats
12 Napkins to use with them
As many everyday luncheon cloths or breakfast cloths as desired

Kitchen Linen

1 dozen Dish Towels
4 Pot Holders
3 Dish Cloths
Bag for lettuce
Cloths for cleaning
Duster, oil- or wax-treated cloth
Silver Cleaning Cloth

BEDROOM LINEN

Our mothers or grandmothers felt themselves very fortunate if they could own linen sheets. Some still prefer them, but they wrinkle much more quickly than cotton. The loosely woven linen pulls in laundering, so unless you can afford the very best grade of linen it is wise to avoid it. Percale sheets are smooth to the touch, are woven from fine cotton threads and are the best buys for long wear and luxurious use. Muslin sheets are woven of heavier cotton threads, with a texture feel in the hand. All sheets are labeled according to the "thread count." The best sheets are the finest woven, the ones with the highest thread count, the greatest number of threads to be found in a square inch. If the sheet is not labeled, hold it up to the light to see the closeness of the weave. Check to be sure the threads are uniform in size, for if they vary from thick to thin, the sheet may wear out in spots.

If the sheet feels stiff, and a white powder comes off on your hand when the fabric is rubbed, it has been heavily sized. This makes it seem as though it has more body than it really has, and this sizing will "come out in the wash." If the color is not pure white, this means it has not been properly bleached, and it will be difficult or impossible for you ever to achieve the dazzling whiteness you want when you launder it.

Check the selvages to see that they are strong, thick and substantial. Without strength here the sheet will be apt to tear. Be sure the hems are straight. Good sheets are torn with the grain of the fabric before being hemmed. Cheaper ones are cut, not torn, and the hems pull off-grain to cause trouble later.

Check the label for size. Buy all sheets in the 108" length to provide sufficient tuck-in allowance at top and bottom of the bed. The width of the bed will determine the width of the sheet, as follows:

For a double bed ...... 90" wide
For a three-quarer bed .. 81"   "
For a twin bed .... 72"   "
For a single bed .... 63"   "
For a day bed .... 54"   "
For a cot, one labeled "cot" or "narrow"

Housekeeping authorities recommend six sheets for each bed and four pillowcases for each pillow. If you like the pillow to be firm, buy a case that fits closely to the measurement of the pillow. If you wish the pillow to seem soft, buy one amply large. Take the dimensions of your pillow, then check with the measurement of the case. You will find the measurement tells you the amount of the fabric folded over the pillow before sewing. Silly, but that's the way they do it, so you will just have to do a little multiplying by two before you go shopping for a pillowcase to fit your pillow.

Have a mattress pad for each bed, with a mattress cover if desired. Plan on two pairs of blankets for each bed, with more or less according to the climate in which you live. It is wise to have one pair of summer weight and one pair of heavy winter weight. You can also add a comforter, if desired, or an electric blanket for cold weather. You will need a summer bedspread and a winter bedspread, or if you have made one to suit the decorations you may substitute a "blanket cover" for a temporary bedspread while the other is being laundered or dry cleaned.

BATHROOM LINENS

The number of bathroom linens you will need depends on the size of the family, the number of bathrooms that will need supplies and the frequency of laundering rotation. It is wise to plan on quite a stack of towels so there will always be enough. When they return from the laundry always place them on the bottom of the pile, so they will wear evenly. Otherwise the stack will remain as is, with the lower ones getting no wear, and the top ones tired and bedraggled.

Here Is a Bathroom Check List for an Average Family

1 dozen Large Bath Towels
1 dozen Small Bath Towels, for hands and face
1 dozen Linen Face Towels
1 dozen Linen Guest Towels
1 dozen Wash Cloths
2 Shower Curtains
2 Bath Mats
2 Bathroom Rugs

Monograms

Bathroom linens may have large monograms, or single initials, or they may have a large flower of the bedroom chintz appliquéd for a spot of color. Most bath-towel monograms are sewn with French knots of coarse, color-fast embroidery thread placed together.

To make a French knot, draw the thread up from under the fabric, twist the thread around the needle five or six times, using that part of the thread nearest the material, rather than the part near the needle. Turn the needle down into the fabric close to the spot where the thread came up. Bring the thread through to the right side and repeat.

The letters used for a monogram may be simple block letters as shown in the sketches herewith, or they may be gay, swirling italic letters. Choose the type you like the best. There is a new style trend that makes sense.

Some of the towels are monogrammed with the husband's initials in a block letter that looks masculine, while some of them are lettered with the wife's initials. This makes it easier to tell which towel is which. In a family with children this could be carried further, and each child have his name on his bathroom linen.

Chain stitch is easy to use for such labeling. It may be used on either bath towels or face towels. The thread is brought up to the surface of the fabric on the right side. Then the needle is pierced through the fabric in the line of direction desired, the thread looped around it to form a "buttonhole stitch" loop. (See diagram.) This is repeated, spacing all stitches evenly, starting each stitch inside the end loop of the last stitch, to form the chain effect that gives this stitch its name.

This chain stitch may be used in a single line, or a double or triple line. It may even be used in combination with French knots to form a firm, even edge.

Satin stitch is used for more formal monograms on linen face towels or guest towels. This is simply an over-and-over stitch, with each stitch close to the one preceding. In order to achieve a raised surface the area is often padded with chain stitch before the overlay of satin stitch is made. This is also used for monograms on table linens or bed linens.

Cross-stitch is a quick stitch, and may be used for monograms on linen in daily use. It is also found on guest towels which are bought with a printed transfer design ready to embroider. In making this stitch the finished effect will be better if all the under stitches slant in one direction, all the upper stitches in the other direction. Then it is a simple matter to have the stitches on the back unobtrusive short perpendiculars.

BLOCK CAPITALS and block small letters

SCRIPT CAPITALS and small letters

OLD ENGLISH

Use these types of letters to make your monograms

X

HOW TO DO ALL THE THINGS YOURSELF

MANY PEOPLE feel that the person who can go to a luxurious and expensive decorator, who can order all the things done for him will have a more attractive home. This is not true at all. There is far more personality shown in the home that is "homemade" than one that is "custom-built." If you make many of the draperies, bedspreads and slip-covers yourself, you will have far more pride in them and they will be far more individual than ready-made ones. They will also cost less, for labor is always an expensive part of any purchased article.

Many of the magazines feature style ideas of things you can do yourself, so by watching their pages you can gain many fresh ideas. They also show photographs of things other people have made. These will give ideas of things that you also can make. There is fun in working out these ideas, in seeing how original you can be. One of the features that attracts most attention in a small country home is a console table on a screened porch painted pottery blue, with a matching console table in "antique white" in the living room. This is really an old-mahogany dining table sawed in half and refinished. In another room of the same house a strip of mirror glass forms the top of a painted bit of wrought iron taken from an old house. Another mirror strip hangs on the wall above to make a lovely console table arrangement.

Another young homemaker used cast iron from a country graveyard fence to form the

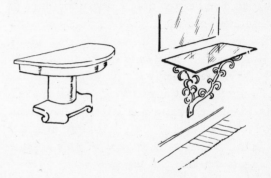

base of the long narrow dining-table. She set a huge oval of wood on top of her trunk, then covered it with a fabric "skirt" to form a hall table. Still another homemaker separated one large room into two smaller ones by folding partitions that started life as shutters on a country house. Try to see how many clever ideas you can think up.

REFINISHING FURNITURE

Some of that old furniture that you bought at the second-hand furniture store or at auction is pretty sadly in need of refinishing. Maybe it has had that ugly shiny varnish added to give the real wood the look of an overpainted hussy. It is easy to strip this off with varnish remover and to rub the wood down to its own natural beauty. It does take patience and elbow grease. Place the piece of furniture on a thick pad of protective newspaper or, better still, work out of doors. Most varnish remover is pretty smelly stuff. Use a brush to apply it, working it well into the interstices of any carving. Allow it to remain until the varnish is softened; then wipe off with old rags or use a dull knife to scrape off the goo. You may need several applications to get down to the wood.

Repeat until the wood looks clean. Then use strong soap powder dissolved in warm water to wash off the wood and rinse in clean water. *Allow to dry thoroughly*. Sometimes this treatment "raises the grain" of the wood. This shows a high and low surface, which is sometimes apparent to the eye or sometimes just to the "feel" when the palm of the hand is rubbed over the surface.

Bleaching Furniture

If you plan to bleach the wood, a raised surface is an advantage, for it offers better contrast than too flat a grain. In fact, oak looks far more attractive if the grain is treated so, and for this purpose one of the acid bleaches is excellent. Ask at your paint store for one that will accomplish this.

All bleaches come with clear directions on the package. These should be followed carefully, or if you are in doubt, you should experiment on an under side of the table, or a place where your trials will not show. For an effect that imitates a bleach, paint over the

Removing old finish

bare wood with a white, pale gray or pale tan paint. Allow it to soak into the wood, but not to dry. Before it is dry, wipe off with soft rags so that the wood grain shows in natural colors on the top surfaces, with the lighter paint gleaming in the lower surfaces of the grain. This technique is often used to gain odd two-color effects. One color is used first, then wiped off, and a second color rubbed on the upper surfaces with a cloth dipped in diluted color.

Much of the old bleached wood used in paneling or furniture is called pickled, because the pale effect was created by using a compound of which vinegar was an important part. For present-day purposes acid bleaches are quicker and easier to use.

Wax Finish

Many of the more attractive pieces of furniture are treated only to a wax finish. This is particularly suitable for provincial type furniture, either French, English or Early American. The best wax to use is beeswax dissolved in turpentine. This is a favorite with museum curators. There are many good commercial polishing waxes available. For a proper patina the furniture should be well polished at least once a week, and with hand rubbing acquires the glow that is so attractive. Many formerly varnished chairs or tables look very well after they have had the varnish removed, and have been waxed into new beauty.

Painting Furniture

There has been quite a vogue for peasant painted furniture lately; all kinds of unlikely chests of drawers or hat racks are appearing with a new color and new trim. Some of these are attractive and amusing to have around. Others just look messy. You must decide

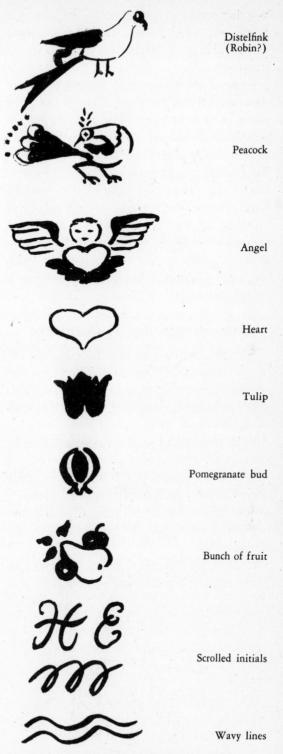

Distelfink
(Robin?)

Peacock

Angel

Heart

Tulip

Pomegranate bud

Bunch of fruit

Scrolled initials

Wavy lines

Pennsylvania Dutch motifs to use in painting or stencilling furniture whether this type of decoration fits into your home, and whether you have the necessary artistic ability to design the decorations attractively.

Most of the furniture is treated to an undercoat of flat white paint. Do not use gloss paint or enamel paint. Then the undercoat is rubbed down with fine sandpaper and a second coat applied. This may be "antiqued." That is, either umber brown or black paint is mixed in a saucer and some of it is brushed lightly across the surface, paying particular attention to the corners. With a soft cloth the areas that are in the center of the panels, or of the drawers, are then wiped off, with the cloth swishing lightly along to give a "feathered edge."

Stencil Painting of Furniture

The peasant designs may be stenciled on, or may be painted freehand. There are also peasant-type decalcomanias that are easy to apply by just following directions. If you wish to stencil them, look in your paint store for peasant-type stencils. If you wish to make your own stencils you will find that only a few motifs are necessary. After cutting these they can be applied variously to create a group design that is charming. The sketches will suggest individual stencils and group arrangements.

Peasant figures are easy to stencil, too. These require slightly more complicated sten-

cils, for several colors will need to fit together. In this case draw the design on one tracing paper; then cut a different stencil for each color.

The system of stenciling on a design requires a short-bristle brush or a tampon with which to apply the color, and a shield with a design cut out of it through which the color is applied. For this shield use either stencil

board, stiff wax-treated drawing board, or butcher's paper. Draw or trace the design on the treated board or paper. Then use a razor blade or a sharp knife to cut out the design. Take care to remove bits of fuzz at the corners, so the design will be clear and sharp.

Mix the color of paint desired in a shallow saucer, thinning it so it has the consistency of thick cream. Apply the shield with cut-out design to the surface of the cabinet, chair or table that is to be decorated, and attach it with Scotch tape so it will stay in place. Now use the short-bristle brush to apply the color, using a tap-tap treatment rather than brushing it on. See that the color goes right to the edge of the stencil, fitting well into each

wish a #1 for fine work and a #10 for larger sections. Mix the paint in a color desired on an artist's palette, or a flat enamel tray, or on a piece of glass. Stroke on the color in a free bold stroke, twisting the brush at the end of the stroke to give the tapered end usually required. Swirl the leaves gracefully, use the tip of the brush for dots, and apply quick even pressure for petals. For long swirling stems draw in the outline with chalk, practise

corner. Do not force it under the edges of the shield. Allow it to dry, then lift the shield, and place it over the next spot to be treated. If the paint is too thick, it will ridge up around the edges after the shield is removed. If it is too thin, it will run under the edges and make a messy stencil.

Always allow the stencil of the first color to dry thoroughly before laying on the stencil for the next color. Use chalk to mark the position or to test it before painting.

Freehand Painting of Furniture

To paint designs similar to stencils on furniture use an artist's brush. Size #5 is satisfactory for most work, although you may also

the sweep before making it, then stroke it quickly as nearly on the chalk line as is possible. Don't worry if it is not exact. The casual look is what you are after for this work.

Many cabinets have gay phrases painted on them. These look more attractive if they are done in your own handwriting. Write on the name or phrase in chalk, then paint over the outline. Stroke all the up and down lines, then work on the rounded ones.

Attractive painted trays may be done with these techniques. The same things sell for terrific prices in the stores, but you can create them yourself at home for a fraction of the cost. If you have an antique tray, you can refinish it in the same design. Trace off the design first, then paint over a fresh undercoat of dull black. Rub this smooth with oil and rottenstone. Paint on another coat and rub down again after it is thoroughly dry. Then trace on the design. Some of the old trays had stenciled designs that were powdered through a mask, using gilt powder thickly in some spots, sparingly in others. Direction books suggest laying the stencil on

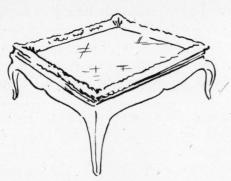

Coffee table of old picture frame painted antique white
and mounted on legs

while the undercoat is tacky, then finishing
the design before lifting the stencil. It seems
obvious that the stencil would stick under
such conditions, so the preferable way is to
lay the stencil on a dry surface, then make the
stencil area sticky by using a transparent
varnish in that area alone before dusting on
the gold powder.

Gold Leaf

Gold leaf may be applied to trays or furniture with the stencil method. The sticky
preparation is laid on the area where the leaf
should adhere, then the stencil mask lifted,
and a thin sheet of the gold, silver or alu-
minum foil laid on, using a soft brush for
the application. After this has thoroughly
dried the excess leaf is brushed off lightly,
taking care to keep a smooth crisp outline for
the design.

"Picking Out" the Design

Some eighteenth-century furniture has a
slightly raised molding. A present mode is
to paint this furniture in light pastel tones,
then to "pick out" or paint the molding in
a contrasting color. This may be done with
the same artist's brush that is mentioned in
the paragraph on freehand painting. If the

edges are to be even, or if the design is not
represented in a raised molding, it is easier to
outline the area with shaped pieces of Scotch
tape. These are carefully placed on the furniture so that the space between is the area
to be painted. The contrasting color paint is
then applied, allowed to dry thoroughly and
the tape removed.

This method of applying strips of Scotch
tape before painting is particularly useful if
a straight stripe is desired. It is far easier to
paint in this way than to try to hold a steady
hand.

Covering Furniture with Fabric
or Paper

Some old furniture has the surface so badly
scarred that it is wiser to apply a surface covering of some sort. Many chests of drawers
look attractive if they are covered with a
flowered chintz, or a dainty wallpaper, or
even a lovely bit of marbleized paper.

The best way to do this is to carefully cut
the various sections of paper or fabric to fit
before starting, leaving enough excess where
there is to be a lap-over to turn inside a
drawer or under the cabinet base, for instance. Then the cabinet is painted all over
with varnish or shellac. This is allowed to
dry partly until it reaches the "tacky" state.

The material is then laid on carefully, smoothing as you go. This tacky varnish forms a smooth and lasting bond. The material will not work loose, indeed will be impossible to remove.

If you prefer to apply the fabric so that it can later be changed, then the wallpaper paste method will be better. Buy a package of wallpaper paste (wheat paste). Mix this powder carefully with water, gradually adding enough water so that it has the consistency of very heavy cream. Use a large brush to apply the paste smoothly to the furniture, then lay the fabric or paper on and smooth it out, brushing out all air bubbles as you work. A wallpaper seam roller will help to press the surfacing in place. This may be finished with a coat of protective wax or thin shellac.

This is an attractive way of finishing the inside of bureau drawers or of bookcases. A striped wallpaper makes an attractive lining for the shelves and inside of a cabinet that is designed for the display of dishes or decorative accessories.

One attractive display room in one of the leading stores had a large wardrobe that had been converted into a de-luxe dressing-table by setting a large mirror inside the upper part. The shelves and the rest of the inside of the cabinet were covered with a white glazed chintz printed in bouquets of violets. The same chintz upholstered the Victorian chair used with it. The wood frame of the chair and the outside of the wardrobe had both been painted a soft dull green to match the color of the violet leaves.

See illustration above.

Painting Unfinished Furniture

Many of the stores carry furniture in pine made up as bookcases, chests of drawers, desks, chairs, and dressing-tables. This has

no finish whatsoever, and the store either delivers it "as is" for you to finish or will have it painted or lacquered at an additional charge. Some of the stores sell the right materials for finishing, or you can purchase them from the local paint store.

Enamel-painted furniture is far less popular now than it was a few years ago. The high gloss of the surface is difficult to apply smoothly, it is apt to chip off and it does not look as well as painted furniture finished in other ways.

Since the wood is slightly rough and porous, it must be prepared for painting. Rub all surfaces with #0 sandpaper, working with the grain. Then rub with #00 until the wood feels smooth to the palm of the hand. Wipe off, cover any knots with shellac, then sandpaper smooth. If there are any surface nicks, fill them with plastic wood, allow to dry hard, sandpaper smooth, and treat with shellac as for the knots.

Stained Furniture

If the wood is to be rubbed with an oil stain, apply without any undercoat. The oil stain may be home-mixed, made of linseed oil and color. Use soft umber tones for natural wood effect, gray for the weathered look,

Van Dyke brown for the red cedar appearance that is so popular for outdoor furniture. Or you may buy an oil or wax stain from the paint store. This is already mixed with the color dissolved in it.

The furniture may then be finished with a rubbing of wax, continuing with weekly wax treatments until it has the sheen desired.

Undercoat for Painted Furniture

If the furniture is to be painted, a thin coat of the same color may be diluted and painted over the furniture like stain. This forms an undercoat that prevents white spots showing if the surface paint becomes scarred or chipped.

If the furniture is to be finished with a pastel color of paint, a surfacing of undercoat or priming paint will be advantageous.

Painting Furniture

You can use either flat or gloss paint for painted furniture although the former is preferred. Mix the paint well so there are no color streaks, straining it twice through clean cheesecloth. Turn the table or chair upside down and paint all the under surfaces first.

It is only too easy to miss spots if you are crawling around under it on your hands and knees. Be sure to brush around spokes first, to fill tiny crevices, then stroke up and down to smooth out brush marks. The object in painting furniture is to have the brush marks show as little as possible. The best way to do this is to stroke the color all one way, then stroke back across it.

Allow one coat to dry thoroughly, then rub down until it is satin smooth, using fine sandpaper, then finishing with oil and pumice or rottenstone. Clean off the surface thoroughly. Paint another coat. Allow to dry thoroughly and rub down again. The more coats of paint applied, and the more thorough the "rub downs" in between, the better the finished product will be.

Lacquered Furniture

Lacquer is better sprayed on, and many vacuum cleaners have spray attachments. Experiment with yours first to be sure it sprays evenly and you can create a smooth unspotted area with it before you try it on the furniture. If you wish to brush on the lacquer, use the directions above as for painting, carefully rubbing down the surfaces between each coat. Five layers of lacquer are recommended. Some very attractive nested tables are finished with each table of the group in a different color. This is very gay, and easy to do at home. An attractive effect is also possible by lacquering a bureau frame black, with the drawers lacquered either soft green or vivid vermilion.

Painting Wicker Furniture

Wicker furniture is inexpensive, and looks very attractive when painted in such gay colors as canary yellow, chartreuse, turquoise, or shocking pink. It is easy to do if the flat paint is mixed thin and a long-bristled brush is used to work the color well in between the strands of the wicker. This is a spattery job, so be sure the surroundings are well protected, and wear some old clothes yourself. This paint sprays on well, so if you can use your vacuum attachment or rent a sprayer from your paint store, you may find it worth while.

Painting Metal Furniture

Metal garden furniture may frequently be had at reasonable prices. It is attractive when painted either white or a soft pastel color. Before painting old black wrought iron, it is wise to paint it with an undercoat of the red specially prepared to keep it from rusting. This should be allowed to dry thoroughly, then two coats of the color desired painted on. Allow the first coat to dry thoroughly before applying the second coat.

Enameling Furniture

You may wish to enamel some furniture for the kitchen, bathroom or the baby's room. In that case proceed as for painting furniture, applying one coat of enamel after the undercoat of stain. Rub down this enamel with steel wool. Allow to dry thoroughly before repeating. Four coats are best; two the absolute minimum.

SEWING FOR THE HOME

There are many things that can be made for the home by the woman who is clever with her needle. In the past every homemaker was expected to make even such things as her sheets and blankets. Then it became easier to buy things ready-made. But today there is a lack of attractive ready-made things; and there is far less individuality in the majority of things found in the stores than in those that are made at home.

Most of the sewing required is of the simplest; machine-stitched seams or hems, simple hand-sewn hems, or gathering. The large draperies and bedspreads may be made more easily with the aid of a sewing machine, for the long seams are rather tedious to sew by hand. If you do not own a sewing machine you will find it possible to rent one from the neighborhood sewing machine store or perhaps from a community center.

Since much of this sewing must last a long time and must go through frequent launder-ings, it is well to know what thread will be satisfactory for the weight of the article and for the fabric. Most people prefer the mercerized sewing thread that comes in a variety of colors to match almost everything. They use this for all sorts of sewing. For heavy work there is the heavy-duty thread, now made in a variety of colors, but formerly made only in black and white. For really heavy work, such as sewing on curtain rings, do use the very strong carpet and button thread.

OTHER SEWING MATERIALS

Besides the needles and threads you will need other sewing equipment to do a professional-looking job. A large table for measuring and cutting the fabric, a yard stick, a tape measure, chalk and marking crayon, lots of pins, and sharp shears are on the top of your list. You will also need an iron and ironing

NEEDLE AND THREAD CHART FOR QUICK CONSULTATION

FABRIC	Needle		THREAD	MACHINE GAUGE
	Hand	Machine		
Sheer fabrics for glass curtains, gauze, organdie, net, ninon, muslin, or voile	9	Fine	100 cotton A silk	Coarse for nets Fine with tissue paper under fabric for soft fabric
Medium weight curtain fabric, chintz, cretonne, percale, gingham, piqué, taffeta, satin, etc.	8	Medium	50 or 60 mercerized cotton A silk	Fine
Heavy curtain fabric, twill, gabardine, rep, ticking, sailcloth	4	Coarse	24 cotton 50 mercerized Heavy duty	Medium
Slipcovers of any fabric	4	Coarse	Heavy duty 50 mercerized 24 cotton	Medium
Top stitching on slipcovers	5	Medium	50 mercerized	Medium
Machine stitching on upholstery fabric		Coarse	36 cotton 16 cotton	Coarse
Hand sewing on upholstery	Curved Upholstery Double-ended		Linen Shoemaker's Waxed Button or carpet	
Sewing on snaps, hooks, curtain rings, etc.	4		Waxed linen Heavy duty Carpet or button thread	

board right alongside the sewing machine, for the more frequently you press your work while it is in process of construction the better it will look. It is wise to get all these materials together before you start work. There is nothing so unpleasant as to have to stop work and dash downtown for some small item.

If you plan to do a great deal of sewing in your home, it is smart to have a sewing closet in which you can keep all your equipment. If this closet is not possible, you will find it convenient to use a large flat drawer which you can pull open while you work, thus having all the material right at your side.

TRANSPARENT GLASS CURTAINS

Glass curtains are so called because they are hung close to the window glass, rather than outside the window frame. Usually they are of transparent fabric, allowing those inside the house to look out, but providing them with privacy from passers-by. Many new homemakers have discovered the economy of making glass curtains first to give the home a lived-in look, waiting for a day when the budget is eased to buy the other fabric to make the overdraperies.

Because of this they take their choice in the placement of the curtains, sometimes hanging them in front of the window frame rather than inside it. One very clever young couple pasted wall paper around the dining-room windows in a deep, mitred border, and then used sheer net curtains falling clear to the floor. This made a finished, colorful and inexpensive window arrangement.

Plain hemmed panels are the easiest to make. A straight length of fabric is hemmed around the four sides, with a wide hem along the lower edge, the same width along the long edge that is to be placed at the center of the window, and usually a narrower hem along the other perpendicular edge. Lately there has been a tendency to make this hem the same width as the others, for then smart homemakers can switch the curtains around every time they are laundered to equalize the wear.

These hems are often sewn by hand, as hand sewing shows up less when the panel is hung against the light. Use fine thread and a dainty needle, and take a catch stitch under the edge of the fabric before sliding the thread along under the turn of the fabric. (See diagram.)

If you prefer to sew on the sewing machine, set the gauge for a loose, rather long stitch if the fabric is coarse net. Hold the material firmly with both hands, so the stitching will not pucker the drapery. (See drawing.) If the fabric is fragile, soft or thin, cut strips of tissue paper and baste along under the fabric where the stitching is to be. Then stitch, and after the hem is pressed you may remove the tracing paper by gently tearing it away.

Some of the new plastic-treated materials or the "unsupported" film are being used for glass curtains, or for bathroom or kitchen curtains. Inasmuch as pinholes or punctures from the needle will show, it is necessary to use paper clips instead of pins to hold the turns in place before sewing. Then use a long, loose stitch and work slowly, so that no mistakes will be made. (When ruffles are made, these may be shirred by hand. Do not

hem the edges; cut with plain scissors or pinking shears; leave plain or roll under the fingers.)

The corners of the hems should all be mitred. This means cutting away the "kitten-ear" of excess fabric so it won't show through heavy against the light. Sew the hem right up to the corner. Fold together the excess fabric and trim with scissors as shown. (See sketch.) Flatten out, turn under raw edge, and fell by hand. Press.

Top Finish of Glass Curtains

Along the top of the curtain there is usually a slot for the rod. This should be sewn after the two long hems up the sides are finished. If there is any possibility of the fabric shrinking when it is laundered—if you have not already soaked it well and hung it on the line to pre-shrink it—then you had better sew this top turn by hand, and allow enough material in the turn to permit the possible shrinkage. Nothing looks worse than

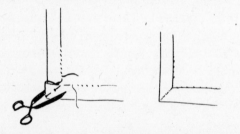

a curtain which hangs an inch or two shorter than it should.

Fold over the top edge, making a double turn for extra strength as well as shrinkage allowance. Baste this in evenly, and slide onto the rod. Be sure it is the right length before sewing. To sew by hand use running stitches, anchored at intervals with a back stitch. (See diagram.)

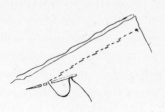

Back stitch

To sew by machine, set gauge for a medium-length stitch, and stitch along close to the edge. Take great care that this slot allows enough of an opening so the rod slides through easily. It is bad for the fabric and for your temper to make this too tight. If the rod sticks, remove it, rub with wax and slide through easily. Or put a thimble over the cut end of the rod to make it run through the slot more easily.

Stand-Up Heading

If no over-draperies are planned, if, instead, the glass curtain panel is hung in front of the window frame, you may wish to have a stand-up heading above the slot through which the rod is run. In order to do this allow for 2″ or 3″ extra. Add this to the amount necessary for the slot, and stitch two rows across the top of the curtain panel instead of only one. Slide the rod through the lower slot, between the two rows of stitching, and a dainty ruffle of 1″ or 1½″ will stand up above the rod. If the fabric is very stiff, you may make the heading wider. A wide head-

ing in a soft fabric has a tendency to flop
unless it is starched.

Ruffles for Glass Curtains

For informal rooms and for bedrooms
many prefer their glass curtains with stiff,
starchy ruffles. These are easy to make, and
may be added to any plain drapery or glass
curtain. The present style calls for a flounce
across the bottom and on *both* up-and-down
sides. This is an attractive finish, and makes
it possible to switch the panels around for
better wear as mentioned in plain hemmed
glass curtains. In many cases there is a ruffle
sewn to the front of the panel just under the
slot stitched for the rod. This makes an attractive finish for the curtain and makes it
possible to dispense with a separate shirred
valance ruffle.

If the fabric does not fray easily at the
edges, the ruffles may be cut with pinking
scissors and the attractive zigzag edge left as

a trimming. If the fabric does fray easily, a
hem will be necessary. This may be a narrow
double turn, so the raw edge is hidden,
stitched by machine or run by hand.

If the ruffle is to be mounted under the
hemmed panel only one edge will require
hemming. If the ruffle is to be sewn on front
of the glass curtain, with the line of shirring
showing along the edge, you will find it more
satisfactory to hem both edges.

In order to have each ruffle edge pleasantly
full, hem enough ruffling to be twice as long
as the distance to which it is to be mounted.
If the curtain is 90″ long each perpendicular
edge will require 180″ of ruffling, while
across the 36″ lower edge there will be required 72″ of ruffling. Another 72″ strip
would be used across the top under the slot
for the rod.

*Never Split the Fabric for Either a Glass
Curtain or a Drapery.* Use the full 36″ panel
at each side for the average size window
(36″). For a wider window than this, seam
together two widths of fabric, and press the
seam flat before making either glass curtains
or draperies.

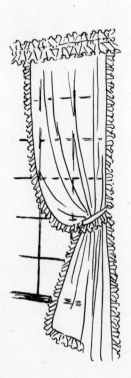

A Ruffled Valance

It is easy to make a gay ruffled valance. All that is necessary is to have a straight strip of fabric twice as long as the window is wide. This should be hemmed along top and bottom, and have a slot for the rod. The slot may be placed anywhere desired, although it is usually placed within an inch or two of the top. The best way to make this slot is to make a deep turn as suggested in the section on "Headings," with a double row of stitching to hold the slot for the rod, and a double thickness of material to stand up above the rod.

If preferred, an extra strip of fabric or a strip of cotton tape may be sewn at the back of the valance ruffle to form the slot for the rod.

This ruffled valance may be made of a different material from the drapery fabric, if desired. An attractive effect may be obtained by having a deep ruffled flounce of the same material as the gathered ruffle around the edge of the curtain.

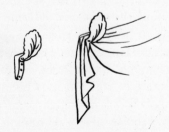

Swag draped over supporting arms

DRAPED SWAG MADE FROM STRAIGHT STRIP OF FABRIC

While draped swags are very attractive, making the shaped ones is rather too complicated a procedure for the average homemaker to enjoy. The straight strip of fabric, cut about 10" longer than half the width of the window, with as much "end hang" allowed for each side as desired, is easy to make.

Cut one straight length of fabric 36" wide and as long as desired. Line it with contrasting fabric, stitching around three sides and most of the fourth side. Leave a foot-long opening for a turning vent. Turn right side out, press flat and sew together the opening vent by hand.

Use plastic or wood rings, or plastic leaf arms as sketched to drape the fabric over. Shape the end sections so part of the lining color shows. (See sketch.) Fasten the fabric firmly together at the arms so it will stay put, by using a few stitches of heavy-duty thread. You will find that it is necessary to take tucks of the fabric to shorten the top edge in order that it will not sag low. These should be taken up behind the arms.

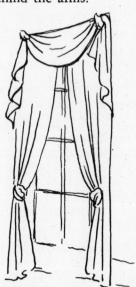

Straight fabric draped swag-like over plastic leaf; other leaves hold back straight draperies

UNLINED OVERDRAPERIES

Unlined overdraperies are made in much the same manner as the glass curtains. These may be of printed dress cottons, gingham, piqué, or of percale, chintz (either plain or glazed), glosheen, sateen, taffeta or satin. For any of these follow the directions preceding.

MEASURING FOR GLASS CURTAINS OR OVER-DRAPERIES

It is necessary to take careful measurements before making either the glass curtains or the draperies. As has been mentioned before, glass curtains are usually hung inside the window embrasure. Therefore the distance measured is from points *a* to *b* as shown on the diagram, with sufficient material added to make the upper turn and the lower hem. (The former is usually 3½" with 2" to 2¾" for the lower edge.) If the glass curtain or the unlined drapery is to hang in front of the window frame, the measurement is taken from point *c* to point *d*, the top of the window frame to the lowest edge of the "apron" of the window. Then the hem allowances are added.

If the sheer panel, the unlined drapery or the lined drapery is to hang to the floor (and this latter is best for all but informal treatments), then the measurement is taken from point *e* to point *f*, or from the top edge of the window frame to the floor. Then the same or deeper hem and top allowances are added.

PATTERNED OR BOLDLY PRINTED FABRIC REQUIRES MORE MATERIAL

When making overdraperies of boldly printed material or fabric with a "bouquet repeat," it is necessary to plan on purchasing more material than would otherwise be necessary. These spots must be evenly placed in all the drapery panels, otherwise the effect would be very dizzy. (See sketch.)

When cutting the drapery panels, all must be laid out on a large flat surface, and the bouquet repeats carefully placed together, before the upper and lower edges are cut. The material removed is seldom wasted. It can usually be used for the tie-backs or for appliqué spots to trim pillows.

HOW TO MAKE TIE-BACKS

Informal glass curtains or overdraperies are often tied back to permit more light and air to enter the room. This may be done with

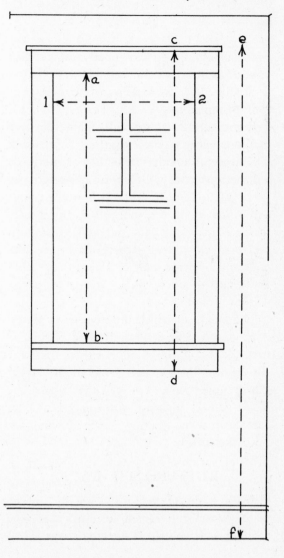

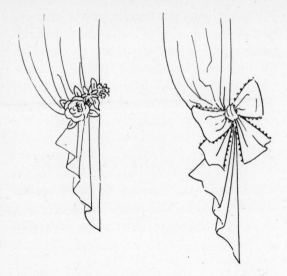

take a hemmed ruffle strip the same width as the other ruffles, and twice as long as the edge it is to decorate. Shir and stitch along the edge of the tie-back as shown in the sketch.

If you prefer to have the edge of the ruffle hidden inside the folded fabric of the tie-back, first complete the shirred ruffle, making it the desired length. Then fold the strip of fabric over it, with raw edges tucked in, and sew by hand. (See diagram.) Or stitch one edge of straight strip to the gathered edge of the ruffle, fold the fabric over and fell the other edge down by hand. (See sketch.)

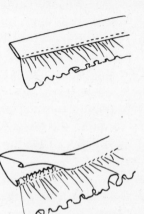

a ribbon sash, or with a looped cord, or with a wired bouquet of imitation flowers, but it is usually done with strips of matching or contrasting fabric.

If the curtain is very full, made of more than one width seamed together, the tie-back will need to be longer than 12" or the folds will be too bunchy. Otherwise cut a strip of fabric 12" long by 8" wide. Fold in the center and stitch along the long edge, right sides facing. Turn right side out and press with the seam along one edge. Tuck in the raw ends and overcast. Sew to a ring or a hook, and attach to a "cup hook" screwed into the window frame.

The height at which the tie-back is placed depends on your wishes. It may be placed low, almost at the window-sill, or halfway up the window, or high at about the center of the upper sash. You can even place the inside tie-back high up, with the outside ones low down when treating a pair of windows. (See sketches.)

RUFFLED TIE-BACK

If you wish to have a tie-back with a ruffled edge to use with ruffled curtains, make the straight tie-back strip as directed above. Then

SASH CURTAINS

Sash curtains are popular for kitchens, and may be made with the upper section tied back and the lower section carried all the way across the lower sash of the window. Together with a ruffled valance, they are called "cottage curtains" when sold in the stores. These are easy to make, by following the preceding directions, permitting the lower section to hang straight, with the upper section overlapping by about 2".

A French provincial style, which is gaining great popularity in this country, uses the sash curtain panel only across the lower sash of the window. This is hung from a metal

rod or even a painted wooden pole. The top of the curtain is pleated in group pleats sewn at intervals with a ring or a hook sewn to each. To exaggerate the curve at the top the sections between are sometimes trimmed out in an inverted scallop, then bound with bias tape of matching cotton. (See sketch and detail diagram of finish of the curtain top.)

These sash curtains may be used without other curtains, or may be substituted for glass curtains where privacy with light is desired. In that case they are often used with peasant chintz overdraperies.

OVERDRAPERIES WITH LININGS

For the living-room, or for more formal rooms it is well to make overdraperies with linings, carrying them with a full sweep from the top of the window to the floor. These have more dignity and richness than any

other type, and the linings make them hang more beautifully. The linings also protect the fabric from dust and soil, and from fading in the sunlight.

A recent trend is to have the drapery rod placed above the window with its ends extending well out along the wall. Then the overdrapery will not cut out any of the light. The window will also become a more important part of the decorative scheme. In many cases the drapery extends all along one wall, with openings left for the windows.

In many modern homes large plate-glass window-walls are curtained with draperies that draw across the window to provide privacy at night. These require lining to give them sufficient body and to make them prac-

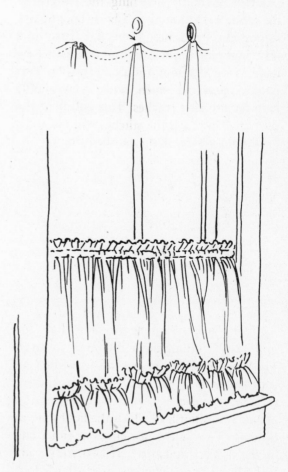

tical for this purpose. Where there are several widths seamed together to provide enough fabric to cover the space, the rod should be extended well out on the wall, so that when the drapery is open in the daytime none of the view will be obstructed. (See sketch.)

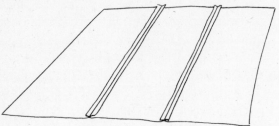

Seam together as many widths as will be required, carefully matching the pattern of the fabric so the seams will be as unobtrusive as possible. Press these seams flat. Turn up a hem along the lower edge and catch-stitch by hand. (See diagram for catch-stitch.) This is a loose zigzag stitch, with a buttonhole loop on alternate stitches. This will hold the turn-up firmly, and the stitches will not show on the right side of the finished drapery.

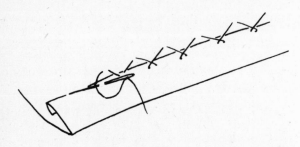

Place a strip of lining crinoline along the upper edge, turning down the fabric to cover. This strip may be bought in 4″ widths, or you can buy it by the yard, 36″ wide, and cut the strips yourself. This is necessary, for it makes a firm finish to which the hooks are to be sewn. Turn in the raw edges at either end of the drapery and baste. If two widths are being hung at one window in a balanced ar-

rangement, there should be a wider turn at the center of the window.

Now you are ready for the lining. Piece together the same number of widths of lining sateen. This may be white, tan, ivory, or a color to match or contrast with the drapery fabric. Press the seams flat. Lay this lining on the finished drapery panel, and catch each perpendicular seam piecing to the matching seam. This will prevent the lining fabric from sagging. Turn under the raw edges along the top and fell—with a loose hemming stitch—at the edge of the drapery fabric turnover. (See diagram on page 143.) Fell the perpendicular edges of the lining fabric to the perpendicular edges of the drapery panel. Then catch-stitch a hem to the inside of the lining, taking care to have this short enough so it will never hang below the front of the drapery when hung in place.

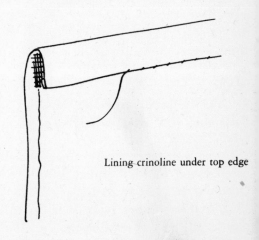

Lining crinoline under top edge

This is the proper way to make a lined drapery. Now here is an easier way that you may prefer. Lay the lining on the length of drapery fabric, with right sides together. Stitch along the edge on three sides—the two long sides and the top. Turn in a hem at the lower edge of the drapery fabric and catch-stitch. Then catch-stitch a hem along the lower edge of the lining, *keeping both hems separate.* Turn the drapery panel right side out and press, after felling crinoline stiffening along the top edge by hand.

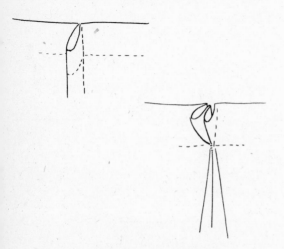

Or, you can get, by the yard, a very clever strip of crinoline-stiffened tape with holes pierced at intervals. This strip is stitched to the back of the drapery panel at the base of the 4″ top turn. When the rod is threaded through the slots the panel automatically pushes into even pleats.

TO MAKE PINCH PLEATS

Many of the ready-made draperies have nice crisp pleats along the top edge, to which the drapery rings or hooks are sewn. These form a very attractive finish and one that may easily be added at home. Thread the needle with heavy, strong thread. Mark off the top of the draperies at even intervals. Baste a 4″ or 5″ deep tuck. Then divide this tucked fold into three smaller group pleats. (See diagram.) Sew firmly together at the base of the fold—4″ from the top edge. Open out the pleat at the top as much as desired, and sew either rings or hooks to the pleat at the back of the drapery.

TAPE SLIDERS

Another very clever invention has metal sliders already fastened on at intervals to a strip of cotton tape. When this strip of tape is sewn to the top of the draperies, and the sliders run through a groove in a special molding placed above the window, the curtain falls into even folds. This dispenses with the necessity for a rod. The molding and tape may be purchased to fit your windows. You may buy a grooved molding, or a grooved cornice board, or one that will carry drapery and valance in two parallel grooves.

This molding may also be used around a dressing-table, along the under edge of the bed or in numerous other places where a gathered "skirt" is desired.

DRESSING-TABLE SKIRTS

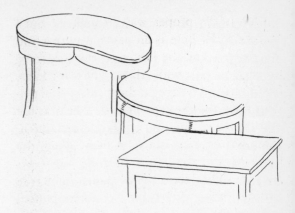

Dainty dressing-tables are attractive and so thoroughly feminine that every woman wants one. They are easy to make. You can cover an old table or a shelf that has been attached to the wall with a strong bracket, or you can buy an unfinished wood dressing-table in the unpainted-furniture section. These come in a "kidney shape," or in oval or oblong shapes. (See sketch.) There are paper patterns you can use to guide you in making these covers, or you can make a cover quite simply without a pattern.

There are two parts to a dressing-table "slipcover." There is the gathered or draped skirt and there is the cover for the top. To make the skirt, follow one of the styles shown in the sketches.

For the skirt section use the directions for making window draperies; for the straight gathered panel with hemmed edge, see directions on page 143. To make the panel with ruffled flounces around the edge follow the directions on page 145. To measure the depth for the skirt, take the distance from the table edge, or the frame under the table—the point where you plan to attach the skirt—to the floor. For the usual table this will measure 30". For a plain hemmed skirt, therefore, you will need lengths 34" long.

To discover how many lengths you require, use the tape measure to find the distance around the table where the skirt is to be attached. Carry the tape well around toward the back so that no awkward gaps show between wall and skirt. Extend the tape around the front of the table to the like spot on the other side. (See diagram.) For a

Scalloped band on edge of dressing table top falling over gathered skirt; window valance to match

softly gathered flounce, piece together enough widths for twice this distance. For a very full skirt or for one made of transparent material over an underskirt, plan on 2½ to 3 times the distance.

If the table has swinging arms at the front, the skirt must be split at the center so you can use the drawers under the swinging arms. If there are drawers shown on the front of the table, the skirt sections may be attached to them, and pull out when the drawers pull out, or they may be attached below the drawers, and a shirred panel mounted on the drawers themselves. (See sketches.)

Most skirts are gathered, then sewn to a firm band. This band is then tacked to the edge of the table, and can be removed for laundering. In some cases the skirt is gathered on a drawstring, either hidden in a casing slot or designed as part of the decoration. This drawstring may be released when the skirt is removed for laundering. (See sketches.)

To make a skirt that is mounted on a band, shir skirt; three rows of running stitch for gatherings. (Diagram at top of next column.) Cut a straight strip of firm fabric such as sateen or white cotton sheeting, 4″ wide and as long as the finished skirt is to be. Lay this strip on the gathered band, with right side facing the right side of the gathered strip. Distribute the gathers evenly. This will

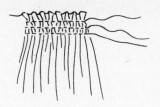

be easier if you have marked the halfway point and other intervals on both the band and the gathered strip. When these marks are matched, draw up the gatherings and baste the two together. (See diagram.) Stitch on the sewing machine. Turn the band over

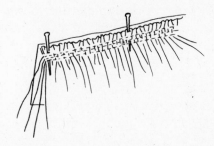

the edge, tuck in the raw edges and sew flat by hand. Press.

This finish should not show. The upper part of the dressing-table cover should come over the edge of the table sufficiently to hide

Dressing-table skirt gathered on a ribbon drawstring

it, as in the styles shown on page 152. To make the top section with the scalloped banding, cut one flat piece of fabric large enough to fit the top of the table and extend over the edge 1″ along the back and ½″ all the rest of the way around. Cut a matching piece of fabric from lining sateen.

Cut a straight strip of fabric 6″ deep and long enough to extend around the front and sides of the table. Use a saucer to cut a paper pattern for a scallop, then trace this pattern all the way around the bottom of the 6″ strip. Lay this strip on a piece of lining sateen (or fabric of contrasting color), right sides facing, and stitch along the line shown. Cut out around the scallops and slash almost to the line of stitching in the corner of each scallop. (See diagram.) Turn this right side

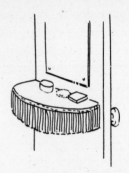

out and press. Lay the right side of the scalloped strip down on the right side of the top, with the band's straight edge matching the front and side edges of the top fabric. Stitch these two together. Stitch the lining sateen to the lining sateen edge of the scallop band, then turn the whole thing and sew along the back edge by hand. Be sure to tuck in the raw edges to make a neat finish. Place thumb tacks in this over-the-edge turn to hold the cover neatly in place.

The gathered band is made very easily, too. Here a 10″ deep strip of fabric is hemmed along one edge, then stitched to the fabric top cut to fit the table. At 8″ intervals rip open tiny slits in the stitching and, when the cover is in place on the table, tie tiny ribbon bows at these openings, gathering up the band softly to form a dainty swag effect.

These are but two of the many suggestions

Sew gathered skirt to top
fitted section

Large circle of fabric covers living-room table

you can carry out in your home, either in bedrooms, or in a corner of the bathroom or for a powder table inside the door of a downstairs closet. If this is small, mount a narrow shelf inside the door, cover it with a wipe-clean coated fabric, then tack a deep fringe around the edge.

LIVING-ROOM TABLES

Many living-room tables, or even hall tables, take kindly to special covers, although these should be simpler and more tailored. Cut a huge circle of fabric, edge with deep upholstery fringe and drape over the ugly old table you rescued from Aunt Hattie's attic. Or, if the legs are too nice to hide, but the top is battle-scarred, cut a smaller circle and hem around the edge. If it's summer camouflage you are after, piece four squares of striped ticking or denim together, then cut the big circle.

To measure for an all-covering circular table cover, carry the tape measure from the floor up to the table edge—usually 30″—then across the table top, then down to the floor. The cover should just clear the floor. So if you plan on a hem any deeper than ½″ all around, better remember to add seam allowance. If you are making the quartered striped job, just cut four squares of fabric,

stitch them together so the stripes meet and match, press the seams open flat, and then cut the big circle. This same arrangement could be done in two different colors, or even four different ones to be used in a game room or play room.

To make the smaller table cover, fit the fabric to the table top in the same way you did for the dressing-table (see directions on page 154), and allow the ½″ for seam all around. Edge with a scalloped band using the directions on page 154, or with a gathered ruffle. Line with sateen or cambric to provide sufficient body.

Slipcovers for small tables

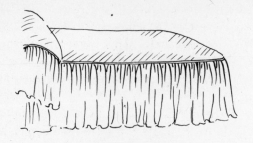

BEDSPREADS

Bedspreads are easy to make, consisting as they do of a large covering piece of fabric and the side overhang. The latter may be gathered, pleated or plain. To make the top you will require one width of fabric, bordered on both sides by another strip of fabric for all but the narrowest beds. Since the average material used for this is only 36" wide (34" by the time seams are sewn), it is easy to see that a 40" bed, or a 50" bed or a wider one will require the center strip, plus a fairly important side strip. Thus plan on 4 yards for the top section. If the sides are tailored into a neat flounce, with just a slash

at the corners for the end posts, then you will require a split length of fabric 2 yards long. If you are planning on a ruffle to extend all around the two sides and across the bottom, you will need enough widths pieced together to make up twice this distance. (See the bedspread sketches for ideas.)

Always introduce a band of trimming, such as piping or welting, or even insertion run with ribbon along the joinings of the fabric. It provides a better finish that way.

Use plain hems, or bound edges or add ruffle flounces at the end of the side panels. Make the spread as simple or as feminine as you wish. Whatever style you choose, do have a feeling of harmony of design between draperies, bedspread and dressing-table cover. If one is simple and tailored, they should all be; if one is daintily ruffled, have the others harmonious.

GATHERED "DUST RUFFLE" FOR BEDS

Many prefer to have a gathered flounce hanging from under the mattress edge, with a rare old woven or crocheted spread tucked in close around the mattress. Or the bedspread may be left hanging down over the

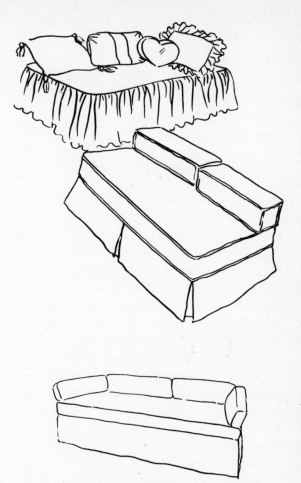

Studio couch covers

top of the flounce. (See sketches.) To make this, prepare a plain flat piece of lining sateen or unbleached muslin almost as large as the box spring of the bed. If it is just as large, the white fabric sometimes shows at the edge, so it is therefore wiser to cut it two inches narrower all around. Add this extra amount to the flounce depth. Make each side flounce and the bottom-of-the-bed flounce separately if there is a corner post. If not, make one long continuous flounce to go around the three sides. Remember the rule about allowing plenty of fullness by making the hemmed flounce long enough for twice the distance required. Gather it with three rows of shirring, and stitch to the edge of the sateen. Place on the spring, then place the mattress above, and make the bed as usual, allowing the spread to hang down or tuck in.

STUDIO COUCH COVER

Many people prefer to have the bedrooms decorated to look like studios or sitting-rooms, so they may serve a dual purpose. To this end, many arrange to have the sleeping bed covered by day with a tailored cover of heavy upholstery fabric. This may have the corners boxed neatly as shown above, or may have an inverted corner box pleat, or may even have a box-pleat flounce all around.

The easiest cover to make is the one with a single piece of fabric covering the top of the couch and a deep gathered flounce for the sides. This is popular with young girls, and is often used in career-girl apartments. The tubular bolsters may be made easily by seaming a straight strip of fabric together, then sewing to circles at each end. One of these may be made with a placket closing along the straight side, so that the sleeping pillow may be put inside by day.

For a living-room couch, sew a 6″ boxing band to the edge of the piece that covers the top of the couch; then have a flounce below with box pleats set in at intervals as shown

in the sketch. This style looks well with the oblong pillows that are sold with a studio couch, or you can have large oblong bolsters made to help it look more like a couch. (See sketch.) Some find it more comfortable to sleep on a wide couch bed, but do not find it so comfortable for sitting during the day. To this end they have a built-in cabinet frame made with a storage cabinet to hold blankets during the day. The couch is on casters, and so slides under the cabinet part way during the day, to pull out quite easily at night. See sketch for an arrangement that you and your husband can easily make yourselves.

Another comfortable arrangement is to have two studio couches covered alike and placed with their heads together against a square cabinet. This is made table-high to

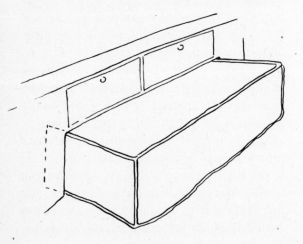

hold an attractive lamp. If the couches are pushed together without a corner cabinet, then piled with cushions, they make a luxurious banquette. (See sketches.)

If the fabric used for the couch is heavy enough, you will not need to make it with a

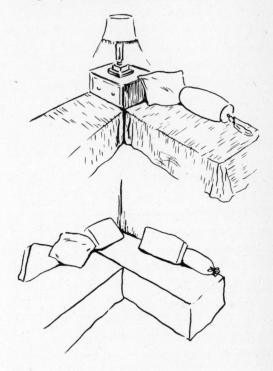

lining. If it is fairly thin material, a chintz or gingham, you will find it will look better and hold its shape longer if the top section is lined with a matching strip of sateen.

It also helps to hold the cover firm on the couch if there is a snap or button flap on the side sections that turn the corner to fasten to an extension from the top of the cover. (See diagram.)

An easy way to cover a studio couch is to have one "super-large" piece of fabric, finished at the edge and draped casually over the couch to fall in soft folds at the corner. Usually the corners are trimmed off into a curve so they will not drag on the floor. If the fabric is not wide enough to cover the

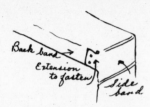

couch and hang clear to the floor, an extension strip may be stitched to it, taking care that the seam of the extension strip is placed along the edge of the couch.

A tailored box-cover looks well in living-rooms, too. This has a plain fitted section for the top of the couch. Welting or other trimming is set around the edges of this top section between a straight boxing, which covers all the side of the couch and extends clear to the floor. This may be hemmed along the bottom edge or trimmed to correspond with the top. The trimming may carry up the seams at the corners of the couch, or these seams may be omitted. (See sketches on pages 157 and 158.)

Group pleats or circular flares may also be set in at these corners to add attractiveness and style. (See sketches below.) To cut the circular flare take a square the size of the depth of the side boxing (usually 18″). Seam adjoining corners to the side and end strips of the cover, then cut off excess along the lower edge so the curve hangs even with the other strips.

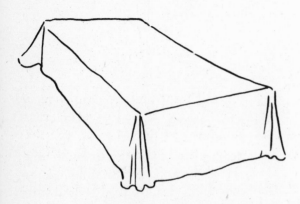

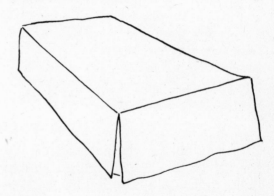

SLIPCOVERS

It is only an easy step from making a bedspread and covering a studio couch to making slipcovers for other sofas and chairs. There are paper patterns for these available, manufactured by three of the leading pattern companies. If you prefer the ease of sewing with a pattern, investigate their style sheets to find whether there is a pattern available for your particular piece of furniture. These patterns are made for the usual chairs such as Lawson, club, wing, boudoir, open armchair, armless upholstered chair, as well as for such sofas as Lawson, club, Chippendale and Duncan Phyffe styles. There is a pattern for an ottoman as well as for dressing-table stools to go with the dressing-tables.

You can easily make your own slipcovers without patterns. You will need 5 yards for the smaller chairs, 7 yards for the living-room chairs, and 9 yards for the wing chair, with from 10 to 16 yards for the couches, depending on the flounce you decide to use.

The safest way to determine the amount of material you will need is to measure the chair. To do this carry the tape measure from the upholstery edge at the back of the chair up over the back and down to the seat. Form an 8″ loop, carry the tape measure across to the front edge of the seat and down to the edge of the upholstery. Make a note of this measurement, for this is the first length of fabric. Start with the tape measure at the upholstery edge on the side of the chair, carry it up over the arm and down to the chair seat, make a 4″ addition. Double this to include the other arm, and add to first measurement. (These additions are for the tuck-ins that are necessary to keep the cover from pulling out of place or the seams from bursting when fat Uncle Ben plops down.)

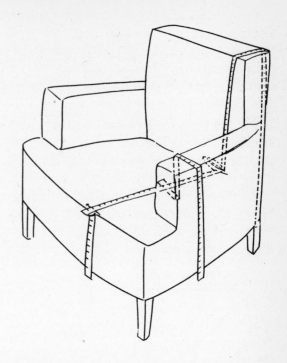

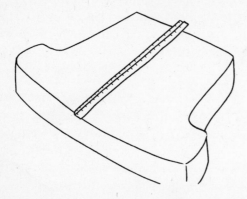

For the cushions, measure across the top, then add the same amount so that both sides of the cushion are covered with the same pretty fabric, and can be turned frequently for longer wear. The boxing section around the edge of the cushion can usually be squeezed out of the sides of the first strip. If, however, you have chosen a fabric with a definite pattern, this strip will have to be cut across the width of the material and strips pieced together. So measure and allow enough 4″ deep strips to extend all around the cushions.

The flounce may be deep enough to go from the edge of the chair seat, or only deep enough to go from the bottom of the upholstery. The deeper flounces are new and fashionable, and also easy to make. They also have the advantage of making the cover so

easy to fit that many times you can eliminate the placket opening at the back of the chair. Such flounces are either 14″ or 16″ deep when hemmed, so allow for strips of fabric 16″ to 18″ deep. For the shorter flounce, 12″ deep when finished, allow for 14″ deep strips.

A gathered flounce should be made two to two and a half times the distance of the circumference of the chair in order to have it sufficiently full. Piece together enough widths, matching fabric carefully so the pattern is even. Press open seams and hem the lower edge before gathering the top edge. If the chair measures 18″ across the front, 20″ at each side, and 16″ across the back, the circumference is 74″. Therefore 148″ or more of fabric will be required for the flounce. This means you will need five widths of 36″ fabric or three widths of 50″ fabric.

For a flounce with box pleats all around, measure three times the circumference of the chair. Then figure out the number of widths required. Piece together, matching pattern of fabric carefully. Hem along the lower edge, measure pleats and press carefully in place before stitching the flounce along the top. The best effect will be obtained if the pleats come out evenly on the front and sides of the chair. So measure the distances carefully, then decide whether the pleats will be two inches or three inches wide to come out evenly. (See sketch.)

The pleats at the corners require 10" extra for each pleat, added to the circumference of the chair when computing the number of widths of fabric that must be seamed together. Thus if the same chair mentioned above has a flounce with a box pleat at each corner, add 40" to 74", plus 2" for the end turn-under. (See diagram accompanying.)

Measuring for Couch or Love Seat

The same method will be followed when measuring for the fabric required for a love seat or a sofa. Since a love seat is twice as

wide in the back and seat as a chair, these measurements are doubled. Since a sofa is three times as wide, these measurements are tripled. The distance for the flounce also increases proportionately, but there are still only two arms, so this measure remains the same as for a chair.

To Fit the Slipcover

To cut and fit the slipcover without a pattern requires plenty of pins. Lay the fabric over the piece to be fitted with the right side down. Take care to center the fabric, particularly if there is a predominant design such as a flower bouquet. (See sketch.) Start at the top of the back. Carry the fabric down to the seat. If the seat is straight across the back, the fabric will not need to be cut here. Make a deep fold to serve as tuck-in (4" minimum fold, or 8"), then carry the fabric

Deep flounce from edge of chair seat to floor

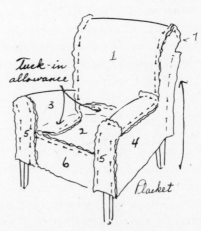

(Numbers refer to cutting order.)

across the chair seat to the front of the chair. Add a row of pins here, placing them so the points are in, and the heads out in an even row. (See sketch.)

If the seat is not straight across the back, cut the fabric and add a shaped piece to cover the seat and extend 4″ out beyond the back of the seat.

To form a tuck-in at the sides of the chair back, add some excess fabric, gradually tapering it from the ½″ seam allowance to around 2″ or 3″ at the sides. Add tuck-in allowance of 4″ at the side of the seat section.

Next cut the arm inside section. Start the fabric at the very outside edge of the top of the arm, carry it down to the seat with an extra 4″ for tuck-in allowance to match the flap at the side of the seat as mentioned above. Place pins as directed before and cut along the line of their heads, thus forming an even ½″ seam allowance. To shape the front of the arm to cover any rounded fulness, place several small tapered tucks, wider at the seam, gradually ending in nothing. (See diagram.) Baste these in place. Form the same type of small tapered tucks at the top of the back if fulness is necessary. *Make sure that all tucks face up* on the side you are fitting. Then they will face down on the right side; they will lie smoother and shed the dust when the cover is finished. (Section 3 on diagram.)

Attach the outside arm section to the top edge of the inside arm section with a row of

(Numbers refer to cutting order.)

pins placed lengthwise rather than crosswise in the fabric. Carry the fabric down, ending it either just below the chair upholstery or at the point where the flounce is to be attached. To repeat, the flounce may be 12″, 14″ or 16″ deep. (Section 4 on diagram.)

If the chair is a Lawson or club type, there will be a section of fabric necessary between the outside and inside sections of the arm. Cut and fit this small piece from some of the left-over bits of fabric. Place the design attractively, so the print shows up to best advantage. If the material is striped, this section may be horizontal to contrast with perpendicular stripes of the rest of the cover. If the body of the slipcover is plaid, you may wish to cut this section on the bias. If you do this, and the fabric is at all stretchy, you will need to line it with a matching section cut on the straight of the goods in order to have the cover hold its shape. (Section 5 in diagram.)

When these two or three pieces are cut to fit one arm, remove them from the chair, and lay right side down, facing matching fabric sections. *Be sure the design is placed equally for each section, and that you have facing sections to form a right and left arm.* Cut out, and place back on chair for fitting.

Cut the small front section above the flounce—unless the flounce carries up from the floor to the front edge of the seat. (See piece 6 on the diagram of cutting order.)

Now cut the back section. This part is usually hidden if the chair sits against the

Modern fabrics show more vivid colorings and larger size designs as in this Camelia used for draperies and slipcovers. One chair is covered in stripes that repeat the colors of flowers and leaf.

Neatly tailored slipcovers of textured plain cotton cover these matching chairs and ottomans. A drapery of boldly patterned flowered glosheen pulls all across the window wall while the same chintz is pasted to the adjoining wall like wallpaper.

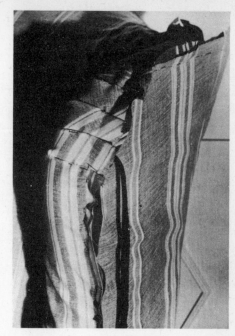

If the tucks required for fitting any shaped sections are turned up on the wrong side they will face down on the right side and thus will not gather as much dust.

Fit the slipcover fabric to the chair wrong side out as you cut. Place all pins close together to hold half-inch seams firmly until they have trimming inserted, then baste before removing the cover from the chair for stitching. Notice the wider seam allowance around chair seat and inside back so the cover will have give, and will not split open at the seams.

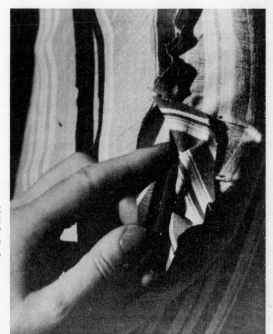

Open the seam one pin at a time and insert the welting strip before repinning for basting. Be sure and hold all raw edges together, fitting the welting tightly and evenly between the fabric thicknesses, having curved edge down and line of pins right on the stitching of the welting strip.

wall. In this case it may be cut of contrasting fabric, if you are running short of material. It must have extra allowance for a placket at one side of the back, to join to a placket band attached to the corner of the front chair-back section, or the outside of the chair arm. (Section 7 on diagram.)

Since most plackets look best on chairs if they are held flat, use an extension of fabric rather than adding an extra straight strip as is usually done for dresses. Make this placket 1½" to 2" deep if you are planning to use grippers, eyelets for lacings, or buttons and buttonholes. You will require only a 1" turn if you are planning to use a slide-fastener closing.

Fit this back section to the adjoining sections, pinning the pins in the fabric lengthwise to form the seam. Pin the placket together temporarily.

The Seam Trimming

Any cover looks far more professional if there is piping or cording, fringe or welting introduced in the seams as they are stitched together. The only exception to this rule is for bedroom slipcovers. These may be made without such seam trimming. The cover is simply basted together, then stitched once along the seams on the wrong side. Then the cover is turned right side out, and another row of stitching is added close to the edge, ridging up the edge of the other stitching. This is like a French seam, but in reverse. It is called a boxed seam.

Welting may be purchased by the yard, and is so reasonable in price that it hardly pays to go to all the trouble to make it. It comes in a variety of colors, and may be had in glazed chintz or twill or plain woven cotton. If you prefer to make your own, cut bias strips of the same fabric as the cover of the chair or of contrasting fabric. These

Proper spotting of design motif—centered in each chair section

should be about 3" wide. Seam the angle ends together, and press the seams open flat. Then lay soft cotton cording at the center along the wrong side, lay the fabric over, and stitch along close to the cord. (See diagram.) You will find it easier to stitch close to the cording if you use the special cording foot attachment of the sewing machine.

Piping is made of the bias fabric, folded and stitched as in welting, but without the cotton stuffing cord. This is far finer, and is not as popular a trim as the welting.

Usually the fringe trim is reserved for slipcovers that are to be dry cleaned. The puffy cotton moss fringe must be rubbed up after it is laundered. The rayon moss fringe and other styles do not come through the laundry so well; so use these only as seam trimming on the very luxurious covers.

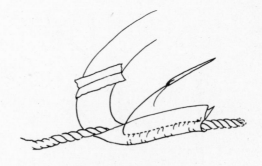

Making welting finishes
Bias strips pieced together
Cording set inside folded bias strips

Inserting the Trimming Along the Seams

After the cover is completely pinned to-together—before the flounce or the back placket finish is added—is the time to introduce the trimming into the seams. Release the pins that hold the seams together one by one; insert the trimming "finish side" down with the rough edges of the fabric up toward you parallel with the other raw edges of the slipcover seam.

Pin the seams again as the trimming is introduced. At the end of the strip, carry the welting through so there will be a smooth tapered ending on the right side. Do this at seam crossings also. Baste the seams before removing the slipcover from the chair.

Stitching the Seams

Stitch all the seams with heavy-duty thread or with matching mercerized cotton. Use the cording foot on the sewing machine so you can stitch along the line of bastings, right close to the puffy part of the welting. If you hold the fingers of your left hand on the fat part as you run it through the sewing machine, you will be able to hold it close and keep the stitching straight.

Be sure to stitch across the seam corners

Diagram of placket

firmly so there will be no gaping holes there. If there are several thicknesses of fabric and cording, go very slowly or you may break the sewing-machine needle. It is sometimes necessary to push each needle insertion through, in order to make it pierce the heavy folds. Always use a strong, coarse needle.

Setting in the Placket

After the cover is completely stitched, press the seams. Then put it back on the chair. If a slide fastener is to be used for the placket opening, buy one long enough to go from the top of the flounce to the point on the chair back where the cover opening ends. *This point depends entirely on the chair.* Naturally a longer one is necessary for a wing chair than for a low-back club chair. The slide fastener does not need to carry down through the flounce, but may do so if you prefer.

Open the slide fastener. Baste one edge to the extension from the side of the chair. Turn the fold edge under along the side edge of the back. Lay this fold over the other edge of the slide fastener, and baste in place, taking care that this flap completely covers the fastener.

This makes a simple placket closing and one that will lie flat. Stitch in place with a line of machine stitching.

For gripper closing you will need a strong double fold of the fabric. These fasteners are "riveted" into the material, using a spool of thread and a pencil as the tools. Full directions for applying come with each package of grippers. Their top rings which show on top of the fabric fold may be had in a variety of colors to match your slipcovers. (See diagram.) These are easier to attach than sewn-on snap fasteners and, if properly applied, will stay firmly in place for the entire life of the cover.

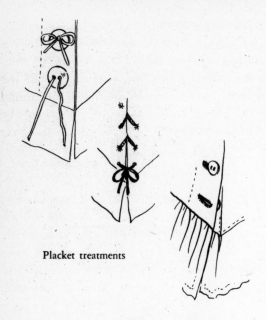

Placket treatments

Buttons and Buttonholes

Many slipcovers look attractive with buttons and buttonholes used as closings, and forming attractive trim at the same time. The buttons may be sewn in place in the usual way. However, if the buttons have large "porthole" openings, tape may be sewn to the slipcover fabric and the button tied in place with an attractive bow. (See sketch.)

These tapes may be led through eyelet holes embroidered in the fabric, or the buttonhole may be embroidered in a horizontal slit. (See sketch.) If preferred, a tailored bound buttonhole may be made. These may be taken to a tailor shop, with the usual charge for large ones about 20¢ each, or they may be made at home.

To make a bound buttonhole, sew a square of fabric on the top or right side of the fabric. Stitch onto the fabric in an oblong as shown, leaving a strip down the center and a fair amount of fabric around the edges. (See diagram.) Slash for the buttonhole opening as shown. Push the fabric around the edges through the slot thus slashed, and tug sharply

at the ends, working now from the wrong side of the material. This tug will cause a small pleat to form at the end of the folds. Adjust the right side so that there is a bound edge of equal size at each side of the slash. Baste in place. Turn under raw edges on the wrong side of the fabric, and overcast flat. (See diagram of finished buttonhole as seen from both the right and wrong sides.) Be sure to press all buttonholes after you have completed them.

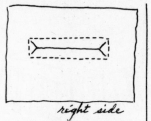

Stitch facing strip (oblong)—then slash as shown

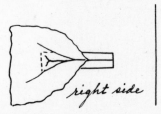

Pull facing strip through to wrong side, leaving neat folded edges equal on each side

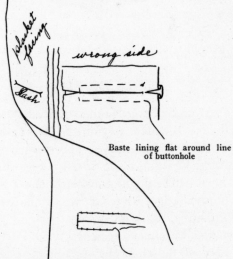

Baste lining flat around line of buttonhole

Fell down raw edges of slash on placket facing to leave fold showing equal distances each side

Bound buttonholes

Boudoir chair with 3 covers showing changes of style
in fabric and in flounces

1 Gathered   2 Pleated all around
         3 Pleated at corners

Adding the Flounce

After the cover is otherwise completed the
flounce is added. A gathered flounce should
be divided into quarters and marked with a
colored basting-stitch thread before shirring.
Then gather the hemmed strip along the unfinished edge, using at least three rows of
gathering. Mark off a strip of welting, indicating each measurement of the circumference of the chair, having the first for the
side of the chair nearest the placket, next the
front, next the other side, and then the back.

Gather the shirrings to fit these distances,
and pin the top row of shirrings to the
marked welting. Baste. Then stitch the welting to form a firm finish at the top of the
flounce. Always have the finish, or round
edge, of the welting facing down toward the
hem of the flounce.

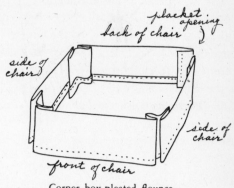

Corner box-pleated flounce

Adjust this finished flounce to the chair
slipcover, turning the raw edges down as you
pin the flounce in place. See that the flounce
hangs evenly all around, just clearing the
floor.

Baste the slipcover flounce in place, remove from the chair and stitch around just
below the welting edge.

The flounce with the box pleats at the four
corners is completed before being hung on
the slipcover. Lay the corner pleats—making
each 10" deep—according to the required
measurements of the chair. Check to be sure

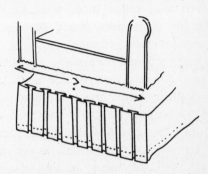

Number of pleats must divide evenly across front of
chair no matter what the measurement

that any piecing seams fall inside the pleats rather than in the center of the flounce. Press these seams, stitch a strip of welting along the top edge, hang on the slipcover while the finished cover is on the chair, and then sew in place. This flounce also should just clear the floor.

The box-pleated flounce should be completely made, with the pleats evenly spaced and pressed, then stitched to the top welting strip that has been marked off to fit each section of the circumference just as directed in the gathered flounce. After this has been done the flounce is attached to the finished slipcover, basted in place and then stitched just below the welting edge.

Covering Loose Cushions

Most chairs, love seats or sofas have loose cushions on the seat, and some of them have them at the back also. These are covered separately. The boxed cushions are the easiest to do. They require only two flat pieces of fabric cut to the shape of the cushion, stitched together with welting strips to trim, and a boxing band to fit the width of the cushion between.

Lay the pillow down on the fabric, taking care to arrange printed material so the center of the design falls in the center of the cushion. Draw around with dressmaker's crayon. Cut out, allowing ½" for seams along all sides, with 1" along the back edge where the placket opening will be. In a straight cushion this will need to be across the back edge only. In a T-shaped cushion it will have to extend around the sides as marked for ease in pushing the cushion into its cover. (See diagram.)

Lay this piece of fabric on another section of fabric, faces together, designs matching, and cut. This will mean that you will have two sides to the cushion just alike. After the

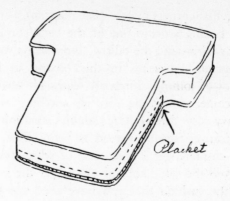

cover is made the pillow may be reversed each time you houseclean, for longer wear of both pillow and cover.

Measure the depth of the boxing band, and then measure the distance around the cushion. Cut a straight strip of fabric to these dimensions, adding seam allowances, of course. If the fabric does not have a definite pattern, or if it is a stripe you wish to contrast, this strip may be cut lengthwise of the fabric along a selvage edge, rather than crosswise. If the design is of flower bouquets, it will be wise to cut and piece crosswise strips, taking care to match the patterns on the seams.

Baste a welting strip around the large fabric sections at inside edge of seam and placket allowance, taking care to see that welting finish edge faces in and raw edge follows along raw edge of the fabric. Baste boxing strip to this section, then baste the other edge of boxing strip to the other section. Make

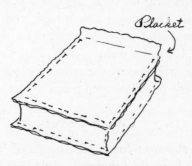

Pillow pinned together

sure that corners match. (See diagram.) Start the boxing strip at one of the back corners, carry all around the pillow, and make a short perpendicular seam in this boxing at the point of joining. Stitch all seams on sewing machine, using one row of stitching with heavy-duty thread. Use double stitching if mercerized sewing thread is being used, as the cushions get a great deal of seam strain.

Add the same kind of closure at the back of the cushion that you have used for the cover. This may be a slide fastener or a row of buttons, snaps or grippers. Make a firm placket, and be sure the fasteners are close enough together so the placket never gapes.

If the cushion is a puffy one, you may cover it with two pieces of fabric without the boxing strip between. Use the upholstery as your guide. Add the fulness, or fit it in by means of the same tapered tucks you used when fitting the slipcover itself. (See sketch of finished cover with controlled fulness.)

Sometimes these pillows have a long tapered strip set in at the lower edge of the pillow. This makes a neat base, and fits into the seat and side-arm section of the chair well. Carry the welting trim along both sides of the strip, hiding the opening placket along one side of this shaped piece.

Couch Covers

A slipcover for a sofa, couch or love seat is made in the same way. The fabric is pin-

fitted to these and basted, then stitched together with welting set in to the important seams. The only difference is that several widths of fabric pieced together will be needed along the back of the couch. In a love seat two widths are pieced together, in a couch three widths. Each is edged with a strip of welting, and this trimming corresponds neatly with the edge of the pillows on the couch. (See diagrams on page 161.)

The flounces are put on in the same manner as on the chairs, except for the flounce with the corner box pleats. That one has the box pleats at the four corners, but also should have extra ten-inch deep pleats corresponding to the breaks between the cushions. (See sketch.)

10" pleats

CHAIR-SEAT UPHOLSTERY

Many dining-room or side chairs have "pad seats." These are made of a flat wooden sheet, padded with hair or cotton, and covered with muslin and upholstery fabric. They are usually held in place in the chair frame with long screws that go up into the pad edges from the frame underneath.

If the covering is soiled or worn, it is an easy matter to replace it. All that is necessary is to take the pad out, pry loose the upholstery tacks around the edge and remove the old cover. Use this cover as a pattern to cut a new one from fresh material, and tack the new cover on the pad. Start by placing one tack in the center of the front turn and the center of the back turn. Smooth evenly, and gradually add tacks to these sections, working out toward the corners of the pad. By doing both front and back at the same time the fabric is kept smooth and even. After these are completed, do the sides, again starting at the center of each side, and tacking both simultaneously.

When you come to the corner, cut off the excess fabric in smooth mitring, then fold over the edges and tack so there is a tight corner, with all raw edges hidden or turned under.

Replace the seat in the chair, screwing firmly in place with the same screws that were removed.

Side chairs fitted to all-over slipcovers

SMALL SLIPCOVERS FOR SIDE CHAIRS

Dining-room chairs or extra chairs that are used in the living-room look well with short slipcovers. These consist merely of a top cover, fitting the seat area, a box band that carries around the edge of the seat, with or without a pleated flounce set on below. (See sketches.)

These may be made easily after the other covers have been completed and you are a real expert. They need only about a yard of fabric for each chair seat. The tabs for fastening come at the back of the seat, with flaps fitting around the uprights that form the chair back. (See sketch.) These short flaps may have gripper fasteners or snaps or tie-tapes.

The chair backs may also have short slipcovers. These may slide on and off without any placket opening, if the back of the chair is fairly straight. If there is much taper to the back and the cover fits closely, you will need to make a placket, as in detailed description on page 164, along the back edge. (See sketches.)

STOOL COVERS

Living-room ottomans or low stools or dressing-table stools take kindly to slip-covers, too. These can be fitted to the furniture easily, for there is only the top, boxing

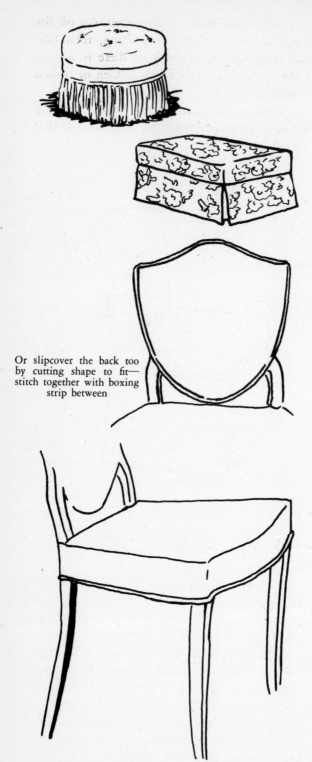

Or slipcover the back too by cutting shape to fit— stitch together with boxing strip between

Slipcover just the seat of dining-room chairs

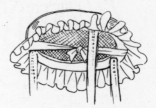

Tie-on stool slipcover

and flounce to consider. These usually do not need any placket closing, but they may need a strap band or anchoring tie-tape to pass under the stool top and hold them firmly in place. (See sketches.)

COVERING LAMPSHADES

Lampshades are easy to make. You can make paper ones or fabric ones, or you can slipcover old lampshades that would otherwise look dingy and soiled. All lampshades require a stiff frame of some sort, usually of wire. This may be bought without covering, or you can use the frame of a discarded shade as the basis of the new one. You will find it easier to handle if there are wire uprights or spokes between the two wire circles than if the wire circles come apart when you remove the stiffened section between.

Paper Shades

If you are making a new paper lampshade from an old one, it is easy to use a discarded section as a cutting guide or pattern for the new section. Or the shade may be twirled slowly over the paper while you draw in the outline to be cut. Don't forget that you will need an extra "seam allowance" to turn over the edge of the shade. This should be about ½" wide. (See diagram for the usual shape of the shade paper with the turn-over edge indicated.) Cut along the outside edge, making sure to leave also a ½" over-lay flap at the end of the shade.

Use paper clips to fasten the paper in place over the wire frame, then sew with over-and-over stitches. Cover this edge with pasted-on trim of ribbon or upholstery braid or anything you desire. If you prefer not to sew along the edge, carry a strip of passe-partout tape or sticky paper tape along the edge, fold over to the inside of the shade and stick in place. This will hold the shade around the wire.

For an unobtrusive lampshade that blends in with the wall behind it, cover stiff drawing paper with wallpaper attached with wallpaper paste. (See directions on page 42 for making and using wallpaper paste.) Then make the shade as directed above. Very attractive formal shades may be made from metallic paper or marbleized paper in the same way.

Butcher's paper may be used to cover shades. When stretched over the wire frame and waxed or varnished, it closely resembles more expensive parchment. Wrapping paper may be crumpled in the hand and dipped in dye, then smoothed out and used to cover lampshades.

Plain paper shades may be trimmed with attractive cut-outs of flowers, ships or children's toys. The shades may be decorated to suit the scheme of the room in which they are to be used.

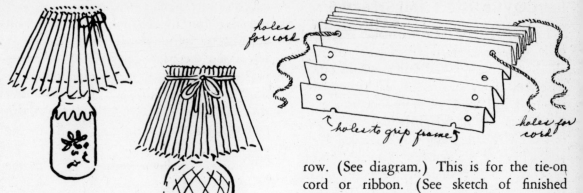

row. (See diagram.) This is for the tie-on cord or ribbon. (See sketch of finished shades.)

Pleated Paper Shades

Pleated paper shades are attractive looking, easy to make and fit onto the frame. A straight strip of stiff paper or of fabric mounted on paper stiffening is first prepared. This may be made with or without a turned hem edge at top and bottom. Try the material plain or turned and stitched, before you decide which you wish to use. Make the strip more than twice as long as the circumference of the shade *taken around the center*. Since most of the shades flare out at the base, this gives you the average. If the pleated strip is to be applied to a drum-shaped frame, the measurement around the middle will be the same as the upper and lower frame.

Fold the stiffened paper back and forth to form 1″ deep pleats. Press every few pleats as you make them. Carry these pleats all the length of the strip. Fold and tie in bundle as shown. Mark along one edge where the wire of the frame will come, indicating the top edge, then the lower edge. In order to have the shade grip the wire rings firmly, use a paper punch to punch holes along the edges where marked at the under edge of each pleat.

Punch another row of holes in the center of each pleat a little way below the upper

Fabric-Covered Lampshades

The easiest way to cover a shade with fabric to match your decorative scheme is to make a slipcover for it. This may be neatly fitted, cut in two or four sections. Choose whichever fits the contour of your shade the

better. Lay the fabric over the shade, wrong side out, and pull taut. Pin the seams together. Trim to ½″ from the line of pins. Remove from the shade and stitch these seams by sewing machine. Bind the upper edge with bias binding to prevent its stretching out of shape, and do the same at the lower edge. Or if you prefer, use decorative trimming similar to that used on the draperies or slipcovers of the room where the shade is to be used. The shade slipcover may have a gathered, hemmed ruffle of organdie, or a pinked ruffle of taffeta, or it may have a band of ball fringe.

If the skirt of the dressing-table is gathered, then it will be in keeping to make a gathered "slipcover" for the lampshade. Simply cut a straight strip of fabric at least twice as long as the circumference of the shade, and 2″ to 3″ deeper. Sew short ends together, and press seam flat. Bind the strip along both edges with a narrow binding of contrasting fabric. Have the lower edge binding wider than the upper binding. About 1½″ from the top, stitch a strip of cotton tape ¾″ wide on the wrong side of the shade, or add a strip of the contrasting fabric the same width to the right side, tucking in raw edges as you baste in place before stitching. This band serves as a slot through which a ribbon drawstring may be run to be tied with a bow.

Sewing fabric right to the wire frame is a bit more difficult. If the frame is made of wire so treated that it will not rust, the fabric may be sewn directly to the bare wire. Otherwise the frame will require that rayon seam binding be wound over the wire. Any natural rust is absorbed in this binding and therefore will not penetrate through to the surface fabric.

Fabric may be fitted in quarters or in halves, depending on the size and shape of the shade. Some big shades have one piece

used for each half. Others have an extreme slope, or flare, and therefore the fabric will not pull off grain as much if four separate pieces are cut and shaped to fit together at the quarter spokes. *All seams should come directly over a wire upright.* This makes them show up less when the light is on, and also makes it easier to fit the fabric and sew the seams.

If there is a special print pattern, lay the design attractively before beginning the sewing. If there is a stripe or a plaid, take care to match the design attractively. All sorts of materials may be used for lampshades. See charts on pp. 115–118 for suggestions. You should determine before starting whether the material is transparent enough to show some light through. A shade that does not diffuse light makes a lugubrious effect, and is hard to use for reading or sewing. It is all right for hall lights or other places where the light is to serve a purely decorative purpose.

If the fabric is transparent, a lining fabric must be used with it. It is most unpleasant to be able to see the bulb clearly through the shade.

To Fit the Outside Fabric

Lay the fabric on the shade, taking care to see that the straight of the goods is in the center. This means that the threads run perpendicular and horizontal, not on the diag-

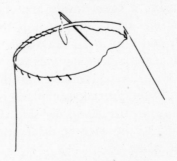

Overcast edge on lampshade

onal. Pin the fabric over the wire at top and bottom center. Add pins toward the right and left, stretching the fabric taut as you pin. Carry these pins toward the side. Pin at top and bottom simultaneously, and when finished pin along the side upright spokes. Thread needle with matching mercerized cotton and sew. If there is to be a trimming braid added after the material, then use overcasting at the edges. (See diagram above.) If there is to be no trimming, use a stab stitch, spacing each stitch evenly, carrying the needle in and out of the fabric to make what appear to be tiny running stitches. (See diagram below.) You will find these stitches hold more tightly if you occasionally take a small back stitch.

Stab stitch edge on lampshade

After the upper and lower edges are sewn, trim the fabric along the edges close to the line of the stitches along the inside of the shade. Use the stab stitches to sew the fabric over the uprights, and trim off excess material. If the shade is to be unlined, you will find it makes a better inside appearance if you trim the fabric first at top, bottom, and sides and turn in all raw edges as you sew. This may be done quite easily.

Turn the shade and complete the other side to match, sewing first along top and bottom, then cutting to size along the side uprights and felling to the edge of the fabric sewn along the spoke.

This completes the outside of the shade.

To Make the Shade Lining

Use shantung, china silk, or other lining fabric that is soft and will allow light to pass through. Pin-fit to the inside of the shade, cutting in two or four sections, depending on which was done for the fabric on the outside of the shade. Pin the sections together carefully, then remove from the shade, baste, and stitch together on the sewing machine. Press seams flat after trimming as close as possible. Replace the lining in the shade, and adjust carefully around upper and lower edges. Pin in place, and sew with blind stitches such as are used to sew a hat lining in place, taking a tiny bit of each fabric in the needle, then sliding the needle along under the edge, and coming up to take another stitch.

Trimming for Fabric Shades

Many formal shades have rich upholstery braid or fringe used to trim the edges. In many purchased ready-made shades this is glued or pasted in place. Thus when the shade is dry-cleaned or laundered it comes off. You will find it far more satisfactory to sew on your trimmings. This may be done with a blind stitch as above described, or with a sort of long and short basting stitch that just catches the trimming in place.

Another nice edging, and one that goes well with simple shades, is bias binding of matching fabric. These bias strips are cut rather narrow, only $3/4$ to $1/2$" wide. They are sewn on as all bias bands: one edge sewn first, close to the edge, then the band turned over evenly, raw edge tucked in and the fabric turn felled flat. All these things you can do yourself for your own home. They take time, but you will enjoy doing them more if you don't rush them—if you allow the feeling of creating your own masterpiece to influence your enjoyment.

There are many other touches of individuality that you can add. Many will be suggested by these ideas. You will find other ideas in the art needlework department of your store, or in the magazines devoted to homemaking ideas. Perhaps you don't feel that you are expert enough to try them, but the old adage of "practise makes perfect" is really true. The more things you make, the more attractive and professional-looking they will become. Don't grow discouraged if the very first efforts are not what you have visualized. Later ones will be.

XI

NOW FOR THE DOING

Here in this volume is the information that many future homemakers go to courses of interior decoration to learn; some of the information that they could only discover by spending time to interview buyers and manufacturers. It is our hope that it will answer all your questions and help you in making your house into a home. We know that you have an ideal in your mind of just what you want. Don't let us or anyone else change that ideal. You will be happy and "feel at home" only if the house suits *you*.

Style in decoration doesn't matter nearly as much as style in clothes. Everyone feels out-of-date if wearing the wrong length skirt or sleeves that looked well in mother's or grandmother's day. But in decoration if you want to have furniture and accessories that were in style then, do—by all means. No one is an arbiter of style in decoration. No one demands you should follow *their* ideas.

Do consider, though, whether the furniture, fabrics and accessories you choose are the ones you will like five, ten, fifteen years from now. The reason that styles in clothes can afford to change is that the investment in a suit is far less than the investment in furniture. In these larger things more careful consideration is necessary before buying.

If there is an argument in your family between modern and traditional, don't go overboard for either one. Try them both out, have a few pieces of the more conservative examples of each in your starting arrangements. Then as you buy extras to complete the decorative scheme you will have your mind more made up. You will know by *living with* these things whether you really like them.

Pictures in a magazine are one thing. There the simplicity of modern chairs and couch look swell, and you think you want them. But in your own home, they all of a sudden are just not what you want with Great-aunt Mehitable's corner cupboard alongside them. It would be ridiculous to throw them out. The couch cost $250 and the big chair $140. What to do? It's too late to turn them in on a new model as you do an automobile, *so do make up your mind first, before buying.*

Scrapbooks or clipping files are valuable investments in your evening hours. Clip and paste all your favorites together long before the house is finished. You'll find home-building pictures in a scrapbook will help you when you yourself build. Look all the pictures over, and you may be surprised to discover that the pictures that looked just right when you cut them out just have to be torn out and discarded some time later. YOU have changed. Your ideas may have matured.

So let your ideas change all they want to BEFORE you decorate. It costs lots less then than it does after. Maybe you think the range of prices of your second-hand furniture dealer means you can turn in mistakes to him and get some of your money back. But, dearie, you've forgotten that mark-up he takes which pays his rent and keeps him in business. He has to give you from 40% to 50% less when he buys from you than he charges when he sells to you.

Don't let that 40% be your loss. It needn't be if you plan every little detail carefully in advance. Then your house will be a home of which you and all the family will be truly proud.

Here Are Some Books You May Enjoy

A Key to Pottery and Glass, B. Rackham.
American Glass, G. S. and H. McKearin.
Beauty Treatments for the Home, Kay Hardy.
China and Glassware, F. J. Ringo.
Decorating for You, Florence Terhune.
Decoratively Speaking, Gladys Miller.
Early American Pressed Glass, R. W. Lee.
Glass and Glassmaking, E. Singleton.
Home Planning Scrapbook, Elinor Hillyer.

Let's Set the Table, E. Lounsberry.
Personality of a House, Emily Post.
Pottery and Porcelain of the U. S., E. A. Barber.
Practical Book of Chinaware, Eberlein and Ramsdell.
Romance of Textiles, Ethel Lewis.
Setting Your Table, H. Sprackling.

Booklets That May Be Purchased from Manufacturers

(or will be sent on request)

How to Be a Successful Hostess, Reed and Barton, Taunton, Mass.
Entertaining the Sterling Way, Gorham, Providence, R. I.
Guide for the Bride, Wamsutta, New Bedford, Mass.
How to Buy Blankets Intelligently, Chatham Blankets, Elkin, N. C.
How to Decorate Your Dream Room, North Star Blankets, Minneapolis 1, Minn.
How to Make Your Towels Last Longer, Cannon, 70 Worth St., N. Y. C.
How to Get the Most for Your Money, Martex, 65 Worth St., N. Y. C.
Your New Home and Your Pocketbook, General Electric, Bridgeport, Conn.

Color Tricks Galore with Fabric, Waverly Fabrics, 58 West 40th St., N. Y. C.
Decorating Your Home with Glass, Pittsburgh Plate Glass Co., Pittsburgh, Pa.
It's Fun to Do Over with Color, Alexander Smith Carpet Co., 285 Fifth Ave., N. Y. C.
Where Little Things Matter So Much, Thomlinson Furniture Co., High Point, N. C.
Thumbnail Decorator, Bigelow Carpets, 136 Madison Ave., N. Y. C.
Let Tables Glisten, Fostoria Glass, Moundsville, W. Va.
Spode, the Fine English Dinnerware, Copeland and Thompson, 206 Fifth Ave., N. Y. C.

Magazines That Will Help You with Your Home Planning

American Home
Better Homes and Gardens
Charm
Glamour
Good Housekeeping

House and Garden
House Beautiful
Ladies Home Journal
Mademoiselle
McCalls

Woman's Home Companion

INDEX